INDIA
ITS CULTURE AND PEOPLE

Anne Ferguson Jensen

Longman
New York & London

Consultants:
Gwen R. Johnson
Scarsdale High School, New York
Beverly Smit
The Spence School, New York City

India: Its Culture and People

Copyright © 1991 by Longman Publishing Group.
All rights reserved.
No part of this publication may be reproduced,
stored in a retrieval system, or transmitted
in any form or by any means, electronic, mechanical,
photocopying, recording, or otherwise,
without the prior permission of the publisher.

Longman, 95 Church Street, White Plains, N.Y. 10601

Associated companies:
Longman Group Ltd., London
Longman Cheshire Pty., Melbourne
Longman Paul Pty., Auckland
Copp Clark Pitman, Toronto

Executive editor: Lyn McLean
Production editor: Halley Gatenby
Production supervisor: Anne P. Armeny
Photo/illustration credits appear on page viii.

Library of Congress Cataloging-in-Publication Data

Jensen, Anne Ferguson.
    India : its culture and people / Anne Ferguson Jensen.
        p.   cm.
    Includes bibliographical references and index.
    Summary: Examines the geography, climate, culture, religions, and
current problems of India.
    ISBN 0-8013-0343-5
    1. India–Civilization. [1. India.] I. Title.
DS423.J43   1991
954–dc20   90-23051
                                                                CIP
                                                                 AC

1   2   3   4   5   6   7   8   9   10-HA-95 94 93 92 91

CONTENTS

LIST OF MAPS

v

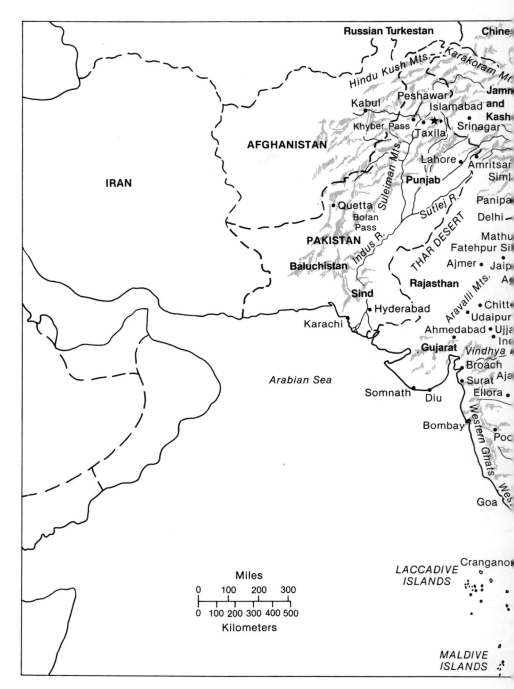

The Indian Subcontinent

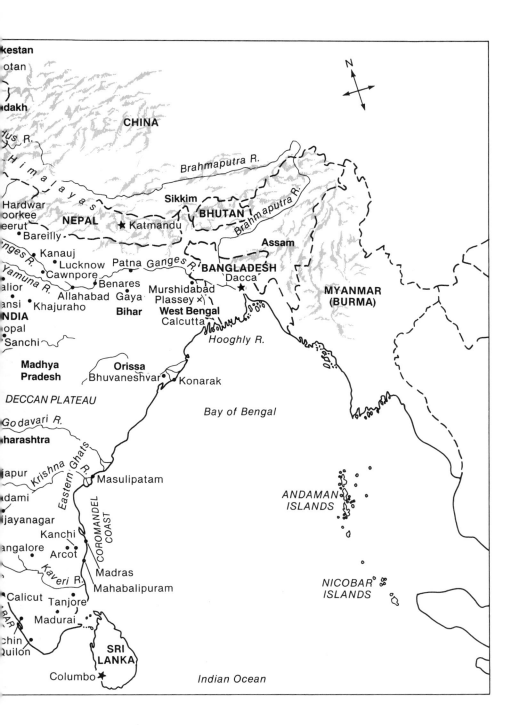

Credits

Grateful acknowledgment is made to the following institutions and individuals for research assistance and for permission to reproduce the photographs in this book. (*Note:* Abbreviations for frequently cited sources are indicated in parentheses.)

Air India Slide Library, New York City (Air India); Archaeological Survey of India, New Delhi; Bettmann Archive, New York City (Bettmann); Freer Gallery of Art, Smithsonian Institution, Washington, D.C. (Freer Gallery); India Office Library and Records, London (IOL, London); Indian Tourist Office, London (ITO, London); Information Service of India, New York City (ISI, New York); Magnum Photos, New York City; National Museum, New Delhi; Photo Researchers, New York City; PIB Photo Library, New Delhi (PIB, New Delhi); Rijksmuseum voor Volkenkunde, Leyden; Victoria & Albert Museum, London (V&A); Wide World Photos, New York City (Wide World).

Cover photo: Karnataka—road near Halebid, Bernard Pierre Wolff, Magnum Photos; **Chapter 1: 2, 6,** ITO, London; **5,** Steve McCurry, Magnum Photos; **9,** IOL, London; **11,** Henri Cartier-Bresson, Magnum Photos; **14,** Air India; **15,** Photo Researchers; **Chapter 2: 25,** Air India; **28** (Vishnu painting and Shiva bronze), V&A; **29** (Krishna and Radha), National Museum, New Delhi; (Ganesha sculpture), Archaeological Survey of India; **Chapter 3: 47,** Frances Mortimer, Photo Researchers; **48, 51,** National Museum, New Delhi; **55, 60,** PIB, New Delhi; **Chapter 4: 74,** Freer Gallery; **77** (stupa), Archaeological Survey of India; **77** (gateway), ITO, London; **88,** V&A; **Chapter 5: 101, 104,** IOL, London; **107** (top left), National Museum, New Delhi; **107** (top right and bottom left), V&A; **107** (bottom right), Freer Gallery; **113,** National Museum, New Delhi; **Chapter 6: 119,** Rijksmuseum voor Volkenkunde, Leyden; **124,** Bernard Pierre Wolff, Photo Researchers; **126,** ITO, London; **135,** V&A; **Chapter 7: 143,** ITO, London; **149, 161,** V&A; **155** (Jahangir), Freer Gallery; (Nur Jahan), V&A; **157, 158, 159,** IOL, London; **Chapter 8: 176, 184, 188, 189,** IOL, London; **181,** V&A; **Chapter 9: 207, 211, 221,** Bettmann; **212, 213, 214, 216, 223,** Wide World; **217, 224,** Henri Cartier-Bresson, Magnum Photos; **Chapter 10: 229, 247,** Wide World; **232, 237** (Shankar cartoons), Children's Book Trust, New Delhi; **232** (nuclear power plant), Henri Cartier-Bresson, Magnum Photos; **232** (Bombay lunch pails), Air India; **235,** ISI, New York; **248, 249, 254,** Bettmann.

The following illustrations are from previously published material: **28** (Kali), Donald A. Mackenzie, *Indian Myth and Legend* (London: Gresham); **137,** John Lockwood Kipling, *Beast and Man in India* (London, 1891); **182,** 19th-century looseleaf etching; **111, 242,** maps adapted from Stanley Wolpert, *A New History of India,* 2d ed. (New York: Oxford University Press, 1982).

Maps: **vi–vii, 46, 102, 109, 173, 183,** by Circa 86.

Interior and back cover illustrations: Joseph DePinho.

GEOGRAPHY AND CLIMATE OF THE INDIAN SUBCONTINENT

India stretches from the tropics right up to the temperate regions, from near the equator to the cold heart of Asia.
Jawaharlal Nehru

The nations of India, Pakistan, and Bangladesh occupy the great triangle of land known as the *Indian subcontinent*, or *South Asia*. The subcontinent is separated from the rest of Asia by the majestic *Himalaya Mountains*. The Himalayas are the tallest mountains on earth, with 30 peaks that rise more than 24,000 feet above sea level. (Mount Everest, the tallest of all, is 29,028 feet.) From east to west, the Himalayas form a graceful curve extending from northern Assam to Kashmir—a distance of more than 1500 miles. There, the mountains angle to the southwest to form another range known as the Hindu Kush and the Suleiman Mountains.

From the western Himalayas, the countryside descends into the high steppe land known as Turkestan, or central Asia. This region, which is now divided between Russia and China, has an extremely cold climate and a rugged terrain. Because of its short summer season and the dryness of its land, it cannot support a society of farmers and city dwellers. Instead, in ancient times, central Asia became the homeland of the Huns, the Mongols, and other nomadic peoples.

In ancient times, Indians pictured Asia as a lotus flower, with the mountains separating the four petals: to the north was Turkestan; to the west, Persia (now known as Iran); to the east, China; and in the south,

1

The *Himalayas* (meaning "abode of snow" in Sanskrit) form a mighty fortress wall along the northern border of the Indian subcontinent. The mountains have an average height of 19,000 feet and are 125 to 250 miles wide (from north to south). For thousands of years, the people of the Himalayas have trekked through the mountains, in an east-west direction, to carry on trade, find pastures for livestock, and spread religious tidings.

India. In addition to the "four petals," there were the many kingdoms within the Himalayas. (Nepal, Bhutan, and Tibet are the largest of these.) The mountain kingdoms have absorbed many cultural influences from India as well as from China.

Beyond the Hindu Kush range, to the west, is the high tableland of Afghanistan. [1] For many centuries, this region was the hub of the overland routes linking Europe and the Middle East to China. (Marco Polo was one of the many travelers who passed through Afghanistan on the way to China.) From the mountains of Afghanistan a traveler can also reach India, because there are several narrow passes that lead to the Indus valley. (The Khyber and Bolan passes are the ones most frequently used.) To the south of Afghanistan is the plateau of Baluchistan, now divided between eastern Iran and southwestern Pakistan.

---

1. The mountainous territories of Afghanistan and nearby regions are known as *tablelands*. In these elevated areas, even the river valleys are far above sea level.

GEOGRAPHY OF THE INTERIOR

The Indo-Gangetic Plain

South of the Himalayas lies the great plain of northern India. Its two great river systems—the Indus and the Ganges—have had the same importance to Indian civilization as the Nile River had to Egypt. They were the sites of India's first agricultural settlements and are still the most populated areas of the subcontinent. Although this vast area is often called the *Indo-Gangetic plain*, the two river systems are separated by a desert barrier. For this reason, the history of the two regions has often been different. In 1948, when India was divided along religious lines, the Indus valley region went to Pakistan (a Muslim-majority state) while most of the Ganges valley remained in India.

To the east of the Indus River valley are the shifting sand dunes of the Thar Desert. The desert ends in the Aravalli mountain range, which tapers into a series of gentle hills at Delhi. To the east of Delhi, the countryside opens into the great Gangetic plain, watered by the Yamuna, the Ganges, and a host of tributary rivers. Unlike the Indus River, the Ganges can be navigated along most of its length.

Southern India

The southern, peninsular part of India is bordered by the Arabian Sea and the Bay of Bengal. On the upper edge of this triangular wedge are the Vindhya Mountains, which are about 3000 feet high. In ancient times, the Vindhyas were thickly covered with jungle and thus formed an almost impassable barrier between the peoples of the north and the south. Paralleling the coasts of South India are two more mountain chains, the Western and Eastern Ghats. (The word *ghat* means "a staircase descending to the water." The Ghats are so called because of their gentle slopes.)

The area between the two Ghats is called the *Deccan* (meaning "south"). The Deccan is a raised plateau, sloping downward from west to east. The high edge of the plateau is the Western Ghat range, about 4000 feet in average height. The Eastern Ghats, a series of lower hills, form the eastern edge of the plateau. The Deccan is more elevated and hilly than the northern plains, and its climate is more desertlike. The Deccan has a number of rivers that provide water for agriculture—notably the Kaveri, the Krishna, and the Godavari—but they are not as dependable as the snow-fed rivers of the north. Many of the smaller streams dry up during the summer.

THE MONSOONS

The monsoons ("seasonal winds") are the most important feature of India's climate. They bring most of the rainfall that is essential for agriculture and relieve the fierce heat of the Indian summer. During the months of March, April, and May, the northern plains of India become hot and parched. Temperatures may reach 110 degrees Fahrenheit in May and 120 degrees by early June. When winds pass over the land, they merely fan the flames of the desert heat. In his poem "The Seasons," the Indian poet Kalidasa gave a brief but pointed description of summer in the northern plains: "The wind is an angry fan, and the world a furnace." In this parched environment, immense dust storms rise and envelop the villages and cities. Plants wither, and animals lose their normal energy and purpose. Kalidasa noted that even the law of the jungle is overturned: a lion passes wearily by its prey, and a frog sleeps in the shade of a cobra's head.

To the southwest, meanwhile, clouds of moisture begin to develop over the Indian Ocean. As the plains reach their hottest, the winds from the ocean are pulled toward the land. (In meteorologists' terms, the high-pressure system over the water rushes to fill the low-pressure system of the land.) The monsoons and rain clouds pass over the hot earth until they strike the cooler air of the Himalayan peaks. After this sudden contact, the clouds can no longer hold their moisture, and the rains begin. Kalidasa described the first rumbles of thunder as the clouds recoil from the mountains: "The clouds advance [on the land] like mating elephants, enormous and full of rain; they come forward as kings among tumultuous armies; their flags are the lightning, the thunder is their drum."

The torrential rains of the monsoons usually begin in late June and last about three months. Later, in December and January, a second monsoon system—the southeast monsoon—comes in from the Bay of Bengal. These rains nourish the wheat crops that farmers sow in October and November.

The arrival of the monsoons is greeted joyously throughout northern India, even though there is always a danger of flooding and other disasters. The rains signify a renewal of life, for they rescue the crops scorched by the "thousand flaming rays" of the sun. Kalidasa described how the world seems to reawaken during the monsoons:

> Being and nature call in chorus: the rivers move forward and the lovers dream; rain is rustling, the peacock dances;
> the elephants trumpet and apes hunt for each other and the thickets glisten.
> And all things live and are moved and seek out their kind. . . .

In some regions of India, monsoon floods are an annual event. Here, a tailor rescues his sewing machine from the deluge.

Because of the intensity of the sun and of the monsoons, weather has had a central importance in India's culture and mythology. *Heat* and *water* are frequent images in Indian literature. Also, the extremes of climate have inspired some of the most distinctive ideas of Indian philosophy. For instance, from the earliest times, India's philosophers have observed that nature must use both its creative and destructive forces to maintain balance and harmony. Thus, they concluded, the yearly extremes of heat–water, feast–famine, and creation–destruction are not really "opposites" but two different aspects of the same force.

Monsoon Failures

The area that the monsoons reach is roughly a triangle extending south of the Himalayas. In some years, the two monsoon systems miss a particular area, or they bring less rainfall than usual. The area of shortage is always patchy and unpredictable. When the monsoons do not come, there can be no harvest of rice or grain in September, and the ground is too hard to plant the wheat or barley that would be harvested in March.

In the more arid regions of India, deep wells are often the only dependable source of water for agriculture and for household needs.

Most villages can survive one drought but will face the threat of famine if it continues two years in a row. Before the era of modern transportation, millions of people died of starvation when the monsoons failed. Even the building of railroads, in the 19th century, did not completely solve the problem. Under famine conditions, the bullocks, or cattle, that transported grain from the railroad station to a village would have to consume nearly their entire load in order to travel a distance of 50 miles. A historian reported that "even as late as 1877, grain lay rotting at the railway stations in Madras, in the very districts where men were starving, because there were no bullocks with the strength to drag it away."[2]

In today's India, the government has had much success in averting some of the disasters caused by rain shortages. Because of modern agricultural techniques and central planning, there have been no widespread famines in recent years. However, each monsoon failure causes severe hardship in the affected villages.

---

2. C. T. Metcalfe, quoted in Percival Spear, *Twilight of the Mughals*, 3d ed. (Oxford University Press, 1973), p. 117.

Flooding

In low-lying regions of the Ganges valley, the monsoons may cause devastating floods. These are particularly likely to occur in the delta region, where villages and cities are only about 10 feet above sea level. In 1988, an unusually severe monsoon caused one of the worst flooding disasters in history. As the Ganges and Brahmaputra rivers rose above their banks, many of the villages and farms of Bangladesh were swept away. In all, about 25 million people—almost one-quarter of the total population—were rendered homeless. The flooding also brought about an epidemic of waterborne diseases and of insects and poisonous snakes.

THE HIMALAYA MOUNTAINS

The earliest peoples of India realized that the Himalayas are the source of all of the rivers that bring life to the plains: the Indus, the Ganges, the Brahmaputra, and many others. In addition, the Himalayas play two more roles: they isolate the subcontinent from Asia, and they determine its climate. Because of the Himalayan barrier, the cool winds of central Asia cannot penetrate to the Indian plains, and the monsoon rains do not travel north to central Asia. As a result, India has a tropical climate even though it lies within the earth's temperate zone.

The Mountain Rivers

The great rivers that flow from the Himalayas to the northern plains are fed by the snows of the Himalayan peaks. For this reason, they are permanent and flow year-round, in contrast to the rain-fed rivers of southern India. Without the silt that these rivers have deposited on the plains, northern India would be a desert of rock and sand. A geographer has described the seeming favoritism toward India:

> Like two great arms the Indus and Brahmaputra completely clasp themselves round the Himalayan Ranges so that all the rain that falls and all the snow that melts, whether on their northern or southern flanks, is bound to come into India. Geographically the Himalayas belong as much to Tibet as to India, but these river-systems bring all the *benefits* of these mountains to India alone.[3]

---

3. Cameron Morrison, *A New Geography of the Indian Empire and Ceylon* (London: Nelson, 1926), p. 67.

The Mountains as Barrier

For most of history, the Himalayas were an uncharted wilderness to all except the peoples who lived there. During the 19th and early 20th centuries, however, a few Western climbers were able to chart the interior mountains before the region was again closed to foreigners.

In several places, such as the beautiful Vale of Kashmir and the Katmandu valley of Nepal, the mountains open into lush river valleys that have been important agricultural areas for centuries. The 19th-century explorers discovered that it is possible to travel in a west–east direction from Kashmir to Nepal and even on to Tibet, following the valleys cut by the Indus and other rivers. In some areas along this route, the traveler may encounter a tiny village perched on a mountain shelf. In other areas, there is no human habitation, and it is difficult to determine direction. One British explorer mentioned his problems in finding Tibet. "No description could enable me to find my way in a country so rugged and forest-clad, through tortuous and perpetually forking valleys, along often obliterated paths, and under cloud and rain."[4]

In some portions of the Himalayas, the mountain rivers may be crossed by means of high rope bridges. In other areas, the rivers must be forded. During the summer season, one climber recorded temperatures as high as 207 degrees Fahrenheit on the high rock surfaces during the day and subzero temperatures during the night. In addition to these temperature extremes—in fact, because of them—there is always the danger of rock and snow avalanches.

Despite all the difficulties, the traders and sheepherders of the Himalayas have trekked back and forth between Kashmir and Tibet for centuries.[5] The north–south route is another story, however. To travel from central Asia to Kashmir, a person must first climb the Karakoram range of mountains and then negotiate the most desolate regions of the Himalayas. The Karakoram route contains 11 high mountain passes, including one 19,000 feet above sea level. Farther south, the traveler finds no sign of life because the Indus and other rivers have cut ravines so deep that the sun cannot reach them. Several explorers described the powerful emotions that they felt in this barren landscape, where they could see nothing but the sheer granite faces of the mountains. One referred to the region as an "abomination of desolation," and another wrote of its "rugged insolence, its brutal savagery, and its utter disregard of all the puny efforts of man."[6]

---

4. Joseph D. Hooker, *Himalayan Journals*, vol. 2 (New Delhi: Today and Tomorrow, 1969), p. 64.
5. The traders of Tibet and Nepal, for instance, bring their fine wool to Kashmir. There it is woven into scarves and other items, often with a paisley pattern.
6. C. G. Bruce and J. N. Collie, quoted in Jean Fairley, *The Lion River: The Indus* (New York: John Day, 1975), pp. 84, 85.

The uncharted Himalayas were the scene of many bizarre adventures during the 19th century. Here, English explorers disguised as Indians (on yaks at left) encounter two Tibetan traders.

In view of the reports brought back by the explorers, it is not surprising that the exact border between India and China was of little concern to either country for many centuries. During the 20th century, however, with the development of new road-building and airplane technology, both countries have become concerned about their national security. In part because of these anxieties, Chinese troops have occupied Tibet since 1951, and Indian troops are stationed in the peaks of Ladakh.

LANDSCAPES AND PEOPLES

The national boundaries of India, Pakistan, and Bangladesh were drawn in the 20th century and were determined mainly by religious affiliations: Pakistan and Bangladesh are Muslim states, while the vast majority of India's citizens describe themselves as Hindus. These major political divisions, however, give little indication of the great variety and diversity of the people who inhabit the subcontinent.

In later chapters we will discuss some of the many ethnic, cultural, and historical traditions of India's peoples. The languages spoken today in India are one indication of this diversity. In a recent survey, 65 languages and dialects were named, and 11 million people reported that they spoke a language not included in this group. At present, the Indian government recognizes 20 of these as official state languages. (The English language, which is commonly used for communications between the northern and southern states, is not counted among these.) The languages spoken in the north have their roots in Sanskrit, the classical language of northern India. However, many of these languages are as different from one another as German and Italian (which are also descended from a common parent). The languages spoken in the peninsula are derived from Tamil, the classical language of southern India. However, numerous other influences can also be traced.

In Pakistan, the Urdu language—which combines elements of Persian and of Hindi, a language of northern India—is one of the most commonly used official languages. However, most Pakistanis speak the Punjabi, Pashto, or Sindi languages. In Bangladesh, nearly everyone speaks the Bengali language.

The Indus River Valley

The Indus River was the site of India's first great civilization and the source of the names *India* and *Hindu*. [7] In 1948, the Indus valley and the Punjab became part of the new nation of Pakistan.

The first British explorers to enter the Indus valley called it "Young Egypt" because of its resemblance to the Nile. (The Indus valley was not "younger" than Egypt, but it seemed so to the explorers because they discovered it later.) Like the Nile valley in Egypt, the Indus consists of a silty plain paralleled by tracts of desert and hills. Also as in Egypt, the fertility of the Indus valley depends entirely on the river, for the region receives very little rainfall.

Before it emerges onto the plain of Pakistan, the Indus has already traveled about 1000 miles from its source in southern Tibet. Along its course, it has carved out great gorges in the Himalayas and carried thousands of tons of silt from the mountains to the plains. One 19th-century explorer remarked on the connection between the mountains and the river of the plains:

> One glance at the Himalaya, and we cease to be surprised at the volume of the Indus. . . . It is impossible not to venerate the river, to form which ten thousand streams have leaped their waters downwards from some of the most elevated and most interesting regions on the face of the earth.[8]

---

7. Visitors to India named the country and its people after the river; the Sanskrit word *Sindhu* ("sea") became *Hindu* to the Persians, and the Greeks called it the *Indos*.
8. G. T. Vigne, quoted in Fairley, *The Lion River*, p. 204.

During the spring and summer, the Indus is a mighty, fast-flowing river, difficult to navigate or to ford. In the winter, when it no longer carries melting snow from the Himalayas, it becomes somewhat narrower. When the river recedes, it leaves an enormous deposit of silt along its banks, and sizable islands appear in the middle of its wide channel. The temporary islands and the silty banks are both used for farming and for grazing cattle. On the river's shores, palm trees flourish, and farmers grow crops such as sugarcane, wheat, rice, and melons.

Every few years, the river changes direction in parts of its course, abandoning an old curve and creating a new one. When this happens, farmers must move their fields and sometimes their houses as well. Over the course of centuries, this constant changing of course has created a wide valley of finely ground rock and silt. It has also made it difficult to find the sites of ancient civilizations.

Occasionally, the Indus has produced sudden, devastating floods. These disasters occur when the Indus is dammed by a rock avalanche or a glacier in the distant mountains. When this happens, a large lake forms over a period of months, then suddenly breaks through the dam. In one such episode (in 1885), the level of the Indus in the plains rose by 90 feet in one day, washing away whole villages. Today, the government of Pakistan monitors the course of the Indus from its modern capital of Islamabad,

A landscape in the Punjab, one of the world's richest agricultural regions. The Punjab is now divided between Pakistan and India.

near the point where the river enters the plains. Teams of engineers are sent to break up any dams that form in the mountains and to decide where irrigation channels are needed on the plains. Through the use of manmade channels and dams, the government has been able to regulate the course of the Indus and spread its waters over a larger area.

The Punjab. The northeastern part of Pakistan is called the *Punjab*, from the Persian *panj ab*, meaning "five rivers." (The Indus River is not included in this count, although it forms the western boundary of the area.) The rivers of the Punjab also originate in the Himalayas but travel a much shorter distance to the plains. Like the Indus valley, the Punjab has been an important agricultural area since prehistorical times.

The Sind. The lower portion of the Indus valley is called the *Sind*. This region includes the delta formed by the Indus when it reaches the Arabian Sea—a delta that every year increases in size due to the volume of silt deposited by the river. The seaport of Karachi on the tip of the delta is one of the largest cities in Pakistan.

The Ganges River Valley

From prehistoric times, the Ganges River (called the *Ganga* in Hindi) has been considered a sacred river. The earliest settlers of the Ganges valley believed that the river's source was Mount Kailasa, the sacred home of their gods. (Actually, the river begins in a glacier cave several hundred miles south of Kailasa.) The Ganges emerges from the Himalayas a few miles above the ancient city of Hardwar. From Hardwar, the Ganges runs about 1200 miles until it reaches the Bay of Bengal. Throughout its course, it has created a fertile agricultural region. As early as the fourth century B.C., the Greek writer Megasthenes noted that there were so many cities along the banks of the Ganges that they could not be counted. Today, the Ganges valley is still the most populated area of India.

In ancient times, the Ganges valley was considered a paradise on earth. (This reputation even spread to medieval Europe, where scholars believed that the Ganges was the site of the Garden of Eden.) In India, there are several ancient myths concerning the divine gift of this river to humankind. One tells how the god Shiva caught the river as it fell from the Milky Way and channeled it to earth by letting it run through his hair. Another relates that the god Vishnu reached the heavens with three giant strides and brought the river to earth. Because of these associations, the Ganges symbolizes not only life and abundance but also divinity—a meeting of heaven and earth. A modern philosopher has explained the spiritual meaning of the river:

Suppose two men go for a bath in the Ganga. One of them says, ''What is this Ganga that people talk so much about? Take two parts of hydrogen and one of oxygen; combine the two gases—it becomes Ganga. What else is there in the Ganga?'' The other says, ''The Ganga flows from the lovely lotus-feet of Lord Vishnu. She has dwelt in the matted hair of Shiva. Thousands of seers, both ascetic and kingly, have done penance near her. Countless holy acts have been performed by her side. Such is the sacred Ganga, my mother.'' Filled with this bhavana (feeling), he bathes in the river. The oxygen-hydrogen-wallah also bathes. Both derive the benefit of physical cleansing. But the devotee (bhakta) gets the benefit of mental purification as well.[9]

Like other things that people have venerated for many centuries, the Ganges has acquired many different names. A guidebook for tourists lists as many as a thousand poetic descriptions. Among these are ''Daughter of the Himalaya,'' ''Eternally pure,'' ''Having a dazzling white garment,'' ''Sportively billowing,'' ''Flowing like a staircase to Heaven,'' ''Mother of what lives or moves,'' ''Destroyer of sorrow,'' and ''Embodiment of the Supreme Spirit.'' Although most descriptions are of the Ganges' creative force, people do not forget about its destructive side—the devastating floods, for instance, which have swept away whole villages. For this reason, the Ganges is often pictured as both creative and destructive: a beautiful goddess with a crocodile by her side.

One of the most famous art works associated with the river is a sculpture known as the ''Descent of the Ganges.'' This relief is thought to celebrate the great panorama of life—human, animal, and semi-divine—to which the river gave rise.

Several sites along the Ganges are especially sacred in Indian culture. The town of *Hardwar*, located where the Ganges emerges from the mountains, is one of these sites. Water from Hardwar is considered to be especially pure and is carried back to villages throughout India for use at weddings and religious ceremonies.

Another sacred site is the ancient city of *Allahabad* (formerly Prayaga). This is the place where the Ganges and Yamuna rivers meet, and it is symbolically the place where the three worlds—heaven, earth, and the underworld—come together. Every 12 years, millions of Hindus flock to the Kumbha Mela at Allahabad, the largest of India's pilgrimage festivals. (The Kumbha Mela festival also rotates among three other cities besides Allahabad.)

---

9. Vinoba Bhave, quoted in Robert A. McDermott and V. S. Naravane, eds., *The Spirit of Modern India* (New York: Crowell, 1974), p. 118.

The Kumbha Mela, which has taken place at least since A.D. 644, celebrates the immortality associated with India's great rivers. One recent festival was attended by an estimated 15 million pilgrims.

A third holy site is the city of *Benares* (also called *Kashi* or *Varanasi*). The American author Mark Twain remarked of Benares that it was "older than history, older than tradition, older even than legend, and looks twice as old as all of them put together." In fact, Benares may be the most ancient continuously inhabited city in the world.

For people interested in human affairs, a trip down the Ganges offers a view both of the present and of the river's past. In this passage, a tourist describes a short stretch of the upper Ganges landscape:

Women stood in the doorways, silently watching us go by; cows stood equally immobile in the shadow of the mud walls, as if pasted to them, adding to the illusion that this was a film that we had seen before and one that had momentarily stopped; but as we turned the bend it began again. Here, on the other side, the scene was more lively: on the upper ramparts dogs were fighting one another energetically and a woman was laying into them with a stick, while down in the river, where some fishing boats were moored, equally energetic girls were walloping away at their washing, shouting to one another with coarse, cheerful voices. Here we went aground, and to the amusement of the laundry girls got out and pushed the boat. . . . A mile or so further down we came to Gangaganj, also on the right bank at a place where the cliff receded from the river and

Benares is one of the seven holiest cities of Hinduism. Pilgrims descend from the ghats (staircases) along the waterfront to purify themselves in the Ganges.

the land could be seen running back green with young wheat and patches of sugar cane, groves of mangoes and clumps of palms. It was in this pleasant countryside that the Governor of Kanauj, in the last decade of the 18th century, had established a military post and, here on the high ground by the river, he had constructed a garden enclosure. . . .

Inside [the enclosure] there was a Hindu temple with a tall spire on which there was a gilded figure of Hanuman, the monkey god, and in a far corner under some old trees there was a delicate, octagonal pavilion with a bulbous, fluted dome. It made a pleasantly frivolous contrast to the forbidding monolith which rose above it. By it a couple of pallid cows were nibbling the scanty grass and a sadhu [holy man] sat in the shade of a pipal tree.[10]

The Deccan

The Deccan, with its hilly, rugged terrain, has always been the most difficult part of India to control or to conquer, and it has also been a barrier to those who wanted to unify north and south India. The northwestern

---

10. Eric Newby, *Slowly Down the Ganges* (New York: Scribner, 1966), pp. 174-175.

Deccan, known as Maharashtra, or "Great Country," has a rugged desert landscape similar to that of the American Southwest. For centuries, the deserts of Maharashtra—and of nearby Madhya Pradesh and Rajasthan—were the favorite territory of independent tribal kings and their warriors. Many of the greatest heroes of Indian legends were the patriots and "outlaws" who made their home in these regions.

In the higher, wetter areas of the Deccan there are tropical forests and wildlife. Leopards, tigers, monkeys, peacocks, and other wildlife roam these areas; wild dates, bamboo, and teak trees thrive, and cotton and peanuts are cultivated.

The Western and Eastern Coasts

India's western coast is a narrow strip of plain (about 40 miles wide) which rises into the Western Ghats. (The southern portion of the coast is known as *Malabar*.) When the southwest monsoons strike the Western Ghats, they drop most of their moisture on the coast. Consequently, the coastal area has a jungle climate, while much of the Deccan remains dry.

The western coast has been an important center of commerce since ancient times. Its tropical forests were the source of some of the pepper and other spices that medieval Europeans valued so highly: these commodities were loaded onto European ships at the seaports of Cochin and Calicut, among others. During the era of the Moghul Empire, the Europeans established additional trading posts farther north; in Goa, Bombay, and Surat.

The eastern coast, or Coromandel plain, is about double the width of the Malabar plain. It is a prosperous agricultural area and was one of the first sites of civilization in South India. As early as 2000 B.C., this region and the Malabar coast were settled by a group of people known as the *Dravidians*, or *Tamils*. Today, the peoples of South India are known for their distinctive literature and music and the elegant forms of their temple architecture. From South India, this culture also spread to the nearby island of Sri Lanka (formerly Ceylon).

An Outsider's View of India

The two central facts of India's tropical climate are heat and water. Of these two, visitors to India have more often remarked about the heat. Ktesias, a traveler from ancient Greece, noted that in India, "the sun appears to be ten times larger than in other countries." Modern visitors, too, have commented on the dazzling, metallic quality of the Indian skies. One visitor to the Ganges valley took away an impression of "a sky like an inverted brass bowl overhead and the earth like an overcooked omelette beneath it."[11] Yet because of the abundance of water brought by the mountain rivers and the monsoons, the peoples of India have been able to create and sustain one of the greatest civilizations on earth. A viceroy of India during the British Empire described the "enchanted vision" that India's civilization has always presented to the peoples who lived on the other side of the mountains:

> As the traveler leaves the plains of India, and, ascending the lower foot-slopes of the Himalayas, looks back upon the country he has left, and as from his ever-increasing altitude the rich landscape widens to a vast horizon, until at length it resembles an embroidered scarf hung up against the sky, he can appreciate the fascination which those verdant [green] plains, that fair and almost illimitable expanse, with its teeming population, its great cities, its agricultural wealth, its capacities for luxury and ease, must have exercised upon the hardier and more penurious [poorer] peoples of the north.[12]

DISCUSSION AND ESSAY QUESTIONS

1. Working with a partner, list the ways in which the Himalayas have influenced India's climate and history.
2. Describe the natural barriers *within* the Indian subcontinent. Which ones are difficult for a traveler or an invading army to cross?
3. Identify the main agricultural regions of India and Pakistan on a map. Which areas receive monsoon rains, and which depend on river water for irrigation?
4. Imagine that you are an American reporter stationed in a small farming village near Delhi. It is late June, and the monsoon rains have not yet appeared. Write an account of your observations for an evening news broadcast.

ADDITIONAL READING

Jean Fairley, *The Lion River: The Indus* (New York: John Day, 1975). A fascinating account of the geography of the Indus, with many glimpses into the human history of the mountains and plains.

---

11. Ibid., p. 23.
12. Marquess Curzon of Kedleston, *A Viceroy's India* (London: Sidgwick & Jackson, 1984), p. 151.

TWO MONSOON DISASTERS

Sometimes the monsoons strike with unusual force, destroying farmers' homes and newly planted crops. At other times, they fail to arrive at all, and crops wither in the fields for lack of water. In either event, food shortages soon develop. In her novel Nectar in a Sieve, *the writer Kamala Markandaya described both types of monsoon-related disasters.*

A Monsoon Flood

That year the monsoon broke early with an evil intensity such as none could remember before. It rained so hard, so long and so incessantly that the thought of a period of no rain provoked a mild wonder. . . . At first the children were cheerful enough—they had not known such things before, and the lakes and rivulets that formed outside gave them endless delight; but Nathan and I watched with heavy hearts while the waters rose and rose and the tender green of the paddy [rice] field sank under and was lost.

"It is a bad season," Nathan said somberly. "The rains have destroyed much of our work; there will be little eating done this year."

At his words, Arjun broke into doleful sobs and his brother, Thambi, followed suit. They were old enough to understand. . . .

As night came on—the eighth night of the monsoon—the winds increased, whining and howling around our hut as if seeking to pluck it from the earth. Towards midnight the storm was at its worst. Lightning kept clawing at the sky almost continuously, thunder shook the earth. . . .

In the morning everything was calm. Even the rain had stopped. After the fury of the night before, an unnatural stillness lay on the land. I went out to see if anything could be saved of the vegetables, but the shoots and vines were battered and broken. . . . The corn field was lost. Our paddy field lay beneath a placid lake on which the children were already sailing bits of wood.

Many of our neighbors fared much worse than we had. . . . Kali's hut had been completely destroyed in the last final fury of the storm. The roof had been blown away bodily, the mud walls had crumbled. "At least it stood until the worst was over," said Kali to me, "and by God's grace we were all spared." She looked worn out; in the many years I had known her I had never seen her so deflated. . . .

In the village the storm had left disaster and desolation worse than on our own doorstep. Uprooted trees sprawled their branches in ghastly fashion over streets and houses, flattening them and the bodies of men and women indiscriminately. . . .

People were moving about amid this destruction, picking out a rag here, a bundle there, hugging those things that they thought to be theirs, moving haltingly and with a kind of despair about them. People we knew came and spoke to us in low voices, gesturing hopelessly. . . .

At dusk the drums of calamity began; their grave, throbbing rhythm came clearly through the night, throughout the night, each beat, each tattoo, echoing the mighty impotence of our human endeavor. I listened. I could not sleep. In the sound of the drums I understood a vast pervading doom; but in the expectant silences between, my own disaster loomed larger, more consequent and more hurtful.

A Drought

The drought continued until we lost count of the time. Day after day the pitiless sun blazed down, scorching whatever still struggled to grow and baking the earth hard until at last it split and great irregular fissures [cracks] gaped in the land. Plants died and the grasses rotted, cattle and sheep crept to the river that was no more and perished there for lack of water, lizards and squirrels lay prone and gasping in the blistering sunlight. . . .

Then, after the heat had endured for days and days, and our hopes had shriveled with the paddy—too late to do any good—then we saw the storm clouds gathering, and before long the rain came lashing down, making up in fury for the long drought and giving the grateful land as much as it could suck and more. But in us there was nothing left—no joy, no call for joy. It had come too late. . . .

As soon as the rains were over, and the cracks in the earth had healed, and the land was moist and ready, we took our seed to our Goddess and placed it at her feet to receive her blessing, and then we bore it away and made our sowing. . . .

Hope and fear. Twin forces that tugged at us first in one direction and then in another, and which was the stronger no one could say. Of the latter we never spoke, but it was always with us. Fear, constant companion of the peasant. Hunger, ever at hand to jog his elbow should he relax. Despair, ready to engulf him should he falter. Fear; fear of the dark future; fear of the sharpness of hunger; fear of the blackness of death. . . .

Now that the last of the rice was gone it was in a sense a relief: no amount of scheming and paring would make it go any further; the last grain had been eaten. Thereafter we fed on whatever we could find. . . . Early and late my sons roamed the countryside, returning with a few bamboo shoots, a stick of sugar cane left in some deserted field, or a piece of coconut picked from the gutter in the town. For these they must have ranged widely, for other farmers and their families, in like plight to ourselves, were also out searching for food; and for every edible plant or root there was a struggle—a desperate competition that made enemies of friends and put an end to humanity. . . .

"It will not be long before the harvest," Nathan would murmur, and I would agree with him, stifling the query whether our strength would last till then, saying, "Ah yes, not long now; only a little time before the grain is ripe." . . .

But of us all Kuti suffered the most. He had never been a healthy child; now he was constantly ailing. At first he asked for rice water and cried because there was none, but later he gave up asking and merely cried. . . .

When Kuti was gone—with a bland indifference that mocked our loss—the abundant grain grew ripe. It was the second crop of the year, sown on ground which had not been allowed to lie fallow, and so we did not think it would be other than meager; but contrary to our expectations it was a very good harvest. Every husk was filled, the paddy stood firm and healthy, showing no breaks in their ranks. We worked through the days and in the twilight getting in the rice, and then we worked three more days draining the fields and clearing them, and then three more nights sifting and winnowing. . . .

"It is as I said," Nathan exclaimed. "Strength has been given to us. Else how could so much have been achieved by such as we?" He looked around triumphantly, pointing to the neat white hills of rice and the husks in a rustling brown heap. We looked at each other, . . . thin and bony like scarecrows and as ugly, and suddenly what he had said seemed very funny.

SOURCE: Kamala Markandaya, *Nectar in a Sieve* (New York: New American Library, 1982), pp. 43–46; 81–83, 91–92, 106.

1. India's villages have traditionally been self-reliant—that is, each community depends only on its own resources. List the possible advantages and disadvantages of this independence in troubled times.
2. How do the village people cope with the troubles they face?

HINDUISM

The one fact of life in India is the eternal being of God.
S. Radhakrishnan

Originally, the word *Hindu* simply meant "Indian": it was a term invented by foreign traders to describe the civilization and peoples of the subcontinent. This civilization originated more than 4000 years ago, long before the first historical events recorded in the Old Testament. Today, it represents one of the oldest continuous traditions in the world. (Only the culture of China is comparably ancient.)

The beliefs and traditions that have guided India's peoples for so many centuries are known as the Hindu religion, or *Hinduism*. There is no central messiah or prophet in this religion; rather, the wisdom of many different sages and saints is represented.

Over the ages, hundreds of sects have grown up within the Hindu religion, and the contrasts among them are greater than those which divide Catholicism, Protestantism, and Judaism. Yet there are certain beliefs and values that most Hindus share, and these give consistency to all of the various sects and forms of worship. In this chapter, we will discuss these beliefs in general terms. Then, beginning with Chapter 3, we will trace their development from the earliest times to the present.

THE HINDU CONCEPT OF GOD

Alberuni, an Arab philosopher who visited India in the 11th century, was one of the few foreign visitors who could find an underlying unity in the Hindu religion. All Hindus, he discovered, believe in a supreme being, an immortal spirit who created the universe and still exists within it. Alberuni described the Hindu belief in God as follows:

> The Hindus believe with regard to God that he is one, eternal, without beginning and end, acting by free-will, almighty, all-wise, living, giving life, ruling, preserving; one who in his sovereignty is unique, beyond all likeness and unlikeness, and that he does not resemble anything nor does anything resemble him.[1]

From this description, it is apparent that the Hindu concept of God is quite similar to that of the Judeo-Christian tradition and of Islam. But at this point a difference arises. These "Western" religions teach that there are essential differences between God and man and between man and other living things. But in the Hindu religion, there are no such divisions. Rather, Hindus believe that everything in the world was created from the same divine spirit.

An ancient Indian myth explains the origin of the universe and tells how the unity of all living things came about. According to this myth, the universe at first contained only one being, called the Self, or *Brahman*. This divine being suddenly experienced a feeling of great loneliness and so poured forth all of the variety of life on earth in one burst of creation.

The message of this story is quite different from that of the biblical version of creation. In the biblical story (Genesis 1), it is related that God created each part of the world on a separate day and then gave humankind dominion over the earth and everything on it (fish, fowl, and cattle, etc.). But in the Hindu version, creation is described as a spontaneous explosion, or act of division. Thus, in the Hindu view, everything in the world—man, animal, plant, and mineral—is equally a manifestation of *Brahman*. The divine essence, or soul, in each living thing is known as *atman*.

KARMA

The earliest thinkers of India believed that everything in the universe reveals the spirit of *Brahman*. This spirit is the *essence* of every creature on earth: it can never be dissolved or destroyed, but continues to live even

---

1. Alberuni (al-Biruni), *Alberuni's India* (New York: Norton, 1971), p. 27.

after death. When an individual dies, therefore, the individual spirit, or *atman*, does not disappear but enters another form, or body. (In this process there is no division between the human and animal worlds. A person might be reborn in either human or animal shape.) Following from this concept of rebirth, we can see that there is literally "nothing new under the sun." To the Hindu, the world has been continually reborn in different forms, but its essence has never changed.

Although the spiritual quality of each individual is immortal, it may be corrupted by *karma*, or actions. A person who lives in a selfish way or fails to obey the rules of morality is said to have "bad karma." This means that the person will be reborn in a lower state in the next life. But almost any type of action involves karma; it is nearly impossible to avoid. This is one reason why a yogi tries to avoid any contact with the world (see text on pages 24 and 25).

Although a person may hope and expect to be reborn into a higher state in the next life, rebirth is not considered a positive thing. One of the constant themes of Indian philosophy is that *all* earthly existence involves suffering. The ultimate goal is to free the spirit from the cycle of rebirth and bondage to the physical world. The discipline of yoga provides one path to this goal. If a person comes close to a state of enlightenment either through yoga or by living righteously, this "goodness" or "greatness of soul" will be apparent in the next life.

AHIMSA

The idea that there is a bond among all living things follows from the Hindu concept of God and from the doctrine of karma. For many centuries, the cow has been the special symbol of animal life in Hindu communities. Through their respect and veneration for the cow, Hindus express the bond that they share with all members of the animal kingdom. Mahatma Gandhi described the respect for this animal as "the one concrete belief common to all Hindus" and went on to explain its importance as a symbol:

> Cow-protection to me is one of the most wonderful phenomena in human evolution. It takes the human being beyond his species. The cow to me means the entire sub-human world. Man, through the cow, is enjoined [urged] to realize his identity with all that lives. . . . Cow-protection is the gift of Hinduism to the world. And Hinduism will live so long as there are Hindus to protect the cow.[2]

---

2. *Young India*, 6 October 1921.

YOGA

The word *yoga* comes from the same root as the verb *to yoke*, or "bind together." It expresses the highest goal of the Hindu religion: to realize, or become conscious of, the link between humans and God and all living things. A person who pursues this goal is called a *yogi*.

Through the techniques and discipline of yoga, an individual learns to suppress the needs and wants that normally occupy the mind. (These impulses are considered undesirable, for they have the effect of clouding over the soul.) After overcoming all such distractions—a process that usually takes many years of effort—the yogi is able to achieve a higher state of consciousness or awareness. At this stage, the individual *atman*, or soul, recognizes its unity with *Brahman*. The ego, or personality, is dissolved, and the soul becomes one with all of creation—"like a raindrop merging into the ocean." This dissolution is called *moksha*, or release. It represents a type of salvation that is unknown in the religions of the West. Rather than *developing* the personality to meet certain spiritual goals, the worshiper instead tries to *dissolve* all sense of individuality.

In the early 19th century, when knowledge of Indian religion had just begun to reach the West, the English poet Percy B. Shelley described the trancelike state induced by yoga:

> Those who are subject to the state called reverie feel as if their nature were dissolved into the surrounding universe, or as if the surrounding universe were absorbed into their being. They are conscious of no distinction. And these are states which precede or accompany or follow an unusually intense and vivid apprehension of life.[3]

The "vivid apprehension of life" that Shelley noted is the heightened awareness that the yogi experiences during his meditations. In this state, he "knows" things in a way that cannot be experienced by the senses (sight, hearing, and touch). He then understands the "eternal realities" of the universe, which are normally disguised by the world of appearance. This state of enlightenment is called *samadhi*.

The Practice of Yoga

There is evidence that the art of yoga may have been known in India prior to 1500 B.C. The first known manual on the subject was written by a yogi named Patanjali, who may have lived about 200 B.C.

---

3. Percy Bysshe Shelley, "On Life," in *Shelley's Poetry and Prose* (New York: Norton, 1977), p. 477.

In preparation for his meditations, Patanjali says, the yogi must first purify both mind and body by withdrawing from the world. This detachment from material things and from human company is essential, for any type of pleasure (or desire fulfillment) only causes more desires to arise. (In any case, Patanjali notes, pleasure is always followed by pain or disappointment. For this reason, those who pursue pleasure are in a state of ignorance.)

To prepare for supreme efforts of concentration, the yogi assumes a position that is uncomfortable at first but provides greater stability over a long period of time. The familiar cross-legged position is one that is recommended. Now the yogi must stop the flow of thoughts and associations that normally crowd the mind. To help this process along, the yogi begins to breathe in a rhythmic fashion and eventually enters a trancelike state. At this point, he begins the process of contemplation. Often, he will concentrate his thoughts on a single object, such as a stone. After a period of meditation, the yogi begins to "know" this object in an entirely new way; that is, he obtains a special insight into it.

The special insights that a yogi achieves during his meditations are believed to be the source of magical powers. Thus, by meditating on the quality of "lightness," for example, it is said that a yogi can make himself

Eighty-four different positions are recommended for the practice of yoga, most of which require long training to master. One of the more familiar positions is shown here.

as light as wool and float through the air. There have also been reports of yogis who can shrink themselves to the size of an atom or extend their minds far enough to explore the moon. A yogi who has achieved such powers is known as a *siddha*. But to Patanjali, the magical powers of the *siddha* were not the true goal of yoga, only a side effect. To reach *samadhi*, he said, the yogi must renounce his magical powers.

The Concept of *Maya*

The Sanskrit word *maya* refers to the entire material world and everything in it—whether living or inanimate—that has shape or form. Many Indian philosophers have considered *maya* to be a trick or illusion because it disguises the underlying reality of *Brahman*. (In fact, the word *maya* means "magic.") Others, however, have had a more positive view of *maya*. In their view, the great variety of forms and shapes in the material world can help people to appreciate the infinite power and variety of *Brahman*.

Descriptions of Brahman

Those who achieved enlightenment were usually reluctant to put their vision of Brahman, or God, into words. Yet their disciples often begged them to describe what Brahman is. Many resorted to negative answers, if they replied at all, because they felt that positive, concrete words were inadequate. For instance, one ancient yogi gave this description: "The eyes do not see him, speech cannot utter him, the senses cannot reach him." One of the most famous descriptions of Brahman in Hindu scripture is "Neither this, nor that."

THE CYCLES OF TIME

In Hindu thought, as we have seen, the nature of Brahman and of atman are eternal. For this reason, the passing of time is viewed as a cycle rather than a straight line. Each turn of the cycle brings about a renewal of the world in outward forms, but no real "progress" or change.

The early philosophers of India were unusual among ancient peoples in that they could visualize enormous quantities of numbers. In describing the revolutions that the universe goes through, they measured time in immense cycles called *kalpas*. A *kalpa* is 12,000 god-years, and each god-year is 360 human years. Thus, a kalpa is 4,320,000 years long. The life of the universe is called a *Brahma Day*, and equals 1000 *kalpas*. A Brahma Day is followed by a Brahma Night of equal length. During this period, all activity ceases and the universe is quiet. Worshipers of Shiva believe that this god plays a central part in ushering in Brahma Days and Nights.

Kalpa cycles are divided into four cycles of unequal length called *yugas*. The coming of each new *yuga* represents a decline in the quality of human society. The first yuga, for instance, was a golden age lasting 1,728,000 years. During this age, people had a life span of 400 years and enjoyed peace and prosperity because of their wisdom and unselfish ways. In our present *yuga*, by contrast, people live only about 100 years and are constantly engaged in strife.

THE HINDU PANTHEON OF GODS

Though Hindus believe in one all-encompassing God, they worship this divine spirit in many different forms. There are innumerable gods and goddesses in the Hindu pantheon, and most Hindus worship one or more of them. Each of these deities is considered to have some—but by no means all—of the infinite qualities of Brahman.

Brahma, Shiva, and Vishnu

The most prominent gods in the Hindu pantheon are Brahma, Shiva, and Vishnu. They are often referred to as the Hindu *triad*. Brahma, the first god of the triad, is venerated for his role in the original creation of the world. However, he is not often worshiped as a "personal" god: most Hindus choose either Shiva or Vishnu as their main god of worship.

Shiva, the great creator-destroyer, is believed to keep the universe in balance with his cosmic dance. His consort, Parvati-Kali, similarly has two aspects: as Parvati, she is worshiped as the Great Mother, but as Kali (or Durga), her destructiveness and fury are more evident. Shiva and Kali are among the most ancient of Indian gods.

Vishnu, a more kindly deity, is worshiped as the preserver of the universe. His consort, Lakshmi, is also associated with love and mercy. At times when evil threatens to overwhelm the world, Vishnu appears as an *avatar*, or incarnation, and sets things aright. According to one tradition, Vishnu has had nine different *avatars*, with a tenth still to come. One of the most popular of these is the god Krishna, who is noted for his sense of humor and playful personality.

Other Popular Gods

Not all Hindu gods and goddesses are depicted in human form; many of them have animal forms and qualities. The kindly, elephant-headed Ganesha is one of the most popular of these. He is worshiped as a bringer

Hindu Gods and Goddesses

The god Vishnu is shown (*top*) in his first avatar, as a fish. When a great flood threatened to destroy the world, Vishnu rescued the earliest human family by towing them to safety. Shiva, the great destroyer-creator god (*bottom, left*), is often portrayed with long, matted hair. Through these locks, legend relates, the Ganges River was channeled to humankind. No Hindu god is complete without a goddess, for the female supplies the necessary principle of creative energy. Kali (*bottom, right*), is the consort of Shiva.

Krishna, one of the most popular gods in the Hindu pantheon, is the eighth avatar of Vishnu. The pastoral adventures (*left*) of Krishna and his consort, Radha, are one of the favorite subjects of Indian art.

Thousands of temple and roadside shrines are dedicated to the elephant-headed god Ganesha (*right*), "remover of obstacles." Ganesha is an offspring of Shiva and Parvati.

of good fortune and remover of obstacles. The monkey god Hanuman also has many shrines dedicated to him.

INDIAN ART

Many people feel overwhelmed or confused when they first view an Indian sculpture or mural because there is usually no "center" or focal point to concentrate on. Instead, different forms are woven together and layered on top of one another, so that it almost seems that the artist had too many ideas for the available space. But this apparent confusion is, of course, intentional. It portrays the "truth" or "reality" that the yogi sees during his meditations.

In describing a particular carved-stone gateway, one writer explains how the dreamlike, fantastical quality of Indian art is achieved:

> All organic forms look as if they were derivatives of one primal substance, whether they represent vegetable, mineral, animal, or human shapes. Whole buildings seem to grow from the soil; their surfaces blossom with figures, beasts, and foliage, all of which are part of the same plantlike growth.[4]

In many other works, too, the same effects can be observed. Not only are details piled one on another, but each form of life shares the qualities of other forms. People have plantlike shapes—and sometimes even grow in trees; plants take on animallike qualities; and rocks seem to have organic life. In this intermingling of forms, the Indian artist presents the idea that all forms of life manifest the same spirit.

INDIAN MUSIC

The first music was probably a melody, or tune, created by a human voice. Indian music has preserved this simple beginning: it is purely melody. Harmony, chords, and counterpoint are not used. Instead, the melody is often enhanced by resonating "grace" notes and by rhythm and drone accompaniments.

Ragas (Melodies)

The melodies used in Indian music are called *ragas*, from a Sanskrit word meaning "colored with emotion." The ragas are simple tunes of no more than seven notes. They express moods associated with a particular time of

4. Richard Lannoy, *The Speaking Tree* (London: Oxford University Press, 1971), p. 23.

day, a season, or an event in Hindu mythology. Ragas are often played on stringed instruments of the lute family. These are somewhat similar to a guitar, but their longer strings and rounded backs produce far more resonance. The *vina* and the *sitar* are two of the most commonly used lute instruments.

Rhythm and Drone

The second major element of Indian music is *tala*, or rhythm. The tala is more complex than the rhythms of Western music, in part because accented beats do not mark time in the same way. Rhythm instruments include the *tabla*, or double drum, and the tambourine.

In addition to solo and rhythm instruments, a musical ensemble may include a *drone* instrument to supply a background or ground note. A tambura (lute without frets) is often used as a drone.

Performance. It takes many years of study to learn the rules and traditions of Indian music, and to master the techniques of an instrument. But in the end, most concerts are improvised on the spot, without any rehearsal.

In performance, a musician usually chooses a raga that is appropriate to the day and the hour, then elaborates on this theme at great length. This improvisation requires great virtuosity on the part of the soloist and also makes special demands on the other musicians. One tabla player has explained these demands as follows:

> The tabla player . . . is somewhat like a psychiatrist when he's onstage. He has no idea of what the main instrumentalist will do, so what he has to do is sit and wait onstage until the instrumentalist decides to initiate a composition. At that point, he finds out what he's going to do, what kind of mood he's in, what kind of temperament he has. . . . We have to understand on the spot and analyze what he wants to express through his music. Or you might say I'm like a catcher—but if the catcher didn't know what the pitcher was throwing, it would be a very different ball game.[5]

THE CASTE SYSTEM

In ancient India, society was organized so that each specialized job was performed by a specific group, or caste. The *interdependence* of all of the various castes was recognized, and each one was considered necessary to the society as a whole.

---

5. Zakir Hussain, quoted in *The New York Times*, 30 September 1988, C-1.

In the earliest known mention of caste, perhaps dating from about 1000 B.C., the metaphor (symbol) of the human body was used to describe Indian society. This metaphor stresses the idea of *hierarchy* as well as that of *interdependence*. The *brahman*, or priestly, caste represents society's head; the *kshatriya*, or warrior, caste are its arms; the *vaishya* caste—traders and landowners—are the legs; and the *sudra* caste—the servants of the other three—are the feet. These four castes—*brahman, kshatriya, vaishya,* and *sudra*—are the classical four divisions of Hindu society. In practice, however, there have always been many subdivisions (*jatis*) of these castes.

The Four Varna

The word *caste* comes from the Portuguese word *castas*, meaning "pure." This Portuguese word expresses one of the most central values of Indian society: the idea of *ritual purity*. In India, however, the word *varna*, or "color," denotes the fourfold division of Indian society. The word *varna* may have been used because each of the four castes was assigned a specific color as its emblem.

In Hindu religious texts, the *dharma*—the law, or duty—of each *varna* is described. It was thought that this *dharma* was an inherited, or inborn, quality. Consequently, people thought that if intermarriages took place, there would be much confusion as to the *dharma* of the next generation of children. As a result of such concerns, marriage between different castes was strictly prohibited. The practice of marrying only a person of "one's own kind" is called *endogamy* and is still a central rule in many Hindu communities.

The Brahmans. The brahman caste is assigned the highest status of the four varnas but also must live by the strictest rules. In their very name, brahmans are identified with the supreme being, and so are expected to uphold this high honor by their conduct.[6] In addition, they must observe many detailed rules concerning ritual purity in their personal lives. They must avoid contact with dirt, for instance, and may not eat foods such as meat that are considered to be polluted.

Because of the strict rules that the brahmans observe, they cannot perform many of the tasks necessary to everyday life. They cannot obtain their own food, for instance, or use violence to defend themselves. Thus, they must depend on other castes to perform these essential services. This

---

6. The priestly castes of India share the name of the divine spirit, or *Brahman*. Some English-language texts use an alternate spelling, *brahmin*, when speaking of the priestly class.

is one way in which the interdependence of the castes is evident. Without the other castes, there could be no brahmans.

In terms of occupation, the first duty of a brahman is to study the *Vedas*, the ancient scriptures of India. A young brahman boy begins this period of study after going through a special ceremony marking his spiritual rebirth. Kshatriya and vaishya boys also go through this ceremony of "rebirth" at age 10 or 11. After the ceremony, each boy is given a sacred thread to wear around his neck as a symbol of membership in the "twice-born" castes.

After ten or more years of study, a brahman may become a priest of a temple, or he may instruct boys of the *twice-born* castes in Sanskrit and the *Vedas*. If there is no employment available as a priest or teacher, a brahman may enter certain other occupations. He must be careful, however, to observe all of the rules and rituals of his caste.

The Kshatriyas. The kshatriya caste includes soldiers, generals, and kings. Their traditional role is to defend the society from invaders and robbers, and they are expected to be both brave and high-minded. The kshatriyas must study the ancient Hindu scriptures under the guidance of a brahman teacher and are expected to follow many of the same rules of ritual purity that the brahman caste observes.

The Vaishyas. The job specialties of the vaishya caste are agriculture and cattle raising. The vaishyas also carry on trading activities; for example, they bring farm products to market and lend money to keep various enterprises going. Like the brahmans and the kshatriyas, the vaishyas are a *twice-born* caste.

The Sudras. In ancient law, the sudras were given only one occupation: to serve the members of the *twice-born* castes. As servants to the other three castes, the sudras performed many of the tasks that involve "pollution," such as agricultural labor, leather working, disposing of garbage, and laundering. In time, however, many sudras became wealthy farmers or artisans in their own right. When a sudra *jati*, or subcaste, improved its status in this way, it was also able to adopt many of the rituals and habits of the *twice-born* castes. Menial tasks then became the dharma of the "outcasts" of society—the untouchables, or *harijans*.

The Untouchables, or *Harijans*

Inevitably, there were certain people who failed to live up to their caste dharma or who violated the rules concerning marriage between castes. Such people and their children were considered *outcasts* from Hindu society. They had to live apart from other castes and were given the jobs that no one else wanted to perform. Because of their contact with things considered unclean or polluted, the outcasts were believed to be deeply tainted. They came to be thought of as "untouchable" because people believed that their touch—or even the sight of them—would compromise a brahman's purity.

The untouchables were not admitted into Hindu temples and instead formed religious sects of their own. Over the centuries, they also organized into subcastes much like those of orthodox Hindu society.

In the 20th century, Mahatma Gandhi made it one of his life's goals to bring the untouchables back into Hindu society. He renamed them the *harijans*, or "children of God," and tried to convince orthodox Hindus to admit them into their temples and their everyday lives. However, other leaders doubted that upper-caste Hindus would ever treat the *harijans* as equals. Dr. B. R. Ambedkar, a distinguished scholar who had been born an "untouchable," was a leading spokesman for this view. He used the term *scheduled castes* when referring to this group, for he believed that the term *harijans* was demeaning. The scheduled castes, he said, should withdraw from Hinduism altogether and join another religion, such as Buddhism, which does not recognize caste distinctions.

After India became an independent nation in 1947, its new constitution outlawed the practice of "untouchability." The constitution also established affirmative action programs to ensure that the scheduled castes would have access to higher education and better jobs. In contrast to similar legislation in the United States, these clauses actually *guarantee* that a certain percentage of university and job openings will be assigned to disadvantaged groups. Because of these programs, there has been a marked improvement in the status of the scheduled castes. Yet discrimination continues, and the condition of the former "untouchables" is still a major social issue today.

The Hierarchy of *Jatis,* or Subcastes

While the term *varna* refers to the classic, or ideal, division of society, people use the word *jati* when speaking of the thousands of subcastes that exist in practice. The *jatis* perform the many specialized jobs that are considered essential to society—farming, metalworking, pottery making, carpentry, weaving, laundering, marketing, and many others. Relations among these various castes are governed by elaborate rules. Each one is very much aware of its status and duties in regard to the others.

The members of each *jati* are believed to inherit the *caste dharma* necessary to carry out their role in society. In practice, however, each person becomes aware of all the complicated rules regarding *dharma* during childhood—usually by observing the behavior of family members. These rules concern not only the caste specialty but also the many other services and courtesies that are owed to other castes.

The quality of *ritual purity* is the most important factor in determining the rank of a *jati* in society. If a *jati* is to maintain or improve its status, its members must accept food and water only from people of their own caste or a higher caste. (For this reason, brahman priests are often employed as cooks during religious festivals.) A *jati* must also avoid contact with castes who are considered to be pollution-prone.

Mobility of Castes. In practice, there have always been more possibilities for upward (or downward) movement within the caste system than the classic rules of *varna* would suggest. To achieve a higher place in the social hierarchy, the members of a *jati* often take the following steps: enter an occupation that involves less contact with pollution; follow stricter rules of purity in daily life; and learn Sanskrit, the classic language of the holy scriptures.

The Continuity of the Caste System

Countless reformers have attempted to abolish or reform the caste system. However, these reform movements have had little effect. Today, the caste system continues to be the main form of government in villages throughout India. In large part, its continuity depends on two central concepts: *caste dharma* and *karma*.

In Hindu society, *caste dharma* is considered to be a divine law. In the words of Mahatma Gandhi, caste dharma is "the duty one has to perform" and "the law of one's being."[7] Many Hindus believe that this obligation tends to enhance the spiritual development of the individual. Because of it, each person learns from an early age to overcome selfish desires and instead focus on group goals and ideals.

The concept of *karma* helps to explain differences in status that might otherwise be considered unfair. Because one's caste membership is thought to be a result of actions in a previous life, a person tends to accept this status rather than complain about it. By the same token, a successful performance of caste duty will improve one's *karma* and perhaps lead to improved status in the next life.

The caste system also returns certain practical benefits to the individual. Being a member of a *jati* gives each person a sense of identity and of belonging to a well-defined group within society. The members of a jati

---

7. *Harijan,* 28 September 1934.

have much in common. They share a job specialty and abide by the same rules concerning diet and religion. Because of the rules of *endogamy*, each *jati* is also an extended family, for most members are related by blood.

Caste in India's Cities. In the modern cities of India, people daily come in contact with hundreds of strangers in public transportation and in the workplace. In this context, the traditional caste rules of the villages cannot be observed. But many city dwellers nevertheless retain a strong sense of caste identity. Thus, one phenomenon of modern India is the device known as "compartmentalization." During the day, a person may learn to be unconcerned with caste rules. But at home, and in the company of other caste members, the ancient ceremonies and rules continue to be respected.

SUMMARY

Hindu civilization has been described as a system of "unity in diversity." In the Hindu religion, there is no central messiah or founder: instead, the teachings of a great variety of sages and saints are recognized as valid. As a result, Hinduism includes many different sects and traditions. And millions of Hindus have venerated the prophets and saints of other faiths as well as of their own. However, most Hindus have proved to be immune to the efforts of foreign missionaries. Because these missionaries usually expressed intolerance toward other faiths, Hindus considered them to be less enlightened than their own teachers.

The principle of "unity in diversity" is also upheld in the caste system. Because differences between peoples were respected (and even encouraged), new sects and ethnic groups were able to take their place in Indian society without giving up their distinctive beliefs and customs. In the following chapters, we will discuss a few of the many cultural traditions that have grown up in India.

DISCUSSION AND ESSAY QUESTIONS

1. Use each of the following words in a sentence. (You may use more than one word in a single sentence.)
    ahimsa   caste dharma   karma   maya   samadhi   yoga
2. What is the goal of the yogi during his meditations? What experience will he have if successful?
3. Does the doctrine of karma explain why some people are "luckier" than others, either in their ability to master a particular skill or in their circumstances?

4. What values are expressed by the caste system? How can a particular *jati* achieve a high place in the social hierarchy?

5. It has been said that hierarchies exist in *every* human society, even in the world's most advanced democracies. What evidence of hierarchy can you identify in your own society? To what extent are all citizens "equal"? Think in terms of political, social, and economic status.

ADDITIONAL READINGS

Mulk Raj Anand, *Untouchable* (East Glastonbury, Conn.: Ind-US Inc., 1983). A poignant view of the lot of the "untouchables" in India prior to 1950.

Rudyard Kipling, *Kim*. Kipling's famous description of the great diversity of castes of 19th-century India, as seen on the Grand Trunk Road (the main highway of northern India), occurs in Chapter 4 of this novel.

R. K. Narayan, *The Vendor of Sweets* (New York: Viking Penguin, 1967). Chapter 12 of this novel describes the events leading up to an arranged marriage in a fictional village of South India. The author skillfully portrays the mixture of religious, family, and financial issues that preoccupy people at such times.

A HINDU PILGRIMAGE

*Technically, it is not possible for a foreigner to become a Hindu. (A
foreigner could not have the necessary caste identity, for one thing.)
But one visitor found herself caught up in the spirit of Hindu religion
after joining a pilgrimage tour. The following account describes one
of three major shrines that she visited on this tour.*

*Note: Darshan is the blessing believed to be radiated by holy
persons or objects.*

We were soon part of the crowd flocking towards the sanctum of Lord Subra-
maniya. We hurried the last few steps only to find him hidden from us, shut
behind huge silver doors framed with small diyas. Their tiny flames fluttered in
the slight breeze and guided our thoughts towards the secluded deity. We
crowded closer, waiting for the doors to open, our hearts leaping in anticipa-
tion when we heard the sound of a sacred conch. As its last powerful note
faded away the entire temple was suddenly flooded with sound. Bells rang,
nagaswarams wailed and huge drums thundered but although surrounded
and almost deafened by this cacophany our attention was undistracted.

The music swelled to a crescendo and, very slowly, unseen hands opened
the great silver doors. Behind them, on the floor, stood a tiered and intricate
aarti lamp, its myriad lights playing on more closed silver doors. A slight pause
preceded the opening of this second set which again revealed the lights of
another oil lamp and more closed doors. In this way two more sets were
opened, both with similar lamps between them. It was unbelievably beautiful
but the sight of a fifth closed set was almost unbearable. They were elabo-
rately decorated and the lights of all the lamps danced upon them before, in a
sudden moment of silence, they were flung open. Five tall and austere looking
priests lifted the lamps from the floor and in their fire and light we saw, at last,
the image of the god: a great, rearing, hooded, silver cobra. The heart and soul
absorbed, the mind did not think: it was power, it was emotion, it was drama
and it was spiritual bliss. It was, and has remained for me, an extraordinarily
moving moment.

I cannot deny that pilgrimages are hard; they stretch every part of the
mind and body and often reduce the brain to a tiny piece of inertia. This
discomfort is never remembered; all that remains is the aura of these ancient
and primal surroundings, their power. . . .

I never once thought: what am I doing here? Instead I was grateful for the
privileges I was enjoying. What pilgrimages seem to do, or certainly did for me,
was to set free some trapped part, to literally release, even discard, pre-
conceptions, teach acceptance. For there is an irony in darshan. We journey
to see a deity. We crave a glimpse of the image. Yet, when we finally stand
before the sanctum we involuntarily close our eyes in prayer. At the supreme
moment we see nothing. We unconsciously acknowledge that the divine
presence must be sought within ourselves.

SOURCE: Pepita Seth, "On Being a Hindu Pilgrim," in *India Magazine,* October 1988
(Delhi: A. H. Avani), p. 56.

POLITICAL ORGANIZATION OF THE UNTOUCHABLES

During the past 50 years, several efforts have been made to organize the scheduled castes, or untouchables, into a political party that would represent their interests alone. The following newspaper account describes one such movement.

Note: *The Sikhs are a religious sect who follow certain Hindu beliefs but (in principle) reject the caste system.*

New Delhi, June 26, 1988

Anyone who finishes third in a local election in India can usually start thinking about retirement. But the recent third-place showing in a parliamentary race by Kanshi Ram, a fiery champion of the rights of untouchables and other low castes, was strong enough to shake India's political establishment and force the country's leadership to pay attention to his demands.

"Let the upper castes look on us as a creeping poison," Mr. Ram said the other day, savoring his capture of nearly 20 percent of the votes. "We have initiated a new process in a big way. We will not stop until we unite the victims of the system and overthrow the spirit of inequality in our country." . . .

Despite some advances, caste discrimination remains pervasive in India, even though it is illegal. Perhaps a quarter of India's nearly 800 million people are in the lowest castes, most living in the worst conditions of poverty. . . .

Like past leaders of untouchables and other low castes, Mr. Ram deplores the ancient aspect of Hinduism that has enshrined acceptance of caste identity as a kind of religious duty. . . .

Nominally, Sikhism calls for an end to caste, but caste identity is so strong that it persists among many Sikhs, as it does among many Moslems and Christians. In the 1950's, Mr. Ram's family caste was listed as a low caste by the Government, entitling it to benefits.

The action led to discrimination while he was in the army, according to Mr. Ram, and he decided to dedicate himself to the cause, later renouncing the idea of marriage, personal property and family obligations. "Through my actions, behavior and personal style, I must induce austerity," he said. As for ideology, Mr. Ram is less clear, other than to say that the lower castes are entitled to more jobs, education, property and other benefits.

"I have seen capitalism accomplish good things in certain countries," Mr. Ram said. "Communism, socialism, liberalism, all of them have accomplished good things in other countries. But all these four 'isms' have failed in India. As long as there is brahminism, nothing else can succeed."

SOURCE: Steven R. Weisman, "Prophet for the Humble: Will They Inherit India?" *New York Times,* 27 June 1988, p. 4.

1. How was Mr. Ram, a modern leader of the untouchables, affected by India's affirmative action program?
2. Why does Mr. Ram single out "brahminism" as the source of his problems? What attitudes do this "ism" represent?

FESTIVALS OF UNITY

In most societies, there are festivals and holidays in which all members of society may come together and participate. These occasions are a way in which people can recognize their basic unity, despite the differences that are apparent in everyday life. The Holi festival, celebrated every spring in the villages of northern India, is one such event.

The Holi festival honors the memory of Holika, a woman who was martyred by fire for her religious beliefs. During Holi celebrations, villagers often build a bonfire, throw colored powders and engage in role reversals. In this account of a Holi celebration, an American professor playfully contrasts the dry theories of anthropology with the actual events of the festival.

Note: The branch of anthropology referred to in this article is the study of human societies—their myths, institutions, and ways of life.

A Holi Festival

As it happened, I had entered Kishan Garhi for the first time in early March, not long before what most villagers said was going to be their greatest religious celebration of the year, the festival of Holi. Preparations were already under way. . . .

I felt somewhat apprehensive as the day approached. An educated landlord told me that Holi is the festival most favored by the castes of the fourth estate, the Sudras. Europeans at the district town advised me to stay indoors, and certainly to keep out of all villages on the festival day. But my village friends said, "Don't worry. Probably no one will hurt you. In any case, no one is to get angry, no matter what happens. All quarrels come to an end." . . .

The celebrations began auspiciously, I thought, in the middle of the night as the full moon rose. The great pile of blessed and pilfered fuel at once took flame, ignited by the village fool, for the master of the village site had failed to rouse with sufficient speed from his slumbers. . . . A hundred men of all 24 castes in the village, both Muslim and Hindu, now crowded about the fire, roasting ears of the new, still green barley crop in her embers. They marched around the fire in opposite directions and exchanged roasted grains with each other as they passed, embracing or greeting one another with "Ram Ram!"— blind in many cases to distinctions of caste. . . . As I entered a shadowy lane, I was struck twice from behind by what I thought might be barley, but found in fact to be ashes and sand. . . . Impressed with the vigor of these communal rites and inwardly warmed, I returned to my house and to bed in the courtyard.

It was a disturbing night, however. As the moon rose high, I became aware of the sound of racing feet: gangs of young people were howling "Holi!" and pursuing each other down the lanes. At intervals I felt the thud of large mud bricks thrown over my courtyard wall. . . . Pandemonium now reigned: a shouting mob of boys called on me by name from the street and demanded that I come out. I perceived through a crack, however, that anyone who emerged was being pelted with bucketfuls of mud and cow-dung water. Boys of all ages were heaving dust into the air, hurling old shoes at each other, laughing and cavorting. . . .

I was not sure just what I could find in anthropological theory to assist my understanding of these events. . . . But I had not long to reflect, for no sooner had the mob passed by my house than I was summoned by a messenger from a family at the other end of the village to give first aid to an injured woman. A thrown water pot had broken over her head as she opened her door that morning. Protected by an improvised helmet, I ventured forth. As I stepped into the lane, the wife of the barber in the house opposite, a lady who had hitherto been most quiet and deferential, also stepped forth, grinning under her veil, and doused me with a pail of urine from her buffalo. . . .

At noontime, a state of truce descended. Now was the time to bathe, the neighbors shouted, and to put on fine, fresh clothes. The dirt was finished. Now there would be solemn oblations [offerings] to the god Fire. . . . "What is it all going to be about this afternoon?" I asked my neighbor, the barber. "Holi," he said with a beatific sigh, "is the Festival of Love!" . . .

I am now unable to report with much accuracy exactly what other religious ceremonies were observed in the four villages through which I floated that afternoon, towed by my careening hosts. They told me that we were going on a journey of condolence to each house whose members had been bereaved during the past year. . . . I know that I witnessed several hysterical battles, women rushing out of their houses in squads to attack me and other men with stout canes, while each man defended himself only by pivoting about his own staff, planted on the ground, or, like me, by running for cover. The rest was all hymn singing, every street resounding with choral song in an archaic Sakta style. The state of the clothes in which I ultimately fell asleep told me the next morning that I had been sprayed and soaked repeatedly with libations of liquid dye, red and yellow. My face in the morning was still a brilliant vermilion, and my hair was orange from repeated embraces and scourings with colored powders by the bereaved and probably by many others. . . .

"A festival of *love?*" I asked my neighbors again in the morning. . . .

Now a full year had passed in my investigations, and the Festival of Love was again approaching. Again I was apprehensive for my physical person, but . . . this time, I began to see the pandemonium of Holi falling into an extraordinarily regular social ordering. But this was an order precisely inverse to the social and ritual principles of routine life. . . .

Who were those smiling men whose shins were being most mercilessly beaten by the women? They were the wealthier Brahman and Jat farmers of the village, and the beaters were those ardent local Radhas, the "wives of the village." . . . The boldest beaters in this veiled battalion were often in fact the wives of the farmers' low-caste field laborers, artisans, or menials—the concubines and kitchen help of the victims. "Go and bake bread!" teased one farmer, egging his assailant on. "Do you want some seed from me?" shouted another flattered victim, smarting under the blows, but standing his ground.

Six Brahman men in their fifties, pillars of village society, limped past in panting flight from the quarterstaff wielded by a massive young Bhangin, sweeper of their latrines. From this carnage suffered by their village brothers, all daughters of the village stood apart, yet held themselves in readiness to attack any potential husband who might wander in from another, marriageable village to pay a holiday call. . . .

Who were those transfigured "cowherds" heaping mud and dust on all the leading citizens? They were the water carrier, two young Brahman priests, and a barber's son, avid experts in the daily routines of purification.

Whose household temple was festooned with goat's bones by unknown merrymakers? It was the temple of that Brahman widow who had constantly harassed neighbors and kinsmen with actions at law.

In front of whose house was a burlesque dirge being sung by a professional ascetic of the village? It was the house of a very much alive moneylender, notorious for his punctual collections and his insufficient charities.

Who was it who had his head fondly anointed, not only with handfuls of the sublime red powders, but also with a gallon of diesel oil? It was the village landlord, and the anointer was his cousin and archrival, the police headman of Kishan Garhi.

Who was it who was made to dance in the streets, fluting like Lord Krishna, with a garland of old shoes around his neck? It was I, the visiting anthropologist, who had asked far too many questions, and had always to receive respectful answers. . . .

Each actor playfully takes the role of others in relation to his own usual self. Each may thereby learn to play his own routine roles afresh, surely with renewed understanding, possibly with greater grace, perhaps with a reciprocating love.

SOURCE: McKim Marriott, "The Feast of Love," in Milton B. Singer, ed. *Krishna: Myths, Rites, and Attitudes* (Chicago: University of Chicago Press), pp. 200–212.

1. What patterns do the anthropologist see when he attends his second Holi festival? In what ways are the usual rules of society overturned during the festival?

C H A P T E R

T H R E E

THE EARLY HISTORY
AND RELIGION OF INDIA

*Always [in India] there is an attempt to understand and adapt
the new and harmonize it with the old.*

Jawaharlal Nehru

The Hindu religion and civilization was created by the mingling of two
groups of people in prehistorical times. The first group are known as the
Harappans, after the civilization they founded. The second group, who
invaded India many centuries later, called themselves the *Aryas* (Aryans).
In their appearance and in their outlook on life, these two peoples were
strikingly different. But in time they learned to live together and created a
unified culture that has lasted for thousands of years.

Evidence of the Harappan civilization of India was first discovered in
the early 20th century as workers were laying a railroad track in the
Punjab. Archeologists began to search for further evidence of ancient
settlements and soon realized that they were uncovering the remains of a
large and prosperous civilization. They also realized that the Harappans
had followed a pattern of development quite similar to that of other ancient
societies throughout the world. The discovery of the Harappan civilization
has contributed to our understanding of this pattern and has also revealed
many details about the particular character of the Harappans.

THE EVOLUTION OF CIVILIZATION

The word *civilization* comes from the Latin word *civitas*, meaning "city." As the first city builders discovered, human life can be greatly enhanced when a group of people find a way to cooperate with one another, and to pool their skills and experience. Through such cooperation and sharing, the basic needs of each individual—such as for food, clothing, shelter, and defense against enemies—can be supplied more efficiently.

City living is a fairly advanced or late stage in the history of human development; it cannot take place until people have discovered the art of agriculture. This important discovery—that food plants can be planted and harvested—brought about an immediate transformation wherever it took place. It meant that people could build permanent settlements instead of following the migrations of animals over the open plains. And since farmers can produce food more efficiently than hunter-gatherers, it was no longer necessary for everyone to share in the task of food gathering. As village settlements grew up, various specialties such as metalworking, weaving, and pottery making evolved. These crafts and skills greatly enhanced the quality of life for everyone.

In discussing a civilization, developments in technology are often used as a convenient way to define its various stages. The art of metalworking, in particular, is considered an important landmark. The skills needed to extract metal from ore and to fashion it into usable objects are quite sophisticated and require a great deal of cooperation and sharing of information. The end results of this effort—tools and weapons made of bronze or iron—are a vast improvement over those fashioned from pieces of flint. Thus, the Bronze or Iron Age of a society is considered to be a significant evolution from the Stone Age.

The words *civil* and *citizen* indicate another facet of civilization. In nomadic societies, tribal (family) loyalties are the basis of most customs and rules that people live by. But as villages and towns grew up, people had to learn to function as part of a larger group. Laws, institutions, and a central government provided a way to accomplish this transition.

In most early societies, a king or priest was recognized as a supreme authority by the group as a whole. Sometimes, the absolute power of the king or high priest was tempered by written laws. But whatever form the central government took, its role was the same. The government enforced the laws and rules that guided people in their daily interactions, settled disputes and punished transgressors, regulated day-to-day economic affairs, and mobilized the society's resources for common needs such as defense.

Each human civilization has produced a list of glowing achievements—in technology, fine arts, and workable institutions. These achievements are the product of long experience. In examining the artifacts of a civilization, it is possible to see something of the unique outlook that a group of people developed as they adapted themselves to a particular climate and found ways to overcome the many adversities they faced.

THE HARAPPAN CIVILIZATION OF THE INDUS VALLEY

The ancient civilization of the Indus valley is named after Harappa, one of its major cities. There is evidence that several different peoples contributed to this civilization. One of them were the *Australoids*, the same ethnic group as the *aborigines* of Australia. Another were the *Dravidians*, the ancestors of the Tamil peoples of South India.

The Harappan Empire

The Harappan society of the Indus River valley began to flourish about 2300 B.C. At this early date, the Harappans had evolved all of the arts associated with civilization. They had learned how to create permanent dwellings with baked mud bricks and to make tools with bronze. They were skilled pottery makers and textile weavers, and had even invented a system of writing. (The Harappans' script has not yet been deciphered, so we do not know if they used it to communicate their learning and ideas to others. However, it undoubtedly facilitated the business of government and commerce.)

Two of the principal sites of the Harappan civilization are Harappa, in what is now the Punjab, and Mohenjo-daro, in the Sind region. The civilization also included many other smaller towns and villages—about a hundred have been uncovered so far. In all, it was a sizable empire, extending the length of the Indus valley (about 1000 miles) north to south and into Baluchistan to the west. To the east, it extended to a site near Delhi, about 200 miles past the present-day Indian border. During the greatest period of the Harappan civilization—about 2300 to 1750 B.C.—the ancient civilizations of Mesopotamia and Egypt were also flourishing. In Mesopotamia, a number of Harappan objects have been found, indicating that the two civilizations carried on trade with each other.

Harappa, Mohenjo-daro, and other smaller cities are almost identical in plan. Each has a citadel (a fortress on a high platform) and streets laid out in a neat, rectangular pattern. For at least five and a half centuries, houses and streets were built according to a central plan, and even the bricks used in construction were of the same exact measure. This kind of continuity is quite remarkable, and scholars have arrived at several explanations. First, it seems that the Harappans were a very conservative

Sites of Harappan Towns and Villages, c. 2300–1750 B.C.

people who did not easily accept changes in their traditional way of life. Also, it is likely that there was a central authority, or government, which ensured that building standards were maintained throughout the empire. Some people have found it easy to imagine that this same authority might have imposed a systematic control over its citizens' lives.

In one section of the Harappan cities, there are large houses for the more prosperous citizens—all of the same plan, with rooms built around an open courtyard. Most larger houses had indoor plumbing and a fresh-water well. The workers had smaller, barracklike dwellings, separated from the rest of the town by a wall. In each city, there were large halls for storing grain, with air ducts beneath the floor to keep the stores fresh. In Mohenjo-daro, one of the largest buildings was an elaborate bath house with a pool that may have been used for ritual bathing.

Some of the most important clues about Harappan life were found in the clay seals that people used to label their merchandise. The seals contain most of the examples of Harappan writing that have been found. On the reverse side of the seals, and in other works of art, Harappan artists have provided many clues about their everyday life and religious beliefs. Nearly all of these images have striking parallels with Indian life today. In figurines and drawings, women are shown wearing necklaces, bangles, and earrings of the same styles that are worn today. The dhoti and shawl— traditional men's wear—are also shown. Adults are shown playing a game that may be an early version of chess, with movable pieces on a square board. There is also a pair of dice, indicating that gambling took place. One of the most surprising images is that of a horned man or god surrounded by animals. This figure may be an early representation of the god Shiva. There are also many images that may be interpreted as mother-goddess figures. In some portraits, Harappan artists merged the features of animal and plant life, just as later Indian artists did: there is a bull-elephant, for instance, and a horned tree-spirit.

Around 1750 B.C., the Harappan civilization experienced a sudden decline; many of the towns were abandoned, and several groups of more primitive peoples began to occupy them. Coincidentally, this was about

The ruins of a large bath house and pool at Mohenjo-daro give an indication of the Harappans' construction methods. The pool is thought to have been used for ritual bathing.

Seal drawings provide many clues about the Harappans' life style and beliefs. This figure is thought to depict a yogi—possibly a god—in his meditations.

the time that Aryan tribes from beyond the mountains were migrating into India. Until recently, most scholars believed that the invading Aryans had destroyed the Harappan cities and created a new civilization in their place. This is the view that the Aryans themselves provided. However, archeologists discovered that the Aryans' accounts did not quite match the facts. Except for Mohenjo-daro, most of the cities uncovered so far do not show the usual signs of a sudden attack. At some locations, there is evidence to suggest that a sudden flood drove the inhabitants away. In other areas, there may have been a plague, or farmers may simply have exhausted the soil. Thus, it seems that the Harappan civilization was already in decline when the Aryans arrived. But India's earliest peoples did not disappear entirely. In time, their beliefs and values helped to shape the developing religion known as Hinduism.

THE INDO-EUROPEANS AND THE ARYANS

In the late 18th century, a British scholar studying in India discovered that there are many similarities between Sanskrit, the ancient language of the Aryans, and the languages spoken in the Western world such as English,

Greek, German, and the Romance languages. Only one theory could explain these similarities: the languages, and the people who spoke them, must have descended from one "parent." This ancient people—the distant ancestors of many of the peoples of Europe and of western Asia— were given the name *Indo-Europeans*. After finding out that the Indo-Europeans existed, scholars again used language studies to follow their movements. By tracing the vocabulary changes that occurred in Indo-European languages, it was possible to estimate when the Indo-Europeans had lived together as one people and when the different tribes had separated from one another. Other clues, such as archeological finds, were also used in this detective work.

Most scholars now believe that the original home of the Indo-Europeans was to the north—possibly the steppe lands of southern Russia. Beginning as early as 2500 B.C., the Indo-Europeans began to migrate. Several tribes invaded Italy and Greece, mingled with the original inhabitants of those areas, and helped to create the civilizations of ancient Rome and Greece. One tribe, the Celts, traveled as far west as Ireland, while the tribes known as the Gauls and the Germans settled in France and central Europe. The Aryans split into two groups. One invaded ancient Persia (now Iran), and the other descended into India, perhaps around 1500 B.C.

The Aryans

The people who called themselves the *Aryas* ("noble ones") were a nomadic, warlike people. They were capable of destroying cities but had not yet learned how to live in them. Instead, they lived in temporary villages, or camps, and measured their wealth in cattle. One scholar has provided this view of their culture:

> They were a vigorous, fun-loving people whose amusements were chariot-racing, gambling, and fighting. . . . The outstanding characteristic of the Aryan tribes was their mobility. When they pushed into Italy, Greece, Persia, and India they acquired more civilization than they brought, but they always contributed the ingredient of enthusiasm.[1]

But even though the Aryans were slow to adopt the "civilized" life of city dwellers, they did develop certain arts that interested them. For example, they had mastered the skills of metalworking and carpentry and were able to make weapons that were far superior to those of other ancient peoples. One of their proudest achievements was a horse-drawn chariot, built with

---

1. Troy Wilson Organ, *Hinduism* (New York: Barron's, 1974), p. 49.

spoked wheels, which was lighter and faster than other vehicles. Another skill that the Aryans—and other Indo-Europeans—developed was the art of storytelling. To commemorate their exploits in battle and the deeds of their slain heroes, they composed and recited epic poems at their tribal gatherings. The *Iliad* and the *Odyssey* are examples of this art: they were created by the Indo-Europeans who settled in ancient Greece. In India, the Aryans created the *Mahabharata* and the *Ramayana*. These epics have provided much of the information that we have concerning the Aryans' life in India and the development of the Hindu religion.

The Aryans did not adopt the art of writing until many centuries after they invaded India, yet the literature they created in ancient times has survived to the present day. They were able to accomplish this feat by composing their sacred hymns and epic adventure stories in measured, rhyming verses. Because rhymes are easier to memorize than prose, priests and storytellers were able to compose lengthy works and teach them to others. In each generation, pupils spent years memorizing a body of literature so that they could in turn pass it on. Some works, including the *Mahabharata*, were added to and embroidered over the centuries. But the *Vedas*, the ancient hymns of the Aryan priests, were preserved as originally composed. Pupils believed that they had a sacred duty to repeat each verse exactly as they had learned it, for otherwise the "magic" it worked might be lost.

THE GROWTH OF THE HINDU RELIGION

The religious tradition known as *Hinduism* was created through the merging of two very different civilizations. The Harappans were a settled, agricultural people. It is believed that they worshiped deities—both gods and goddesses—whom they associated with the earth's fertility. We can guess that they had also developed the art of meditation, because of the yogilike figures found on ancient Harappan seals. The Aryans had a quite a different view of religion and nature. Their pantheon of gods did not include any Mother Earth figures. Instead, their most popular gods were male warriors, who were associated with the sky rather than the earth.

As the Hindu religion grew, a way was found to reconcile the beliefs of these two cultures, and all traditions were accepted as valid. This process of merging two different ways of thought is known as *syncretism*, and it has been a central aspect of Hinduism from the beginning. An example of this process can be seen in the way the two societies thought about the cow. The ancient Harappans apparently worshiped the cow as a symbol of fertility: its image appears on Harappan seals and other works of art. The Aryans also venerated the cow because it was the basis of their economy.

A great many Harappan seals depict the distinctive *brahmani* cow, which is still held sacred in Hindu culture. Cows were also of central importance to the Aryans.

In the Hindu religion, the cow kept the symbolic importance it had held for both societies. As we have seen (Chapter 2), the cow came to be a symbol of veneration and respect for all forms of life.

The *Rig Veda*

The most ancient religious literature of the Aryans, the *Vedas*, were composed during the first thousand years of the Aryans' life in India. The Sanskrit word *veda* means "knowledge" or "wisdom," and Hindus today accept these works as their most sacred literature. There are four collections of verses known as *Vedas*. The oldest and most important is called the *Rig Veda*. Many of the 1028 verses in the *Rig Veda* are hymns of praise to the earliest Aryan gods and describe in detail their personalities and powers. Other verses are chants that brahman priests performed while conducting sacrifices to the gods.

The Early Aryan Society. The hymns of the *Rig Veda*, composed from about 1500 to 1200 B.C., reveal many details about the early society of the Aryans in India. At the beginning of the Vedic period, the Aryan tribes were loosely organized into three classes: priests, warriors, and common people. The early hymns indicate that these classes were not rigid, and people could freely move from one occupation to another. Gradually, however, the brahman, or priestly, class became much more important and exclusive. One of the last verses of the *Rig Veda* describes the division of society into the four *varnas*. (See Chapter 2.) By this time, the sudras had been incorporated into Aryan society as laborers, yet were excluded from religious ceremonies. The brahmans, on the other hand, had the highest possible status. It was their sacrifices, people believed, that kept the universe going.

The Gods of the Aryans. In the hymns of the *Rig Veda,* the Aryans reveal how they pictured their gods and what they expected from them. The most popular of the gods was Indra, god of storms and of battle: almost one-quarter of the hymns in the *Rig Veda* are devoted to him. Many people have viewed Indra as a portrait of the Aryans themselves:

> He was the personification of the exuberance of life, a boastful thunderbolt-throwing god, a slayer of dragons and a heavy drinker. . . . He was a paradigm [model] of the human qualities the Aryan most admired: vigor, enthusiasm, strength, courage, success in battle, gluttony and drunkenness. Indra slew both his brother and his father. He was a *svaraj* (a king by seizure), not a *samraj* (a king by right of inheritance). In other words, Indra was an upstart who gained sovereignty by force.[2]

One of the most famous hymns of the *Rig Veda* tells how Indra brought the gift of the rivers to the Aryans, and others tell how he destroyed the cities of their enemies. Another important god was Varuna, who represented law and divine order (*rita*). He was responsible for keeping the seasons in their proper order and for enforcing the moral laws of human society. Among the lesser gods, there were two who later became very important in Hinduism. One of these is Rudra, who was greatly feared as a destructive god and yet also had the ability to heal. Rudra is believed to be an early version of the god Shiva. Vishnu is another Vedic god who later became a central deity. A verse in the *Rig Veda* mentions his ability to bound to heaven in three giant steps.

The final verses of the *Rig Veda* indicate that people were questioning their old gods. Several of the hymns, for example, defend the worship of Indra—an indication that some people had doubts about him. There are also hymns which speculate that one divine spirit, or creator, had existed before all of the other gods.

---

2. Ibid., p. 51.

Vedic Sacrifices. To obtain the favor of the gods, the Aryans offered sacrifices of the things they considered most precious—usually cattle or *soma*. *Soma* was a plant, or possibly a mushroom, that grew in the Himalayas. When "sacrificed" by boiling, it yielded a golden nectar that caused intoxication and hallucinations. It was also believed to confer immortality on those who drank it and gave people the feeling of having godlike powers. Because it served as an intermediary between gods and humans in this way, Soma was worshiped as a god in its own right. Agni, or fire, the agent of many sacrifices, was also worshiped as a god. The god Agni was believed to be present in every kind of fire—in lightning, in fireplaces, and in the fires by which sacrifices were offered to the heavens. Today, this ancient god is still commemorated in Hindu marriage ceremonies: a central fire serves as a "witness" as the bride and groom are united.

The Brahmanas

After the *Rig Veda*, another group of religious texts called the *Brahmanas* was composed. In the *Brahmanas*, many new ceremonies are set forth that are intended to preserve the brahmans' purity and ensure the success of their sacrifices. The sacrifices were no longer aimed at pleasing the gods but were thought to be a kind of magic in themselves.

The many instructions contained in the Brahmanas indicate the complexity of the brahmans' rituals and the details that were thought to be essential to the success of a sacrifice. This passage, for instance, tells how to gather the grass that was strewn, or distributed, at a sacrificial site:

> For being used as strewing grass there should be tied up a bunch of *darbha* blades having a circumference equal to the one produced by joining the tips of nails [of the thumb and forefinger]—such is the view of some teachers. A bunch should be tied up of as many *darbha* blades as could be cut off in one stroke—such is the view of some teachers. . . . It should be tied up so as to be as thick as the handle of the sacrificial spoon—such is the view of some teachers. It should be tied up so as to be as thick as the thigh-bone—such is the view of some teachers. It should be tied up so as to be as thick as the thumb-joint—such is the view of some teachers. It should be tied up without being measured—such is the view of some teachers.[3]

During the period of the *Brahmanas* (about 900 to 500 B.C.), thousands of animals were sacrificed to bring about the priests' "magic." Yet, appar-

---

3. Wm. Theodore de Bary, ed., *Sources of Indian Tradition*, vol. 1 (New York: Columbia University Press, 1958), p. 23.

ently, the kings and warriors who supplied the cattle were disappointed with the results. The old answers no longer seemed enough, and people began to search for new wisdom. One result of this search was the collection of works known as the *Upanishads*.

APPROXIMATE DATES IN EARLY INDIAN HISTORY

2300 B.C.	First flourishing of the Harappan civilization of the Indus valley
1750 B.C.	Decline of the Harappan civilization
1500 B.C.	Arrival of the Aryans in the Indus valley; first hymns of the *Rig Veda* composed
1000 B.C.	Aryans move eastward to the Ganges valley; battle of the *Mahabharata*
900 B.C.	First *Brahmanas* composed
700–500 B.C.	*Upanishad* era
300 B.C.	*Ramayana* composed (based on a story that may have originated about 800 B.C.)
A.D. 200	Bhagavad Gita written

The Upanishads

The *Upanishads* were composed not by brahman priests but by the forest-dwelling hermits known as yogis. In some ways, the *Upanishads* built on the knowledge and beliefs of the sacred *Vedas*. For this reason, they are known as the *Vedanta*, or "end of the Vedas." But the *Upanishads* also represent a new way of thinking. To take note of this difference, the older religion of the Vedas and the Brahmanas is called *brahmanism*, while the *Upanishads* are considered to be the first step toward the religion and philosophy known as *Hinduism*. Hinduism was built on both traditions—brahmanism and the *Upanishads*—and later absorbed several others.

In the last verses of the *Rig Veda*, several of the hymn writers had begun searching for a single event or being that could explain all things. In the *Upanishads*, this search continued. The forest philosophers of the *Upanishads* each had a vision of the supreme spirit, or Self—also called Brahman, or God. As we have seen in Chapter 2, many of them hesitated to describe this vision: they did not want to say that the Self is specifically one thing or another because such descriptions would imply that it was *not* something else.

The revelation of the *Upanishads* is that the human soul, or atman, is identical with the Universal Soul. The *Upanishad* philosophers taught their students that in order to realize the "one ultimate reality"—the identity of atman and Brahman—they must first renounce all desires and attachment to the things of this world. They dwelt on the evil effects of karma—the clouding of the soul that comes about through any kind of action. The only true path to knowledge, they taught, was the one that they themselves had taken—a withdrawal from the world.

The Four Stages of Life (c. 500 B.C.)

During the *Upanishad* era, thousands of people left their homes and villages and took up a life of self-denial and religious searching. Many of them joined one of the ascetic sects that were forming at this time. (Two of the most popular of these, Buddhism and Jainism, will be discussed in Chapter 4.)

In an effort to stem this flight of young people from Hindu society, brahman priests put forth a doctrine called the *Four Stages of Life*. According to this life plan, an upper-caste Hindu must first fulfill his duties as a *student* in his early teens. Then it was time to marry and become a *householder*. After raising a family and contributing his skills to society, the householder might choose to retire from society and become a *forest-dweller*. (At this stage, his wife, now a grandmother, might choose to

In the final two stages of life, a Hindu may withdraw from family responsibilities to concentrate on personal salvation. Shown is a modern *sannyasin*, or religious seeker.

accompany him.) Finally, he could continue his spiritual search by giving up all possessions and becoming a *wandering ascetic*.

In describing the Four Stages of Life, Hindu law books acknowledged a person's right to seek individual salvation after other obligations had been fulfilled. This model of life has remained an influential ideal to the present day.

THE *MAHABHARATA*

The great Indian epic the *Mahabharata* is one of the most central documents of Hindu civilization. It started as the story of a specific historical event, a great war between two royal families. But as the tale was composed—a process that took eight centuries or more—a host of other myths, romances, folktales, and religious stories were incorporated into it. It came to be the longest epic in the world, with about 100,000 rhyming verses (200,000 lines).

There are hundreds of characters in the *Mahabharata*—including gods as well as humans—and numerous subplots. These have been the inspiration for many different forms of popular entertainment. Since ancient times, singer-dancers have acted out the stories of the epic in elaborate dramatic performances. Wandering poets and minstrels, painters and sculptors have also portrayed its themes. In modern times, the epic has been dramatized in films and in television serials that have reached audiences of many millions. The central characters and events of the *Mahabharata* are thus known to every Hindu and continue to serve as a guide to daily life.

The great war at the heart of the *Mahabharata* may have taken place around 1000 B.C. By this time, the Aryans had moved east to the Ganges valley and had begun to build cities and kingdoms. The name *Mahabharata* means "Great Bharata." Bharata was the name of one of India's most ancient kings, and the characters in the epic, the Kurus, were his descendants. Today, the name *Bharata* is still very important: it is the Hindi name for India.

One of the central themes of the *Mahabharata* is the moral conflict faced by the king Yudhishthira. In order to live up to his dharma as a kshatriya (warrior) and as a king, he must participate in a great war. However, there is another dharma that he must follow—that of his own conscience. His conscience tells him that nonviolence and truthfulness are the highest duties of man. But the god Krishna comes to earth and tells him that he must fulfill his caste dharma. At every turn, he struggles to do what is right but can never find a way that satisfies both the gods and himself. In the end, he becomes a tragic figure because he cannot resolve this conflict.

The Plot of the *Mahabharata*

The central plot of the *Mahabharata* concerns a dispute between two branches of the royal Kuru family over which should rule their kingdom. The two groups of cousins—the Pandavas and the Kauravas—have about an equal right to the throne. The blind king decides to divide the kingdom in half. One half will be ruled by his own hundred sons, the Kauravas, and the other by his five nephews, the Pandava brothers.

Of the five Pandava brothers, the most notable are Yudhishthira and Arjuna. Yudhishthira, sired by the god Dharma, is renowned for his wisdom and righteousness. Arjuna is known for his bravery and skill in archery.

Yudhishthira and his brothers rule their half of the kingdom fairly and are greatly loved by their subjects. But soon, Duryodhana, the eldest Kaurava brother, becomes jealous of them. Being a shrewd gambler, he challenges Yudhishthira to a game of dice. In this fateful game, Yudhishthira loses not only his kingdom, but also his wife, Draupadi. A compromise is worked out, and the Pandavas agree to give up their kingdom for 14 years.

After spending 14 years in the forest, the Pandavas return to claim their kingdom. But Duryodhana refuses to keep his part of the bargain. Yudhishthira's dharma as a warrior requires him to fight for his legacy, but he is reluctant to do so. He sends his guardian, the god Krishna, to plead with Duryodhana. But all is in vain. The two parties summon their forces for a massive war. While the armies are being arrayed on the battlefield, the famous dialogue of the Bhagavad Gita takes place (see text).

During the 18 days of the great war, all of the Kauravas are killed. The war-weary Yudhishthira becomes king but would prefer to retire to the forest and live the life of a hermit. Krishna, however, informs him that he cannot achieve salvation by living the life of a holy man; he must fulfill his dharma by remaining as king. He rules for 15 years and then finally retires to the forest with his wife and brothers.

Yudhishthira and his family begin to ascend the Himalayas toward heaven, and one by one they drop by the wayside. Finally, only Yudhishthira remains, accompanied by his loyal dog. The god Indra appears and offers to escort Yudhishthira to heaven if he will abandon his dog. (Dogs are considered unclean and are not permitted there.) But Yudhishthira refuses the offer, pointing out that it would be a sin to renounce a being who has been so loyal to him. Suddenly, the loyal dog reveals himself to be the god Dharma, Yudhishthira's own father. Indra then escorts him to heaven. But as soon as he enters heaven, Yudhishthira sees his old enemy Duryodhana feasting and enjoying himself. (Duryodhana, of course, has fulfilled his dharma as a warrior and king.) Then Yudhishthira learns that his own family is suffering in the shadows of hell. At this point, his patience breaks, and he curses the dharma of the gods. Because of this outburst, caused by his continued attachment to his family, Yudhishthira cannot achieve *samadhi*, or release. He must once again enter the round of existence.

THE BHAGAVAD GITA

The Bhagavad Gita was probably inserted into the *Mahabharata* several centuries after the first part of the epic was composed. It is a long conversation between the god Krishna and Arjuna that takes place at a critical point in the great war. As the two armies prepare for battle, Arjuna sees many of his relatives and old friends among the Kaurava warriors and feels that he cannot enter the fight. But Krishna, who is serving as Arjuna's charioteer, tells him that he must enter into battle and explains why. Then he goes on to explain the complexities of the Hindu religion. He reveals the various ways of knowing Brahman and how men and women must act in order to achieve *moksha*, or release. Finally, he lets Arjuna see a vision of Brahman and reveals all of the spendor of the universe.

In his long speech to Arjuna, Krishna states that there are three paths to salvation. The first is the one that Arjuna must take, of performing his caste dharma as a warrior. But Krishna warns that it is not enough simply to perform this duty. Arjuna must also maintain a pure state of mind as he does so, making sure that personal concerns do not enter his mind. "Do your duty, always; but without attachment," Krishna says. By acting in an unselfish, disinterested way, Arjuna can avoid the evil effects of karma and achieve spiritual realization. This path to salvation is called *karma yoga.*

Krishna then goes on to explain the other two paths to salvation. The second is that taken by the yogi—of meditating on an all-encompassing God. Finally, there is worship of a "personal" god. All three paths to salvation are legitimate, Krishna says: "Howsoever they approach Me, so do I welcome them, for the path men take from every side is Mine."

The Bhagavad Gita has the same importance to India as the New Testament in Western culture. Mahatma Gandhi referred to it as his "spiritual reference book," and it still fulfills this purpose for millions of Hindus today.

THE *RAMAYANA*

The *Ramayana*, India's second great epic, may be based on a story that originated about 800 B.C. By this time, the Aryans had cleared many of the jungle forests of the eastern Ganges valley and had begun to explore the lands to the south. Some scholars believe that Lanka, the island mentioned in the epic, is the present-day island of Sri Lanka. Others doubt that the Aryans could have traveled so far south at this early date.

Rama, the hero of the epic, is one of the most respected and beloved figures in Indian culture. He is not only a great king, but also is considered an *avatar*, or incarnation, of the god Vishnu.

The Plot of the *Ramayana*

The setting of the *Ramayana* is the kingdom of Kosala, in the Ganges valley. Rama is the eldest son of Dasaratha, the king of Kosala. Dasaratha decides to announce that Rama is the heir to his throne. The whole kingdom rejoices because Rama is well liked and respected. But Dasaratha's youngest wife suddenly decides that her son Bharata should be king. She asks Dasaratha to keep a promise that he once made to grant her any wish. He agrees. She then states her wish: Rama must be banished from the kingdom, and Bharata appointed as king. Dasaratha sorrowfully agrees to her demands. Rama gives away all his possessions and goes into exile, accompanied by his faithful wife, Sita, and his brother Lakshman. When Bharata hears of what his mother has done, he is greatly upset and tries to get Rama reinstated as heir to the throne. But Rama declines, saying that his father must keep the promise.

While Rama, Sita, and Lakshman are living in the forest, they make friends with the monkeys and other animals who live there. They also get to know the forest hermits and villagers. To help his new friends, Rama destroys some demons who have been bothering them. The great demon king Ravana, who lives in the faraway island of Lanka, decides to avenge the deaths of the demons. He comes to the forest in his flying chariot, kidnaps Sita, and takes her back to his island kingdom. Rama and Lakshman frantically search for Sita but cannot find a trace of her. Hanuman, a general among the monkeys, finally locates her on the island of Lanka. The demon Ravana has not harmed her but wants to take her as his wife.

Hanuman escorts Rama to Lanka. When they reach the island, a great battle ensues. Both Rama and Hanuman have supernatural powers, but so do the demon Ravana and his warriors. Ultimately, Rama is victorious.

After Ravana is defeated, Rama finds Sita. But their reunion is clouded by Rama's doubts about her innocence. Sita is greatly saddened and declares that she will throw herself upon a funeral pyre. The fire is built, and Sita enters it. But Agni, the fire god, rises up and declares her innocence. Rama is delighted at this news and gladly accepts her back.

Rama, Lakshman, and Sita return to their kingdom. Rama rules the kingdom wisely and justly, and everything goes well for a time. But then rumors begin to circulate that Sita was dishonored while she was held captive by Ravana. Rama knows that the rumors are untrue. But it is his duty to maintain peace in the kingdom. He therefore decides, sorrowfully, that Sita must be banished. Soon after her banishment, Sita gives birth to twin sons. Many years later, Rama and Sita are reunited. Sita is once again called on to prove that she has remained pure and blameless. She declares that she has never thought about anyone except Rama. Then, to prove her innocence, she calls for the earth to receive her. The earth opens up beneath her feet and takes her away. Rama is brokenhearted but continues to rule his kingdom for many years. At last, he ascends to heaven to be reunited with Sita, leaving his twin sons and Hanuman in charge of the kingdom.

The great epics are still the center of popular Hindu culture. In this village festival, the triumph of good over evil in the *Ramayana* is being reenacted. Queen Sita (in carriage at left) watches as the demon Ravana (center) receives his comeuppance; he will soon be set afire.

The *Ramayana* provides several important models for Hindu society. Rama is a perfect king, one who always thinks about the welfare of his subjects rather than his own happiness. In times of crisis, he sacrifices his personal life rather than fail in his duties as king. His wife, Sita, illustrates the Hindu ideal of a woman. She devotes herself to her husband, never putting her own interests ahead of his. Even when her husband makes a mistake, she supports him and obeys his wishes. Her dharma is fulfilled by this self-sacrifice rather than by any other qualities.

The animal characters in the *Ramayana* also contribute to its meaning and popularity. Hanuman, a resourceful monkey god who comes to Rama's aid, is one of the central characters of the epic.

SUMMARY

When the Aryans and the Harappans first encountered each other, they had little in common. Yet as their two cultures mingled, the dialogue between them resulted in a new synthesis. The first religion of the Aryans held that people could behave as they pleased and then appease the anger of the gods by offering them sacrifices. But by the time of the *Upanishads*, this idea no longer prevailed. The *Upanishad* philosophers taught that people must offer another kind of sacrifice: they must practice self-denial and fix their thoughts on Brahman.

In the developed religion of Hinduism, all of India's ancient traditions are considered legitimate. A person may worship one personal god, or several, or may worship God in the impersonal form of Brahman. Religion is a matter of individual conscience, or *svadharma*.

DISCUSSION AND ESSAY QUESTIONS

1. Imagine that you are a citizen of the ancient Harappan civilization and have a pen pal in Egypt or Mesopotamia. Write a letter (a) describing your civilization or (b) giving advice on how to cope with environmental or political problems. (Note: Egypt and Mesopotamia are also river-based civilizations.)

2. Compare and contrast the Harappans and the Aryans. What do we know about their "personalities" and life styles?

3. What was the basic message of the *Upanishad* philosophers?

4. The *Mahabharata* and the *Ramayana* are part of the "living tradition" of Hindu civilization. What does the phrase "living tradition" mean? Does your society have any historical heroes or events that still serve as an inspiration?

ADDITIONAL READINGS

Several English-language retellings of the Indian epics are now available. All of these are greatly condensed from the original versions.

Jean C. Carriere, ed., *The Mahabharata* (New York: Harper Collins, 1989). This is the screenplay for a popular film of the epic made by the director Peter Brook.

P. Lal, ed., *The Mahabharata of Vyasa* (Flushing, N.Y.: Asia Book Corp., 1980). A longer (400-page) version of the epic.

John Murdoch, ed., *The Mahabharata* (Columbia, Mo.: South Asia Books, 1986). A short, easy-to-read version of some of the main events of the *Mahabharata*.

William Buck, ed., *Ramayana* (New York: Mentor, 1978). A 350-page version of the epic, written in the style of a novel.

R. K. Narayan, ed., *Ramayana* (Harmondsworth, England: Penguin, 1977). One of India's most popular storytellers recounts some of the main episodes of the *Ramayana*.

HYMNS OF THE *RIG VEDA*

Indra, the god of war and of storms, won first place in the Aryan pantheon of gods during the early Vedic period. This hymn tells how Indra vanquished the demon Vritra, who took the form of a giant serpent. By killing Vritra, Indra freed the seven rivers (of the Punjab) and the cattle that Vritra had been withholding from the Aryan people. Some people have considered this hymn to be a celebration of the Aryans' own warlike character and success in battle. It is also a creation myth; that is, a story that explains how the world was brought into being.

Notes: *The word* mace *refers to Indra's war club—a thunderbolt.* Tvashtari *was the god who manufactured weapons. The* Panis *were a group of people whom the Aryans encountered in the Punjab region.*

How Indra Freed the Waters and the Cattle

Now I shall proclaim the mighty deeds of Indra, those foremost deeds that he, the wielder of the mace, has performed. He smashed the serpent. He released the waters. He split the sides of the mountains.

He smashed the serpent, which was resting on the mountain—for him Tvashtari had fashioned a mace that shone like the sun. Like lowing cattle, the waters, streaming out, rushed straight to the sea.

Eager, like a rutting bull, he took for his own the soma. He drank the soma in the three ceremonial cups. The Provider [Indra] took up his missile, the mace. He smashed him, the first-born of serpents. . . .

When you, Indra, smashed the first-born of serpents, you overcame even the tricks of the tricky. Then you brought forth the sun, the heaven, and the dawn, and since then you have never had a rival.

With his mace, that great murderous weapon, Indra smashed Vritra, the very great obstacle, whose shoulders were spread. Like branches hewn away by an axe, the serpent lies, embracing the earth. . . .

As he lay in that way, like a broken reed, the waters, consigning themselves to man, rushed over him. Whom Vritra in his greatness had once surrounded, at their feet now lay the serpent.

Before this the waters stood still—their husband had been the barbarian, their guardian, the serpent—entrapped like the cows by the Panis. Indra opened up the hidden exit for the waters when he smashed Vritra. . . .

Indra, holding the mace, is the king of both that which stands and moves, of the horned and the not-horned. So, as king, he rules over the peoples. As a rim the spokes of a wheel, he encompasses them.

Varuna, the guardian of order, inspired more fear than did Indra, who was considered a more "human" and friendly god. Varuna was believed to know everything, and was not easily pleased or flattered.
    Note: *The House of Clay was a gloomy underworld where sinners were believed to go.*

Hymn to Varuna

Let me not go to the House of Clay, O Varuna! Forgive, O gracious Lord, forgive! When I go tottering, like a blown-up bladder, forgive, O gracious Lord, forgive!

Holy One, in want of wisdom I have opposed you. Forgive, O gracious Lord, forgive! Though in the midst of waters, thirst has seized your worshiper. Forgive, O gracious Lord, forgive!

Whatever sin we mortals have committed against the people of the gods, if, foolish, we have thwarted your decrees, O god, do not destroy us in your anger!

The "Hymn of the First Man" is one of the most important hymns of the Rig Veda. *It describes the creation of the world and also tells how the caste system came into being. The creation of the world is likened to a sacrifice: the god who existed before all others divides himself to create the universe and all living things.*

Hymn of the First Man

From that all-embracing sacrifice were born the hymns and chants, from that the meters were born, from that the sacrificial spells were born.

Thence were born horses, and all beings with two rows of teeth. Thence were born cattle, and thence goats and sheep.

When they divided the Man, into how many parts did they divide him? What was his mouth, what were his arms, and what were his thighs and his feet called?

The brahman was his mouth, of his arms were made the warrior, his thighs became the vaishya, of his feet the sudra was born.

The moon arose from his mind, from his eye was born the sun, from his mouth Indra and Agni, from his breath the wind was born.

SOURCES: *Rig Veda:* "Indra" (1.32), trans. Joel Brereton;"Varuna" (7.89), trans. A. L. Basham; "First Man" (10.90), trans. A. L. Basham.

1. Contrast the personalities of Indra and Varuna. Why was Indra the more popular?
2. The "Hymn of the First Man" is considered to be central to Indian religion and culture. Why is this so? Describe the myth of creation that it provides. What attitudes and beliefs does this myth inspire?

THE *UPANISHADS*

The word Upanishad *means "sitting down face-to-face." The forest sages of the Upanishad age often engaged in an informal dialogue with their students, rather than delivering lectures.*

In the first dialogue excerpted here, a sage explains to his son, Svetaketu, the nature of Brahman.

That Art Thou, Svetaketu (Chandogya Upanishad)

In the beginning there was Existence alone—One only, without a second. He, the One, thought to himself: Let me be many, let me grow forth. Thus out of himself he projected the universe; and having projected out of himself the universe, he entered into every being. All that is has its self in him alone. Of all things he is the subtle essence. He is the truth. He is the Self. And that, Svetaketu, THAT ART THOU."

"Please, sir, tell me more about this Self."

"Be it so, my child.

"As the bees make honey by gathering juices from many flowering plants and trees, and as these juices reduced to one honey do not know from what flowers they severally come, similarly, my son, all creatures . . . know nothing of their past or present state, because of the ignorance enveloping them— know not that they are merged in him and that from him they came.

"Whatever these creatures are, whether a lion, or a tiger, or a boar, or a worm, or a gnat, or a mosquito, that they remain after they come back from dreamless sleep.

"All these have their self in him alone. He is the truth. He is the subtle essence of all. He is the Self. And that, Svetaketu, THAT ART THOU."

"Please, sir, tell me more about this Self." . . .

"Be it so. Bring a fruit of that Nyagrodha [fig] tree."

"Here it is, sir."

"Break it."

"It is broken, sir."

"What do you see?"

"Some seeds, extremely small, sir."

"Break one of them."

"It is broken, sir."

"What do you see?"

"Nothing, sir."

"The subtle essence you do not see, and in that is the whole of the Nyagrodha tree. Believe, my son, that that which is the subtle essence—in that have all things their existence. That is the truth. That is the Self. And that, Svetaketu, THAT ART THOU."

One of the last Upanishads *was composed by a sage known as Svetasvatara. Like the earlier sages, Svetasvatara saw Brahman as an all-pervading spirit. Yet he chooses to meditate upon certain concrete aspects, such as the beauty and variety of the natural world.*

The Supreme, the Great One (Svetasvatara Upanishad)

He moves fast, though without feet. He grasps everything, though without hands. He sees everything, though without eyes. He hears everything, though without ears. He knows all that is, but no one knows him. . . .

Thou are the fire, thou art the sun, thou art the air, thou art the moon, thou art the starry firmament, thou art Brahman Supreme; thou art the waters—thou, the creator of all.

Thou art woman, thou art man, thou art the youth, thou art the maiden, thou art the old man tottering with his staff; thou facest everywhere.

Thou art the dark butterfly, thou art the green parrot with red eyes, thou art the thunder cloud, the seasons, the seas. Without beginning art thou, beyond time, beyond space. Thou art he from whom sprang the three worlds. . . .

Forgetting his oneness with thee, bewildered by his weakness, full of sorrow is man; but let him look close on thee, know thee as himself, O Lord, most worshipful, and behold thy glory—Lo, all his heavy sorrow is turned to joy.

SOURCE: *The Upanishads,* trans. Swami Prabhavananda and Frederick Manchester (New York: Mentor, 1975), pp. 68–70, 123–125.

1. Why does Uddalaka keep telling his son "That art thou"? What message is he trying to convey? Is Uddalaka's method of teaching effective?
2. What manifestations of Brahman does Svetasvatara focus on? How does a person feel before and after he finds union with the Self?

THE *MAHABHARATA*

This passage from the Mahabharata *describes one of the many episodes in which Yudhishthira must resolve a conflict between caste dharma and his own conscience. His conscience informs him that he must always tell the truth. Yet, at a critical point in the battle, Krishna convinces him that his caste dharma requires that he tell a lie: the fortunes of the Pandavas are at stake.*

Note: Drona was once the Pandavas' beloved friend and mentor; it was he who taught them their skills in archery. But on this day he commands the Kaurava forces and is thus their primary enemy. Bhima is one of the Pandava brothers. He is noted for his brute strength.

Yudhishthira's Lie

As long as Ashvatthaman, the son of Drona, lived it came to be believed that his father would never be conquered, for his love and hope for his son were sufficient to keep him filled with courage and energy. Bhima, therefore, being bent on the defeat of Drona, selected an elephant named Ashvatthaman and slew it with his own hands, and then threw himself in his might on the Kuru front in the neighborhood of Drona, shouting: "Ashvatthaman is dead! Ashvatthaman is dead!"

Drona heard the words, and for the first time his stout heart sank. Yet not easily would he accept the news that was to be his death-blow. Unless it was confirmed by Yudhishthira, who was, he said, incapable of untruth, even for the sovereignty of the three worlds, he would never believe that Ashvatthaman was dead. Making his way then to Yudhishthira, Drona asked him for the truth, and Yudhishthira answered in a clear voice: "Yes, O Drona! Ashvatthaman is dead!" And this he said three times. But after the word Ashvatthaman he said indistinctly each time the words "the elephant." These words, however, Drona did not hear. And up to this time the horses and wheels of Yudhishthira's chariot had never touched the earth. But after this untruth they came down a hand's-breadth and drove along the ground. Then Drona, in his despair for the loss of his son, became unable to think of his divine weapons. Seeing, then, that the time had come, he charged [instructed] the great bowmen who were about him as to how they were to conduct the battle, and laying down his own weapons, he sat down on the front of his chariot fixing his mind on itself. At that very moment Dhrishtadyumna, the Pandava general, had seized his sword and leapt to the ground in order to attack Drona in personal combat. But before he touched him the soul of the Kuru general had gone forth, and to the few who had vision it appeared for a moment as if the sky held two suns at once. . . . Then darkness came on, and wearily and mournfully all departed to their quarters.

SOURCE: Ananda K. Coomaraswamy and Sister Nivedita, eds., *Myths of the Hindus and Buddhists* (New York: Dover, 1967), pp. 184–186.

1. What happens to Yudhishthira's chariot after he mumbles his lie? Does the lie have the effect that Krishna intended?
2. What happens to Drona's soul after he dies?

THE BHAGAVAD GITA

The dialogue of the Bhagavad Gita comes at a critical point in the story of the Mahabharata. *Seeing his grandfather and other friends among the ranks of the "enemy," Arjuna feels that he cannot go to battle. Yet Arjuna is the best warrior among the Pandavas, and their cause depends on him. He appeals to his guardian, the god Krishna, for advice. Krishna tells him that he must enter into battle—it is his dharma—and reassures him that he will not really be killing anyone.*

Next, Krishna explains how a person may avoid the evil effects of karma, or actions, by being indifferent to their outcome. The technique of performing one's duties with an attitude of detachment is known as karma yoga.

The Warrior Slays Not, and Is Not Slain

Your words are wise, Arjuna, but your sorrow is for nothing. The truly wise mourn neither for the living nor for the dead.

There was never a time when I did not exist, nor you, nor any of these kings. Nor is there any future in which we shall cease to be.

Some say this Atman is slain, and others call it the slayer. They know nothing. How can it slay, or who shall slay it?

Dream not you do the deed of the killer, dream not the power is yours to command it. . . .

Not wounded by weapons, not burned by fire, not dried by the wind, not wetted by water: such is the Atman.

Desireless Action

Realize that pleasure and pain, gain and loss, victory and defeat, are all one and the same: then go into battle. Do this and you cannot commit any sin.

I have explained to you the true nature of the Atman. Now listen to the method of Karma Yoga. If you can understand and follow it, you will be able to break the chains of desire which bind you to your actions. . . .

Perform every action with your heart fixed on the Supreme Lord. Renounce attachment to the fruits [of action]. Be even-tempered in success and failure; for it is this evenness of temper which is meant by yoga.

Work done with anxiety about results is far inferior to work done without such anxiety, in the calm of self-surrender. . . . They who work selfishly for results are miserable.

SOURCE: Bhagavad Gita, trans. Swami Prabhavananda and Christopher Isherwood (New York: Mentor, 1972), pp. 36–37, 39–41.

1. Why should Arjuna not grieve for his slain friends and relatives or consider himself a killer?
2. What attitude should Arjuna have as he fulfills his caste dharma?

AMERICAN AND ENGLISH POETS INFLUENCED BY HINDU THOUGHT

Up to the late 18th century, most Western writers expressed a view of the world that centered on human beings and their activities. But after the Upanishads *and the* Bhagavad Gita *were translated into English, a distinctly new attitude appeared. Those who were influenced by these works began to express a new view of the natural world and of humanity's place within it. What Indian influences can you detect in the following works?*

Brahma
Ralph Waldo Emerson

If the red slayer thinks he slays,
or the slain thinks he is slain,
They know not well the subtle ways
I keep, and pass and turn again.

Far or forgot to me is near;
Shadow and sunlight are the same;
The vanished gods to me appear;
And one to me are shame and fame.

They reckon ill who leave me out;
When they fly, I am the wings;
I am the doubter and the doubt,
and I the hymn the Brahmin sings.

The strong gods pine for my abode,
And pine in vain the sacred seven;
But thou, meek lover of the good,
Find me, and turn thy back on heaven.

Leaves of Grass
Walt Whitman

With music strong I come, with my cornets and my drums,
I play not marches for accepted victors only, I play marches for conquer'd
  and slain persons.
Have you heard that it was good to gain the day?
I also say it is good to fall, battles are lost in the same spirit in which they
  are won. . . .

Have you outstript the rest? are you the President?
It is a trifle, they will more than arrive there every one,
and still pass on. . . .

Clef Poem
Walt Whitman

A vast similitude interlocks all
All souls, all living bodies though they be ever so different,
  or in different worlds,
All gaseous, watery, vegetable, mineral processes,
  the fishes, the brutes
All identities that have existed or may exist
  on this globe or any globe
This vast similitude spans them, and always
  has spann'd,
And shall for ever span them
  and completely hold and enclose them.

If

Rudyard Kipling

If you can keep your head when all about you
  Are losing theirs and blaming it on you,
If you can trust yourself when all men doubt you,
  But make allowance for their doubting too . . .
If you can dream—and not make dreams your master;
  If you can think—and not make thoughts your aim;
If you can meet with Triumph and Disaster
  And treat those two impostors just the same . . .
If neither foes nor loving friends can hurt you,
  If all men count with you, but none too much . . .
Yours is the Earth and everything that's in it,
  And—which is more—you'll be a Man, my son!

1. Who is the speaker, or narrator, in Emerson's poem "Brahma"?
2. Do the poets succeed in getting beyond a self-centered or human-centered point of view?
3. Describe the message of one of these poems, and tell what Hindu concept or scripture may have inspired it.

CHAPTER

FOUR

BUDDHISM AND JAINISM

All men love life; remember that you are like unto them, and do not kill, nor cause slaughter.

The Buddha

The era in which Buddhism and Jainism arose—the sixth and fifth centuries B.C.—witnessed many remarkable events in the ancient world. It was a time of unceasing warfare, yet also a time when people realized they should follow their "higher" instincts and find new ways to deal with one another. Throughout the ancient world, religious leaders expressed this new way of thinking. In Israel, the Old Testament prophets no longer prayed to a "jealous and angry God" who called for the destruction of their enemies. Instead, in the midst of great troubles, they began to speak of a universal God who expected right conduct from all peoples. Farther east, Cyrus the Great, ruler of Persia, was following the new Zoroastrian religion. Zoroastrians believe in one universal God and express tolerance toward other religions and peoples. In war-torn China, Confucius (c. 551–479 B.C.) preached the Golden Rule of conduct and suggested that no lasting benefits can be gained by oppressing others. In India, as we have seen, the *Upanishad* teachings about Brahman had radically changed the Aryans' view of the world. Though the Aryans still went to war, they no longer believed that tribal gods such as Indra were protecting their troops.

Buddhism and Jainism—the religions we will discuss in this chapter—continued to build on the wisdom of the *Upanishads*. They were founded on the belief that reality is not what it appears to be, nor is human fulfillment to be achieved by grasping for power and riches. Instead, they taught, people must look further to discover their real interests. A truly wise person recognizes his or her unity with others and does not behave in a selfish manner.

Buddhism and Jainism are unusual among India's religions because their founders are known by name. Siddhartha Gautama, better known as the *Buddha*, and Vardhamana Mahavira, the founder of Jainism, were greatly venerated in their own time. Moreover, their first disciples preserved many details and legends about their lives so that people could revere them as individuals. Just as Christianity was shaped by stories concerning the life of Jesus, Buddhism and Jainism were given form by the life stories of their founders.

At times, Buddhism and Jainism have been viewed as sects, or divisions, in the Hindu religion. But both religions have also had a long independent life of their own. In the centuries after the Buddha's death, Buddhism spread beyond India's borders and became a major world religion.

HINDU SOCIETY IN THE SIXTH CENTURY B.C.

By the sixth century B.C., Indian civilization had little resemblance to the nomadic society depicted in the Vedas. The Aryans had cleared and settled the forests of the Ganges valley and had created great cities and kingdoms all across northern India. There were at least 16 sizable kingdoms, extending from Afghanistan to Bengal. Some of the kingdoms were ruled by maharajas ("great kings"), and others were "republics" that had a more democratic form of government.

Though the kingdoms of northern India were growing and prospering, many people were expressing a spirit of bitterness and disillusionment. We do not know exactly what brought about this mood. But it may have been caused, in part, by the frequent warfare among the northern kingdoms.

During the sixth century B.C., the idea spread that the rise of one all-powerful king could eliminate the warfare and devastation caused by rivalries between kings. The hoped-for universal king was known by the name *Chakravartin*, from the word *chakra*, meaning "wheel," and *vartin*, meaning "he who turns." People imagined that the Chakravartin would extend his rule in an ever-expanding circle until he controlled the whole world from his hub at the center.

Criticisms of the Hindu Religion

By the sixth century B.C., the *Upanishad* teachings about the soul, karma, and reincarnation had been accepted by orthodox Hindus throughout northern India. But at the same time, people were expressing many doubts and reservations about their religion. The number of sects within Hinduism multiplied as people sought answers for their doubts and uncertainties. Then, toward the end of the century, two new religious leaders arose to challenge India's ancient religion. In order to understand the appeal of Buddhism and Jainism, it is helpful to know something about the criticisms that people were voicing at this time.

The Materialists. The most radical critics of Hinduism were a little-known group known as the *materialists*. They referred to the sacred Vedas as the "vomit of brahmans" and even rebelled against the *Upanishad* teachings. They announced that the only end, or goal, of human life is to enjoy the pleasures of the senses and denied that there is such a thing as a soul. Instead, they said, everything is made up of four basic elements: earth, water, fire, and air. Thus, anyone who believes in abstract ideas such as *karma* or *immortality* is simply being foolish.

> There is no [merit in] almsgiving, sacrifice, or offering, no result or ripening of good or evil deeds. There is no passing from this world to the next. There is no afterlife. . . . Man is formed of the four elements; when he dies earth returns to the aggregate of earth, water to water, fire to fire, and air to air, while the senses vanish into space. . . . They are fools who preach almsgiving, and those who maintain the existence of immaterial [spiritual] categories speak vain and lying nonsense. When the body dies both fool and wise alike are cut off and perish. They do not survive after death.[1]

Other critics did not doubt such basic doctrines as the soul, karma, and reincarnation, but they did question the authority of the brahman priestly caste.

Criticisms of "Brahmanism." In the sixth century B.C., the sacred texts of Hinduism were still taught in Sanskrit, a language that people no longer spoke in everyday life. This meant that only privileged members of the brahman and kshatriya castes were able to study and fully understand the message of their religion. Moreover, brahman priests spent much of their

---

1. Ajita Kesakambala, quoted in Ainslie T. Embree, ed., *Sources of Indian Tradition*, 2d ed., vol. 1 (New York: Columbia University Press, 1988), p. 46.

time debating the fine points of theology rather than explaining it to others. (For instance, many hours were spent in discussing the exact means by which souls migrated to other bodies.)

Ironically, both Siddhartha Gautama and Vardhamana Mahavira belonged to princely families and were thus entitled to all of the benefits of their religion. Yet both men found the brahmans' sacrifices and rituals to be empty and meaningless. They taught their followers that salvation depended on their own efforts, not on the guidance of priests. Both the Buddha and Mahavira spoke to people in their own languages, rather than in Sanskrit. Moreover, neither man would engage in scholarly debates or provide any comments on "metaphysical" questions, such as the nature of God and the infinity of the universe.

THE LIFE AND TEACHINGS OF THE BUDDHA

The teachings of Siddhartha Gautama, the Buddha (c. 563–483 B.C.) were not written down until long after his death but were preserved in the memories of his disciples. It is likely that many legends about the Buddha are based on real incidents, while others arose after his lifetime. In one sense, it does not matter exactly which of the many legends concerning the Buddha are historically true: all of them have shaped and defined the beliefs of Buddhists to this day. Most Buddhist sects agree on the basic events of the Buddha's life, and each would also add many more details and legends.

The Story of the Buddha's Life

Siddhartha Gautama, the future Buddha, was born into a royal family who lived near the Himalayan foothills. (His father ruled one of the small "republics" that had not yet been absorbed by the great maharajas.) After his birth, it is said, his father asked some fortunetellers to predict the future course of his baby son's life. They agreed that the boy would have a remarkable life but said that he had two possible destinies. If he pursued a worldly course, he would become a Chakravartin, or world ruler. And if he pursued a spiritual life, he would become a world redeemer. The king preferred the first destiny for his son and did everything in his power to insulate him from the cares and sorrows of the world. According to legend, he went so far as to provide 40,000 dancing girls for his son's amusement. (A possibly more accurate account is this statement later attributed to the Buddha: "I wore garments of silk and my attendants held a white umbrella over me.")

Legends surrounding the Buddha's birth describe it as a miraculous event. This depiction, showing the future Buddha emerging painlessly from his mother's side, dates from the second century A.D.

The future Buddha became a strikingly handsome young man who, at the age of 16, was married to a beautiful princess. After about a dozen years, the princess, named Yasodhara, bore her husband a son, Rahula.

Even after his marriage, the servants of the prince did their best to shield him from all unpleasantness. But occasionally, they failed to clear the road carefully enough when he went riding. One day, he saw a man bent with age, leaning on a cane; another day, a diseased person; another day, a corpse; and finally, a religious wanderer with a begging bowl. After seeing the first three sights, he found it impossible to forget that all living things are subject to age, disease, and death. The fourth sight, the man with the begging bowl, showed him the course he must take. The pleasures of court life no longer attracted him, and even the birth of a son gave him no delight. Late one night, when he was about 29 years of age, he said goodbye to his sleeping wife and infant son and departed from the palace.

In the episode known as the "Great Going Forth," the future Buddha departed from his kingdom with a trusted servant. When he was far from the palace, he exchanged his fine robes for a hermit's rags and sent the servant back to inform his father. For several years, he studied the wisdom of the *Upanishads* with a sage. But this study failed to provide the enlightenment he was seeking. Then he joined a group of five ascetics for several years and fasted so rigorously that he nearly died of starvation. When all of these sufferings still did not lead to enlightenment, he decided to follow a "middle path" and eat a moderate amount of food. The five ascetics left him in disgust.

At around the age of 35, the future Buddha traveled south to Magadha and settled in a park near the town of Gaya. He sat down under a pipal tree and resolved that he would not move until he had achieved enlightenment. As he sat meditating, he was showered with temptations but remained motionless. On the seventh day, he achieved enlightenment. He saw a vision of his past lives, of the sorrow of the world, and of what people must do to overcome their suffering. At this point, he became a *Buddha*, meaning "Enlightened One."

For several days, the Buddha remained in a state of ecstasy, which he called *nirvana*. He later described *nirvana*, which means "blowing out," as the absence of all selfish thoughts and desires; a state of absolute calm and tranquility. After reaching nirvana, the Buddha—technically—no longer had an individual personality, because he had overcome all thoughts of "me" or "mine." However, his followers did not quite see it in this way. In their view, he had achieved a status higher than that of the gods.

The Buddha's enlightenment is considered to be different from the *moksha* of the forest philosophers, for two reasons. First, he did not speak of *atman* or of *Brahman* and would not discuss the relationship between the two. And second, he did not lose all concern with worldly matters after his enlightenment. Instead, he emerged with a desire to help others along the path he had taken.

The first people to hear the Buddha's revelations were his former friends, the ascetics. Finding them at a deer park at Sarnath, near Benares, he unfolded his message. This legendary first sermon set forth his discovery of the Four Noble Truths: that all life is suffering; that the cause of suffering is desire, or craving; that the way to overcome suffering is to eliminate all cravings; and that this cure can be accomplished by following the Eightfold Path (more on this shortly).

The Four Noble Truths, together with the Buddha's later teachings, are called the *Dhammapada*. (*Dhamma* is the Pali language word for "dharma.") The Buddha's followers refer to their religion not as Buddhism but as the *Dhamma*, or Law. From their point of view, the *Dhammapada* describes the basic truths of human life and sets forth guidelines for people to follow. The Buddha's first preaching became known as The Setting in Motion of the Wheel of the Law.

The Buddha's fame soon spread throughout the Ganges valley, and he spent the next 45 years teaching the many disciples who gathered to hear him speak. He soon established a monastic order in which people could concentrate on following the Eightfold Path. Buddhist monks took a vow of poverty, chastity, and nonviolence and wore yellow robes—the traditional color of outcasts and criminals—to signify their withdrawal from the world. In their life style, they followed a "middle way"—eating one meal a day and avoiding extreme fasts and penances. For eight months of the year, they traveled around the country, begging for their daily food and telling people about the *Dhammapada*. Then, during the monsoon season, they settled in one place—usually a refuge provided by a wealthy patron— to rest and meditate.[2] The Buddha guided the practical and spiritual affairs of his monks and was also available to those who sought his advice from the outside world. Numerous stories indicate that he showed equal respect to everyone who approached him, whether king or outcast. But because he devoted most of his attention to his monastic order, it seemed that his message was intended mainly for those who wished to withdraw from the world.

At first, the Buddha did not allow women to join his order. But toward the end of his life, he yielded to entreaties and created a separate order of Buddhist nuns.

Shortly before the Buddha died, he explained to his pupils that his body had become like a worn-out cart that could be patched together only with much trouble. His last advice to them reportedly was: "All composite things pass away. Strive onward vigilantly."

Buddhist Shrines. The towns and sites associated with the Buddha's life have been visited by millions of pilgrims from all over the world. The central shrines are the site of Kapilavastu, the town of his birth; the Bodhi (Enlightenment) Tree at Gaya, where he attained nirvana; the deer park at Sarnath, where he preached his first sermon; and a park near Kusinagara, the scene of his death. (See map on page 102.) Buddhist monasteries are usually situated near a grove of sacred trees and often include a *stupa*, or rounded shrine building.

The Four Noble Truths

Many of the Buddha's followers felt that he had a vast wisdom that he did not try to communicate. Instead, he saw his mission as being immediate and urgent: to diagnose the ills of the world and to propose a cure. Because

---

2. After the Buddha's death, however, many monks gave up the period of homeless wandering and settled in one place year round.

A common memorial to the Buddha is a *stupa* building, modeled on the burial mounds of Aryan warriors. The stupa commemorates the Buddha's *paranirvana*, or final death.

Many *stupas* were adorned with elaborate gateways posted at each cardinal direction. The figures on the gateways depict the worldly life left behind as a pilgrim enters the stupa.

of this emphasis on the practical and the therapeutic, the Buddha's teachings have often been compared to the advice of a physician. One scholar explains the first two Noble Truths as follows:

> He went forth into the world in the character of a doctor diagnosing an illness, to prescribe for his patient a cure. First he asked, "What are the symptoms of the world disease?" And his answer was, "Sorrow!" The First Noble Truth: "All life is sorrowful."
>
> Have we heard? Have we understood? "*All* life is sorrowful!" The important word here is "all," which cannot be translated to mean "modern" life . . . so that if the social order were altered, people then might become happy. Revolution is *not* what the Buddha taught. His First Noble Truth was that *life*—all life—is sorrowful. And his cure, therefore, would have to be able to produce relief, no matter what the social, economic, or geographical circumstances of the invalid.
>
> The Buddha's second question, accordingly, was "Can such a total cure be achieved?" And his answer was, "Yes!" The second Noble Truth: "There is release from sorrow."[3]

The Buddha's message about sorrow is illustrated in the *parable of the mustard seeds*. According to this story, a poor woman named Kisha Gotami had a young son who died suddenly. The grief-stricken mother began to wander about in confusion, carrying the boy on her hip. Finally, a kind passerby told her that the Buddha was preaching nearby and might be able to help. Gotami found him and asked for medicine to bring her son back to life. The Buddha instructed her to go to town and bring back some mustard seeds from a house in which no one had died. Gotami visited every family in town and, of course, discovered that there was no such thing as a house where no one had died. She then realized that sorrow and suffering are universal and became reconciled to her loss.

The cause of the world's sorrow, the Buddha explained, is that people have cravings and desires that can never be satisfied. One of these is the longing for permanence and eternal life. But according to his diagnosis, there is no such thing as permanence. Everything on earth is continually changing and evolving.

One of most drastic of the Buddha's revelations is that people cannot even regard themselves or their personalities as constant. Like everything else in the universe, the Buddha explained, the self, or personality, has no reality or permanence. Instead, it is a *composite* of five separate elements: sensations, ideas, thoughts, moods, and desires. These elements are con-

---

3. Joseph Campbell, *Myths to Live By* (New York: Bantam, 1973), p. 136.

stantly changing and interacting, so that a person is not the same from minute to minute.

To avoid disappointment, the Buddha taught, people must learn to have a detached attitude toward things that are changable, including their own personalities. The Buddha's advice in the *Dhammapada* provides a way to accomplish this. By following the Eightfold Path, practicing Buddhists learn to control the ever-changing mind and find an inner tranquility.

The Workings of Karma. Though the Buddha would not discuss the idea of a soul, he did accept the doctrine of karma. To some people, this presented a major dilemma: to what does karma attach if there is no permanent soul? The Buddha indicated that it is a person's thoughts that provide continuity from one day to the next and from one life to the next. "All that we are is a result of what we have thought."[4]

The Eightfold Path

The Buddha's teachings in the *Dhammapada* offer a practical manual for living, with advice on every step in the Eightfold Path. The emphasis is always on the individual's own efforts, for salvation cannot be gained by knowledge alone.

Right Views. To start on the road to salvation, a person must first accept the realities set forth in the Four Noble Truths. The simple act of recognizing the common suffering of all, the Buddha said, should change a person's behavior. "The world does not know that we must all come to an end here; but those who know it, their quarrels cease at once."

Right Resolve. After recognizing the brotherhood of humankind in suffering, it is time to do something about it. This means resolving to conquer all impulses that would cause harm, even indirectly, to another being. The difficulty of this task cannot be overstated. As the Buddha noted, "One's own self is difficult to subdue."

Right Speech. The Buddha's monks avoided all idle chatter and gossip and were not afraid of silence. All words were to be carefully considered before they were spoken to make sure that they did not arise from harmful or selfish impulses.

---

4. In the second century B.C., a monk named Nagasena used the analogy of a flame to clarify the Buddha's explanation. He pointed out that the flame in a lantern is not the same flame that burned there an hour ago, yet the lantern is the cause of both flames.

Right Actions. A Buddhist vows to refrain from obvious wrongs such as killing, stealing, telling lies, and so on. But it is not enough simply to avoid these actions: a person must constantly examine his or her thoughts to make sure they are free of selfish or evil intent. Since angry or selfish thoughts produce bad karma, they will do a person more harm than any enemy on the outside.

Right Livelihood. The Buddha listed occupations that would not hinder the search for salvation and those that would. Among the jobs to be avoided were butcher, weapons maker, prostitute, and tax collector.

Right Effort. A person must remain vigilant and watchful in order to keep from backsliding. Simply to maintain the necessary degree of concentration and awareness requires constant effort.

Right Mindfulness. Even after overcoming all egoistic and selfish impulses, a person must still keep vigilant. This means being superconscious of all one's actions and their real motives and keeping track of the five elements of the mind. (To keep track of the five elements is to have a "right mindfulness" of them.) While watching the emotions and sensations at work, a person constantly thinks, "This is not mine; this is not me; this is not my soul."

Right Meditation. Once freed from self-interest and craving, the mind harbors no hostility for others because it is no longer engaged in competition. The mind rests and is in harmony with the universe.

BUDDHIST SECTS

The Buddha referred to his teachings as a "raft," or "vehicle," that could be abandoned once the end was reached: he offered no promises or teachings concerning the hereafter. When asked whether he was a god, he said no. Instead, he referred to himself by the name *Tathagata* ("Thus Come One").

In the centuries following the Buddha's death, the Buddhist religion split into a number of philosophical and religious sects, each of which grew in separate ways. Among Buddhists today, there are three major divisions: Theraveda Buddhism, Mahayana Buddhism, and Zen Buddhism. All three sects are solidly rooted in the Buddha's original teachings, yet they are so different from one another that they have the status of separate religions.

Theraveda (Hinayana) Buddhism

The Buddhism we have discussed so far came to be known as *Hinayana* ("Small Vehicle") Buddhism to members of other sects. However, those belonging to this branch of Buddhism have preferred the term *Theraveda*, or "Teachings of the Elders." While other Buddhist sects believe that a religion can continue to grow as people have new insights, Theraveda Buddhists are guided mainly by the original teachings contained in the *Dhammapada*. In one passage of the *Dhammapada*, it is suggested that only a few people will reach the "other shore" of salvation but that these few give an important example to others.

From ancient times to the present, the island of Sri Lanka has been one of the main centers of Theraveda Buddhism. It was here that the oldest and most authentic Buddhist literature was preserved in the centuries after the Buddha's death. Burma and Thailand are also important centers of Theraveda Buddhism.

Mahayana ("Great Vehicle") Buddhism

About five centuries after the Buddha's death, a new spirit of hope and optimism began to spread among the Buddhists of northern India. This new spirit was inspired by the idea that salvation is open to all—that is, every human being is a potential Buddha. Those who held this belief called themselves *Mahayana* ("Great Vehicle") Buddhists. They emphasized the Buddha's compassion toward all people and believed that his mission had been to save and enlighten all humanity. Thus, by acting in an unselfish manner and showing active concern for others, a person could follow the Buddha's example and achieve salvation.

A central doctrine of Mahayana Buddhism is the idea of *bodhisattvas*. A *bodhisattva* is an exceptional being who, following the Buddha's example, has spent many lifetimes searching for enlightenment. During this long search, the bodhisattva shows great compassion for others and performs many unselfish acts. Rather than attaining nirvana, he or she deliberately decides to stay in the world and help others.

Mahayana Buddhism flourished throughout northern India from around A.D. 80 to 600. In the first centuries of the Christian era, Mahayana Buddhism spread from India to central Asia and China and then to Japan and Tibet. Today, there are millions of practicing Buddhists in these regions to the east.

The Buddhist religion did not fare as well in India, however. During the Muslim invasions of the Ganges region (beginning about A.D. 1000), Buddhist monasteries were destroyed and thousands of monks killed.

After about 1200, Buddhism no longer existed as a separate religion in India, though many of its concepts were incorporated into the Hindu religion. In the present day, however, Buddhism is once again emerging as an independent religion.[5]

Zen Buddhism

The Ch'an school of Buddhism[6]—usually known by the Japanese name *Zen*—was developed in sixth-century China and later traveled to Japan. Zen Buddhists believe that the Buddha imparted some of his highest wisdom to only a few disciples—possibly to as few as one. The Buddha's "secret" message was communicated in the legendary Flower Sermon. According to this story, the Buddha on one occasion simply held up a lotus flower to his monks rather than preaching to them. One of the monks grasped the Buddha's message and smiled to indicate he had understood.

Generally speaking, the Flower Sermon illustrates that there are truths that cannot be expressed in words. Like the Buddha himself—the Tathagata, or "Thus Come One"—the flower simply *is*, and its essence cannot be explained in words. Zen teaches people to understand that language is a very inexact and misleading tool. That is, when we think we are describing "reality," our words are actually creating a separate reality of their own.

The Zen goal of seeing and experiencing things *directly*, without relying on words and logic, is difficult to achieve. To help their students break out of their normal patterns of thinking, Zen masters, or teachers, assign them a problem called a *koan*. A *koan* is a seemingly impossible riddle, such as "What is the sound of one hand clapping?" or "What did your face look like before your parents were born?" The pupil meditates on the assigned koan for several months, under a master's guidance. Eventually, the pupil, if successful, will have a sudden flash of enlightenment and begin to see the world in an entirely new way.

Although only a few people have traveled the full distance to Zen enlightenment, this branch of Buddhism has had an enormous influence on the cultures of Asia. By noticing and taking pleasure in the concrete details of everyday life, a person avoids the tendency to rank some activities as more important or more meaningful than others. Arts such as gardening and the tea ceremony help people to celebrate and appreciate the beauty of everyday things.

---

5. In 1990, there were about 6 million Buddhists in India, a fairly small number compared to 689 million Hindus and 92 million Muslims.
6. *Ch'an* is a Chinese translation of the Sanskrit word meaning "meditation." The Ch'an sect of Buddhism, after incorporating many Taoist ideas, traveled to Japan and became *Zen*.

BUDDHISM AND CHRISTIANITY

Because of the parallels between Buddhism and Christianity, many people have wondered whether there is a relationship between the two. Some scholars have suggested that Buddhism inspired the prophesies of a compassionate savior that circulated in Judea before the birth of Christ. Conversely, the idea of a *suffering* savior who takes the world's sins upon himself may have traveled from Judea to the Mahayana Buddhists of India. But to date, no definite influence has been traced in either direction.

There are many similarities—as well as some important differences—between the lives and teachings of the Buddha and Jesus. Like the Buddha, Jesus was concerned with the "real" or inner person, who is defined by thoughts as well as actions. In one sermon, for instance, he suggested that people should do their charitable deeds in secret to avoid being influenced by public opinion. But there are also essential differences between the Buddhist and Christian religions. Christians view Jesus as a uniquely divine messiah, an incarnation of God in human form. The miracles described in the New Testament support this idea. But as we have seen, the Buddha strongly discouraged the idea that he was a god. Moreover, he taught that others could conquer their human failings, just as he had, and achieve enlightenment.

JAINISM

Vardhamana Mahavira ("Great Hero") is the name by which the founder of the Jainist sect is known. Like the Buddha, who was his contemporary, he was by birth a member of a princely kshatriya family. At the age of about 30, he left home and became one of the many ascetics who were then wandering the forests of the Ganges.

The Doctrine of Universal Suffering

After a dozen years of wandering, Mahavira achieved enlightenment. Like the Buddha, he suddenly became conscious of the fellow-suffering of all beings. However, he went farther than the Buddha or any other known religious figure in identifying this suffering. In Mahavira's view, even such objects as rocks and trees participate in it. A scholar describes Mahavira's view of a living world in which everything is endowed with a *jiva*, or soul.

> The whole world is alive. In every stone on the highway a soul is locked, so tightly enchained by matter that it cannot escape the careless foot that kicks it or cry out in pain, but capable of suffering nevertheless. When a

match is struck, a fire-being, with a soul that may one day be reborn in a human body, is born, only to die a few moments afterwards. In every drop of rain, in every breath of wind, in every lump of clay is a living soul.[7]

Mahavira soon acquired disciples and eventually founded an order of monks. The Jainist monks were known as the "naked ascetics"—they did not wear clothing because the making of cloth involves harm to cotton plants and other things. They strained their drinking water to save the microbes that it contained and wore masks so that their breathing would cause less injury to the *jiva* in the air. They stepped lightly when they walked, carefully avoiding ants and other insects. They ate as little as possible and usually obtained their food from other sects. If they gathered their own food, they would wait for a fruit or vegetable to fall rather than plucking it from the plant.

The Jain philosophy required an extraordinary degree of considerateness and unselfishness. To restrain their harmful impulses, Mahavira and his monks constantly reminded themselves of the suffering of others: "Not I alone am the sufferer—all things in the universe suffer! Thus should man think and be patient, not giving way to his passions."[8]

The Workings of Karma. Given the Jainist view of the world, even the most careful monk could not sustain life without injuring others. And each injury caused a buildup of karma that weighed down his soul and kept it from ascending to heaven. The Jains did not believe that good actions or intentions could help to cancel out this karma; only suffering could wear it away. Thus, they constantly subjected themselves to fasting and other penances. At the age of 72, Mahavira deliberately starved himself to death. In the Jainists' view, this final penance confirmed his reputation as a *jina*, or conqueror.

The Many-sidedness of Reality

In addition to the idea of universal suffering, the Jainists developed a second important teaching. The *doctrine of many-sidedness* notes that each person's view of the world is limited and one-sided. To illustrate this idea, the ancient Indian parable of the blind men and the elephant is often cited. A scholar explains how the story goes and how it illustrates the many-sidedness of reality:

---

7. Embree, *Sources of Indian Tradition*, pp. 53–54.
8. Ibid., p. 67.

[The parable] tells of a king who, in a fit of practical joking, assembled a number of blind men and told them each to touch an elephant and tell him what they felt. The man who touched the trunk declared that it was a snake, he who touched the tail, a rope, he who touched the leg, a tree trunk, and so on. The story concludes with violent altercations, each blind man maintaining that he knew the whole truth. So man, incapable of seeing things whole and from all aspects at once, must be satisfied with partial truths. All too often he maintains that he knows the whole truth, and his one-sided approach results in anger, bigotry and strife. The Jain, trained in the doctrine of many-sidedness, realizes that all ordinary propositions are relative . . . and tries to know the objects of his attention as thoroughly as possible by considering them from all points of view.[9]

The Spread of Jainism

After Mahavira's death, a group of Jain monks adopted the custom of wearing white robes. This led to a division of the Jainists into two sects: the "white-clad" and the "sky-clad." Aside from the issue of clothing, however, the two sects have no major disagreements, and both maintain a tolerant attitude toward other sects.

Because the Jains could not engage in farming or manufacturing, many of them turned to commercial activities to make a living. As money-lenders and merchants, the Jains grew prosperous, and their influence spread to central and southern India. At its height, from about 200 B.C. to A.D. 1000, Jainism was supported by a number of powerful kings. Beginning in the 11th century, however, devotional Hindu sects grew more popular, and Jainist sects declined. Today, there are about four million Jains in India, mostly concentrated in the western provinces.

Influence of the Jains on Mahatma Gandhi

Gandhi grew up in the province of Gujarat, one of the main centers of the Jainist sect, and often spoke of their influence on his life and philosophy. In this passage, Gandhi described how difficult it is to pursue the Jainist ideal of nonviolence in general, and especially in his *ashram*, a small farming community:

I know that in the act of respiration I destroy innumerable invisible germs floating in the air. But I do not stop breathing. The consumption of vegetables involves *himsa* [violence] but I cannot give them up. Again,

---

9. Ibid., p. 78.

there is *himsa* in the use of antiseptics yet I cannot bring myself to discard the use of disinfectants like kerosene. I suffer snakes to be killed in the ashram when it is impossible to catch and put them out of harm's way. I even tolerate the use of the stick to drive the bullocks in the ashram. Thus there is no end of *himsa* which I directly and indirectly commit.

Several years later, Gandhi concluded that although the Jainist ideal of *ahimsa* is unattainable, it should remain a goal nevertheless: "Perfect nonviolence whilst you are inhabiting the body is only a theory like Euclid's point or straight line, but we have to endeavor every moment of our lives."[10]

During his long struggle for India's independence, Gandhi often spoke of the doctrine of many-sidedness and put it into practice when dealing with his many antagonists. In 1926, he wrote:

I very much like this doctrine of the manyness of reality. . . . It has been my experience that I am always true [correct] from my point of view, and am often wrong from the point of view of my honest critics. I know that we are both right from our respective points of view.[11]

SUMMARY

Out of the turmoil of India in the sixth century B.C., two major new religions arose. At first, Buddhism and Jainism were just two of the many sects in the Hindu, or Indian, religion. In time, however, they came to have the stature of independent religions.

Both Buddhism and Jainism were originally designed for those who wished to live a monastic life apart from society. However, they also offered guidelines for people in all stations of life. Eventually, their basic teachings were accepted by millions of people and spread to all parts of India. Both religions had great appeal to people who wanted to escape the rules and confines of the caste system.

The Jainist sect founded by Mahavira is still in existence today, little changed after more than 2000 years. Buddhism, by contrast, continued to grow and develop over the centuries.

Although Buddhism eventually disappeared from India, it had an important influence on the Hindu religion. Even today, the foundation of religious life for millions of Hindus is the Buddhist monks' vow of poverty, chastity, and nonviolence.

---

10. Mohandas K. Gandhi, *All Men Are Brothers*, ed. K. Kripalani (New York: Continuum, 1987), p. 83.

11. *Young India*, 26 January 1926.

DISCUSSION AND ESSAY QUESTIONS

1. What criticisms of the Hindu religion did the Buddhists and Jainists express, either by their actions or in their teachings?
2. The Buddhist parable of the mustard seeds is often compared to Jesus' raising of Lazarus from the dead (described in the New Testament book of John). What is similar about these two stories? What differences do they illustrate?
3. Describe how Mahayana Buddhism relates to the original teachings and life story of the Buddha.
4. What are the two main doctrines of Jainism? What practical effects do these teachings have on a person's behavior toward others?
5. Working with a partner, list possible reasons why Jainism did not spread beyond India's borders, while Buddhism did.

ADDITIONAL READINGS

René Grousset, *In the Footsteps of the Buddha* (Salem, N.H.: Ayer, 1932). A fascinating biography of Huan-tsang (c. 604-664), a Chinese pilgrim who traveled to India to visit Buddhist shrines. Huan-tsang's memoirs are the main source of information for this period of Indian history.

Nancy Wilson Ross, *Buddhism: A Way of Life and Thought* (New York: Vintage Books, 1980). A well-written summary of the Buddha's message and of the major branches of Buddhist thought. Numerous black-and-white illustrations.

This relief, dating from about 180 B.C., shows Hindu gods worshiping the Buddha (symbolized by the throne and dharma wheel). About a century later, artists began to portray the Buddha in human form rather than by such symbols.

A PERSON IS THE PRODUCT OF HIS OR HER THOUGHTS

The Buddha gave supreme importance to the thoughts that occupy our minds. It is our thoughts, he said, that provide continuity and define what we are.

All that we are is the result of what we have thought: it is founded on our thoughts, it is made up of our thoughts. If a man speaks or acts with an evil thought, pain follows him, as the wheel follows the foot of the ox that draws the carriage. If a man speaks or acts with a pure thought, happiness follows him, like a shadow that never leaves him.

"He abused me, he beat me, he defeated me, he robbed me"—in those who harbor such thoughts hatred will never cease. For hatred does not cease by hatred at any time; hatred ceases by love—this is an eternal law. . . .

The thoughtless man, even if he can recite a large portion of the law [*Dhammapada*], but is not a doer of it, has no share in the religious life, but is like a cowherd counting the cows of others.

The follower of the law, even if he can recite only a small portion of it but, having forsaken passion and hatred and foolishness, possesses true knowledge and serenity of mind; he, attached to nothing in this world or that to come, has indeed a share in the religious life.

Whatever a hater may do to a hater, or an enemy to an enemy, a wrongly-directed mind will do us greater mischief.

Let a man overcome anger by love, let him overcome evil by good; let him overcome the greedy by liberality, the liar by truth!

Speak the truth; do not yield to anger; give, if you are asked, even though it be a little: by these three steps you will come near the gods.

Make yourself an island, work hard, be wise! When your impurities are blown away, and you are free from guilt, you will enter into the heavenly world of the elect.

The fault of others is easily perceived, but that of one's self is difficult to perceive; a man winnows [sifts through] his neighbor's faults like chaff, but his own fault he hides, as a cheat hides an unlucky cast of the die.

If a man looks after the faults of others and is always inclined to be offended, his own passions will grow, and he is far from the destruction of passion.

SOURCE: E. A. Burtt, ed., *Teachings of the Compassionate Buddha* (New York: Mentor, 1982), pp. 52–65.

1. In the first paragraph, what metaphors (symbols) are used for pain and for happiness? Give a possible reason why the Buddha chose these particular images.
2. How does a person's mind normally behave, if it is not controlled? What benefits come to a person who is able to control his or her thoughts?
3. Debate the question "Thoughts make the person" versus "Actions make the person."

QUESTIONS THAT DO NOT LEAD TO ENLIGHTENMENT

Sometimes, the Buddha's disciples found it difficult to suppress their curiosity regarding the great "metaphysical" questions. One day, the monk Malunkyaputta decided that the Buddha simply must explain whether the universe is eternal or finite and whether an arhat—a saint who has achieved nirvana—exists after death. Malunkyaputta declared that if he could not get answers, he would abandon the religious life and return to the world. The Buddha, as usual, responded that it was profitless to speculate on such matters. Then he went on to illustrate his point with a parable.

Parable of the Man Wounded by an Arrow

It is as if a man had been wounded by an arrow thickly smeared with poison, and the sick man were to say, "I will not have this arrow taken out until I have learned whether the man who wounded me belonged to the warrior caste, or to the brahman caste, or to the agricultural caste, or to the menial caste." Or if he were to say, "I will not have this arrow taken out until I have learned the name of the man who wounded me, and to what clan he belongs—or whether the man who wounded me was tall, or short, or of the middle height." Or if he were to say, "I will not have this arrow taken out until I know whether the bow-string was made from swallow-wort, or bamboo fiber, or sinew, or hemp, or of the milk-weed tree—or until I know whether the shaft was feathered from the wings of a vulture, or of a heron, or of a falcon, or of a peacock—or until I know whether it was an ordinary arrow, or a razor-arrow, or an iron arrow, or a calf-tooth arrow."

That man would die, Malunkyaputta, without ever having learned this. In exactly the same way, anyone who should say, "I will not lead the religious life under the Blessed One until the Blessed One shall explain to me either that the world is eternal, or that the world is not eternal . . . or that the saint either exists or does not exist after death"—that person would die, Malunkyaputta, before the Tathagata had ever explained this to him.

The religious life does not depend on the dogma that the world is eternal, nor does the religious life depend on the dogma that the world is not eternal. Whether the dogma [is true] that the world is eternal, or that the world is not eternal, there still remain birth, old age, death, sorrow, lamentation, misery, grief, and despair, for the extinction of which in the present life I am prescribing. . . .

Accordingly, Malunkyaputta, bear always in mind what it is that I have not explained, and what it is that I have explained. And what have I not explained? I have not explained that the world is eternal; I have not explained that the world is not eternal; I have not explained that the world is finite; I have not explained that the world is infinite; I have not explained that the soul and the body are identical; I have not explained that the soul is one thing and the body another; I have not explained that the saint exists after death; I have not explained that the saint does not exist after death. . . . And why, Malunkyaputta, have I not explained this? Because this profits not, nor has to do with the fundamentals of religion, absence of passion, tranquility, and Nirvana; therefore have I not explained it.

And what, Malunkyaputta, have I explained? Misery have I explained; the origin of misery have I explained; the cessation of misery have I explained; and the path leading to the cessation of misery. And why have I explained this? Because this does profit, has to do with the fundamentals of religion . . . ; therefore have I explained it. Accordingly, Malunkyaputta, bear always in mind what it is that I have not explained, and what it is that I have explained.

Thus spake the Blessed One; and, delighted, the venerable Malunkyaputta applauded the speech of the Blessed One.

1. Give examples of "metaphysical" questions of the type the Buddha will not answer. What reason does he give for not wanting to answer these questions?
2. What questions *is* the Buddha willing to answer?

BUDDHIST MORALITY

In a dialogue with a man named Singala, the Buddha outlined some of the duties that people owe one another. In describing the duties owed to women and servants, the Buddha was far in advance of his time: no other known teacher in ancient times expressed as much consideration for these classes.

A husband should serve his wife in five ways: by honoring her; by respecting her; by remaining faithful to her; by giving her charge of the home; and by duly giving her adornments. And thus served by her husband a wife should care for him in five ways: she should be efficient in her household tasks; she should manage her servants well; she should be chaste; she should take care of the goods he brings home; and she should be skillful and untiring in all her duties. . . .

A master should serve his slaves and servants in five ways: he should assign them work in proportion to their strength; he should give them due food and wages; he should care for them in sickness; he should share especially tasty luxuries with them; and he should give them holidays at due intervals. Thus served by their master they should care for him in five ways: they should get up before him; they should go to bed after him; they should be content with what he gives them; they should do their work well; and they should spread abroad his praise and good name.

SOURCE: Ainslie T. Embree, ed., *Sources of Indian Tradition*, 2d ed., vol. 1 (New York: Columbia University Press, 1988), p. 124.

1. Compare and contrast the Buddha's rules of conduct with current Western ideas about husband-wife or employer-employee relations.

CHRISTIANITY AND BUDDHISM

Many people have seen striking similarities between the teachings of the Buddha and those of Jesus almost five centuries later. To what extent do their messages seem to agree?

Jesus' Sermon on the Mount

You have heard that it was said, "Thou shalt not commit adultery." But I say to you that every one who looks at a woman lustfully has already committed adultery with her in his heart. . . .

You have heard that it was said, "An eye for an eye, and a tooth for a tooth." But I say to you, Do not resist one who is evil. But if any one strikes you on the right cheek, turn to him the other also. . . .

You have heard that it was said, "Thou shalt love thy neighbor, and hate thine enemy." But I say to you, Love your enemies, bless them that curse you, do good to them that hate you, and pray for them who spitefully use you and persecute you; so that you may be the children of your Father who is in heaven. For he makes his sun rise on the evil and on the good, and sends rain on the just and on the unjust. . . .

Beware of practicing your piety before men in order to be seen by them; for then you will have no reward from your Father who is in heaven. Thus, when you give alms, sound no trumpet before you. . . . But when you give alms, do not let your left hand know what your right hand is doing. . . .

Enter at the strait [narrow] gate: for wide is the gate, and broad is the way that leads to destruction, and many there be which enter by it. Because strait is the gate, and narrow is the way, which leads unto life, and few there be that find it.

SOURCE: Matthew 5:27–28, 38–39, 43–45; 6:1–2; 7:13.

1. Analyze the meaning of one paragraph from the Sermon on the Mount. Then compare and contrast this message with the Buddha's teachings.

JAINISM

In the first passage quoted here, a Jainist monk describes the travails that a typical jiva endures during its lifetimes on earth. In the second passage, a Jainist teacher tells how one should react to the world's suffering. A person must constantly be aware of the suffering of others, he says, in order to avoid adding to it. Yet this concern must stop short of active involvement or attachments, since human passions also increase karma.

All Creation Groans in Torment

Helpless in snares and traps, a deer, I have been caught and bound and fastened, and often I have been killed. A helpless fish, I have been caught with hooks and nets. . . . A bird, I have been caught by hawks or trapped in nets, or held fast by birdlime, and I have been killed an infinite number of times. A tree, with axes and adzes by the carpenters an infinite number of times I have been felled, stripped of my bark, cut up, and sawn into planks. As iron, with hammer and tongs by blacksmiths an infinite number of times I have been struck and beaten, split and filed. . . . Ever afraid, trembling, in pain and suffering, I have felt the utmost sorrow and agony. In every kind of existence I have suffered pains that have scarcely known reprieve for a moment.

The Workings of Karma

One should know what binds the soul, and, knowing, break free from bondage. . . . He who grasps at even a little, whether living or lifeless, or consents to another doing so, will never be freed from sorrow. If a man kills living things, or slays by the hand of another, or consents to another slaying, his sin goes on increasing. The man who cares for his kin and companions is a fool who suffers much, for their numbers are ever increasing. All his wealth and relations cannot save him from sorrow. Only if he knows the nature of life, will he get rid of karma.

SOURCE: Ainslie T. Embree, ed., *Sources of Indian Tradition*, 2d ed., vol. 1 (New York: Columbia University Press, 1988), pp. 59, 62–63.

1. In the Jainist view, how should a person behave in order to avoid the accumulation of karma?

THE JAINS IN 16TH-CENTURY INDIA

Duarte Barbosa, a cousin of the Portuguese explorer Ferdinand Magellan, was one of the many foreign adventurers who visited India in the 16th century. In the first paragraph quoted here, he describes the life style of the Jains.

Duarte also described how other groups, especially the Muslims, played practical jokes on the Jains. For instance, a Muslim seeking alms might stab himself with a collapsible knife or beat himself with stones when he saw a Jain approaching. The Jain, even knowing it was a trick, would pay money to prevent this violence. This kind of "ransoming" had many variations.

In their houses they sup by daylight, for neither by night nor by day will they light a lamp, by reason of certain little flies which perish in the flame thereof; and if there is any great need of a light by night they have a lantern of varnished paper or cloth, so that no living thing may find its way in, and die in the flame.

Often it is so that the Moors [Muslims] take to them live insects or small birds, and make as though to kill them in their presence, and the [Jains] buy these and ransom them, paying much more than they are worth, so that they may save their lives and let them go. And if the King or a Governor of the land has any man condemned to death, for any crime which he has committed, they gather themselves together and buy him from justice, that he may not die.

SOURCE: Duarte Barbosa, *The Book of Duarte Barbosa*, vol. 1 (Hakluyt Society Works, 2d series, no. 44, 1918), pp. 111–112.

1. Why were the Jains obvious targets for pranksters? Why did they pay up even when they knew they were being taken advantage of?

C H A P T E R

F I V E

THE RISE OF EMPIRES IN ANCIENT INDIA

Some kind of a dream of unity has occupied the mind of India since the dawn of civilization.

Jawaharlal Nehru

In the centuries after the Buddha's death, or final nirvana, his disciples often wondered what might have happened if he had become a *Chakravartin*, or world emperor, rather than a spiritual leader. One of the monks' favorite tales concerned a legendary Chakravartin who had lived in a golden age many centuries past. This great king did not use violence to impose his rule: instead, the force of his dharma, or righteousness, was enough to establish his authority. At the beginning of his reign, he simply appeared in each of the four corners of the earth and was accepted as king.[1]

Hindus, too, imagined the rise of one all-powerful king. Like the Buddhists, they believed that such a king could unify the world and provide all the benefits of peace and prosperity. However, they did not agree that this great king must be nonviolent. In fact, according to ancient Aryan theories, the very purpose of kings was to organize armies, and their first duty was to defend and enlarge their kingdoms.

In the centuries we will discuss in this chapter, great empires were built and destroyed, both in India and the rest of the ancient world. The

---

1. At this time, Indians believed that the world contained four continents, with India counted as one.

rise of several great kings in India—both Hindu and Buddhist—helped to illustrate how well or ill the ideals of kingship worked in practice.

ALEXANDER THE GREAT IN INDIA

In the year 326 B.C., India had its first contact with a real "universal emperor." This world conqueror was not an Indian king, however; he was Alexander the Great of Macedonia. At the age of 30, having just conquered the great Persian Empire, Alexander crossed the Hindu Kush and descended into the Indus valley. His plan was to travel across India until he reached the eastern limit of the world. During this journey, he would incorporate all the territory he discovered into his vast empire.

After entering India, Alexander made peaceful treaties with the first two kings he encountered and thus established his control over the upper Indus valley. He then crossed the first river of the Punjab in late June of the year 326 B.C. Here, Alexander encountered a great Indian king known as Porus, who was not willing to give up the Punjab without a battle. Porus had assembled an army of 30,000 troops—about double the force Alexander had brought across the river. Moreover, the center of Porus' army was shielded with an imposing array of 200 elephants. According to the account of the battle provided by Alexander's historians, Porus and his troops put up a gallant fight but were outmaneuvered by Alexander's superior tactics.

After the battle, Alexander met with Porus, a tall and handsome king. In recognition of Porus' bravery, Alexander gave him back his kingdom. In return, Alexander asked that Porus make peace with an old enemy, the king of Taxila. Thus, Alexander ensured that all of the kings of the upper Indus and Punjab were loyal to him and at peace with one another.

From Porus and other informants in the Punjab, Alexander learned for the first time of the existence of the Ganges River and of the great kingdoms that flourished along its banks. He was excited by this news and immediately laid plans to make the 12-day march across the Thar Desert so that he could explore and conquer the Ganges. At this point, however, Alexander's luck ran out. His troops, exhausted and homesick, refused to listen to his new plan; they simply wanted to go home.[2] Reluctantly,

---

2. The troops' attitude is not surprising. After conquering the Persian Empire, they had not been given leave as expected but instead had been forced to fight their way across the rugged Hindu Kush so that Alexander could reach India. Then, there had been the great battle against Porus, and since that time Alexander's engineers had kept them constantly busy in constructing bridges, boats and even cities during the height of the monsoon season.

Alexander yielded to their wishes and announced—to great rejoicing—that the army would turn back.

Alexander did not leave India the same way he had come but divided his army into three parts so that he might explore additional routes. One branch of the army sailed down the swiftly flowing Indus and, after many mishaps and adventures, reached the Arabian Sea. At this point, the fleet set out to find an ocean route back to the Tigris River, the center of Alexander's empire. Two other branches of the army, one commanded by Alexander himself, marched across the desert of Baluchistan to explore the land routes to the Tigris. After much hardship and loss of life, the army was finally reunited at Susa, in Persia.

A little more than a year after his return to Persia, Alexander suddenly died of a fever. His great dream of unifying the entire known world then came to an end, for no other leader had the ability to carry out such a grand enterprise.

The Impact of Alexander's Visit

Alexander led the first great invasion of India since that of the ancient Aryans, about 1200 years before. He and his men brought the first detailed news that India had received of the civilizations to the west, including Greece, Egypt, the Middle East, and Persia. Moreover, during their visit, Alexander and his army completely reorganized the kingdoms of the Indus, a campaign that cost the lives of more than 20,000 Indians. However, not a single mention of Alexander has been found in Indian literature. The only traces of his visit are a number of legends that were preserved orally by local peoples.[3]

While Alexander apparently did not make much of an impression in India, his visit had two practical consequences. First, his invasion had the effect of opening up communication between India and the Western world. The land and sea routes that he charted became the avenues of trade and cultural exchanges for several centuries to come.

Also, for those who were interested, Alexander's campaign demonstrated how one man could organize and carry out seemingly impossible tasks. It is believed that a young Indian prince named Chandragupta Maurya was among the interested onlookers as Alexander passed through

---

3. Several tribes in Afghanistan, Pakistan, and the Himalayan foothills believe they are descended from Alexander or his soldiers, based on stories that may have been passed down from generation to generation for 2300 years. The fact that a number of these tribal peoples have light-colored eyes and European features gives credence to the legends.

India.[4] In any case, Chandragupta soon became a "great organizer" himself. With the help of his mentor, Kautilya, an expert in Indian politics, Chandragupta soon completed the work Alexander had begun in India.

A PRACTICAL THEORY OF EMPIRE BUILDING

At the same time that Alexander was in India, a senior brahman minister named Kautilya was composing a work called the *Arthashastra* ("Science of Worldly Success"). Kautilya has often been compared to Niccolò Machiavelli, an Italian theorist who lived 18 centuries later. Both men lived in an era marked by constant strife among numerous small states. In response to these conditions, each wrote a political manual describing how a forceful and ruthless prince could seize power and bring about political unity. Both Kautilya and Machiavelli believed that unity was more important than any other consideration. Thus, each advocated that a prince ignore all normal rules of morality and religion in order to bring it about. Machiavelli's name came to be associated with the doctrine that any type of action may be justified by "reasons of state." However, he did not go nearly as far as Kautilya in stating this position.

It is believed that Kautilya was the "power behind the throne" as Chandragupta Maurya began to build his empire. Thus, the text of his *Arthashastra* provides many hints as to how Chandragupta, who was probably only a minor prince, managed to build the largest empire yet known in India.

Conquest of Northern India

Kautilya's *Arthashastra* does not mention any rules of "fair play" when a king is building a kingdom. Instead, it explains how to play the game of power politics with all of the tools at hand. A king may suddenly start a war without provocation, for example, or he may use deceit to undermine an alliance between other kings. As long as he is certain that the benefits to his kingdom will outweigh the costs, all such tactics are "fair."

We do not know exactly how Chandragupta put this advice into practice, but by 323 B.C. he had conquered the great kingdom of Magadha. After hearing of Alexander's death, Chandragupta then marched west-

---

4. Alexander's historians reported that he met a youth named "Sandrocottus" in the Punjab, who urged him to travel east and conquer Magadha. Many scholars feel certain that this young man was Chandragupta.

ward and conquered the Indus and the Punjab. Thus, in just three years, Chandragupta became master of northern India.

Governing an Empire

Whereas a king must be shrewd and ruthless in dealing with outsiders, Kautilya outlined a much different set of rules for domestic affairs. In governing his kingdom, he said, the king must show himself to be completely trustworthy and just. It must also be clear to his subjects that he devotes himself with tireless energy to the welfare of the kingdom. If not, Kautilya warned, the kingdom would soon fail. For example, if a king is lazy or selfish, people will soon leave his kingdom and settle in one that is better governed. Also, Kautilya said, the subjects of a "bad" king will soon begin to imitate his low character. And once this happens, the kingdom will weaken and soon fall prey to outside invaders.

THE MAURYAN EMPIRE

During Chandragupta's reign, a Greek ambassador named Megasthenes took up residence at his court in Pataliputra. Thanks to Megasthenes' reports, we know many details about Chandragupta's life and government.[5]

Megasthenes reported that the king lived in a splendid palace surrounded by a walled park. When he appeared in public, for his daily hunt or other ceremonies, he was attended by a procession of courtiers and servants. The king himself wore fine robes embroidered with purple and gold, and even the elephant or horse that he rode had trappings of gold. Thus, Chandragupta apparently heeded Kautilya's advice that "the people are pleased to see their king enjoying welfare and prosperity." But at all times, the king busily attended to the affairs of his kingdom, Megasthenes said.

To protect his realm and put down any possible revolts, Chandragupta had a large standing army with as many as 600,000 infantry soldiers, 30,000 cavalry, and 9,000 elephants. And his capital city, Megasthenes said, was surrounded with a wall that had 570 towers and 64 gates. The king was also careful about his personal security. We do not know if his palace contained hollow pillars and secret passages, as the *Arthashastra* advised. But Megasthenes noted that the king often slept on different beds in order to foil assassination attempts.

---

5. Megasthenes' original book about India has been lost. However, many of his accounts were copied by other ancient authors and so have survived to the present day.

To administrate his kingdom and to be ready for any emergencies, Chandragupta had to have a large treasury. Much of his income came from the taxes paid by farmers, who, Megasthenes said, were the largest "caste" in his empire. In each village, the king's tax officials were present at harvest time to collect a portion—usually, one-fourth—of the crops. But except for this transaction, Megasthenes indicated, the farmers seemed to be totally unconcerned with the affairs of the empire:

> The husbandmen are in disposition most mild and gentle. They never go to town, either to take part in its tumults, or for any other purpose. . . . In times of civil war the soldiers are not allowed to molest them or ravage their lands. Hence, while the former are fighting and killing each other as they can, the latter may be seen close at hand tranquilly pursuing their work—perhaps ploughing, or gathering in their crops, pruning the trees, or reaping the harvest.[6]

In the cities, officials collected taxes and duties from artisans and traders. But Chandragupta was careful to avoid ruining his subjects with high taxes. When he needed extra revenue, he may have resorted to some of the unusual methods suggested in the *Arthashastra*. For instance, Kautilya suggested, the state could build a multiheaded serpent and charge people admission to see it.

An unusual feature of Chandragupta's government was an elaborate spy network. All types of people—students, fortunetellers, family men, beggars—were recruited as spies. Their reports allowed Chandragupta to find out what people were thinking and doing in all parts of his realm. After receiving the reports, the king and his ministers quickly dealt with troublemakers. Severe punishments, including the death penalty, were enforced for crimes such as rebellion and tax evasion.

Conquest of the South

At the age of about 50, according to legend, Chandragupta retired from public life and became a Jainist monk. His son Bindusara, who succeeded him as king, decided to expand the Mauryan Empire to the south. South India, at this time, was divided into three prosperous kingdoms. Most people in the south spoke the Tamil language and were probably related to one of the ancient peoples who helped to build the Harappan civilization of the Indus (see Chapter 3). As we will see in Chapter 6, South India readily adapted to the culture of the north and soon began to make its own contributions to it.

---

6. Megasthenes, quoted in Arrian's *Indika* 11:39.

Assessments of the Mauryan Empire

The first two Mauryan kings ruled India for about 65 years and introduced many of the benefits that people had hoped a Chakravartin would bring. Their empire was secure, peaceful, and efficiently maintained. Roads were safe and well kept, allowing people to carry on trade with faraway regions. The people of India grew more prosperous and could afford such luxuries as fine pottery, jewelry, and clothing. Demand for new luxuries led to an increase in commerce, and the taxes collected from trade helped to swell the royal treasuries. During the Mauryan age, Hindus began to say that the king is the "maker of his age." Due to the strong leadership of Chandragupta and his son, a new era of peace and prosperity had dawned.

However, the Buddhists were less enthusiastic. In general, Buddhist stories illustrate the moral that when a person is indulged in his selfish desires—as a king is above all—there will be no limit to his harmful impulses. Many Buddhist stories tell of kings whose violence, greediness, or intolerance made a misery of their subjects' lives.

A "good" king, Buddhists believed, must follow the Buddha's example: he must have conquered his own passions and desires. And in his conduct toward others, he must be nonviolent, kind, and honest. But could these spiritual values be developed amid all the luxury and ceremony of a king's court? As we have seen, the Buddha himself apparently thought not. In his Great Going Forth, he had renounced his kingdom and had chosen to live in poverty.

In the reign of Ashoka, the third Mauryan king, Buddhists were able to resolve some of the questions that had troubled them. Ashoka, a devout Buddhist, did not renounce the prerogatives and luxuries he enjoyed as a Mauryan king. Yet both Buddhists and Hindus eventually gave him their highest praise.

The Reign of Ashoka

Ashoka, the third king of the Mauryan empire, is the best known of India's ancient kings. One reason for his enduring fame is that he "published" his messages to his subjects on durable materials. Throughout his empire, his words were carved on sandstone pillars and on rocks so that people might read the king's messages as they carried out their everyday activities. Many of these carvings can still be seen today. (Only one of the surviving messages contains Ashoka's name, however: he usually referred to himself as "Beloved of the Gods.")

In the first years of his reign, Ashoka apparently carried out the same forceful policies that his father and grandfather had used. In 261 B.C., he decided to conquer Kalinga (present-day Orissa), a province that had

This sandstone pillar, still at its original site, contains one of the messages Ashoka wrote to his subjects. The carving of a lion atop the pillar was one of Ashoka's "signatures."

resisted Mauryan rule. But the battle for Kalinga turned into a full-scale war. In the end, Ashoka won the war, but he was horrified by the violence of the campaign. In his 13th Rock Edict, he expressed his great regret at the bloodshed. Moreover, he said that he had decided to follow the dharma, or law, of a Buddhist:

> Kalinga was conquered by the king, Beloved of the Gods, when he had been consecrated eight years. 150,000 people were taken captive, 100,000 killed, and many times that number died. But after conquering Kalinga, the king began to follow dharma. Now the Beloved of the Gods regrets the conquest of Kalinga, for when an independent country is conquered people are killed, they die, or are taken captive, and this is a matter of profound regret and sorrow to the Beloved of the Gods. . . . So now, even if the number of those killed and captured in the conquest of Kalinga had been 100 or 1000 times less, it would be a matter of regret to the Beloved of the Gods.

In this edict, Ashoka went on to say that he wanted all his subjects to have "security, self-control, peace of mind, and joyousness." To achieve these goals, Ashoka began to teach people how to live by the rules of dharma. In his rock and pillar messages, he asked his subjects to show respect and compassion toward all living things. Also, he asked them to

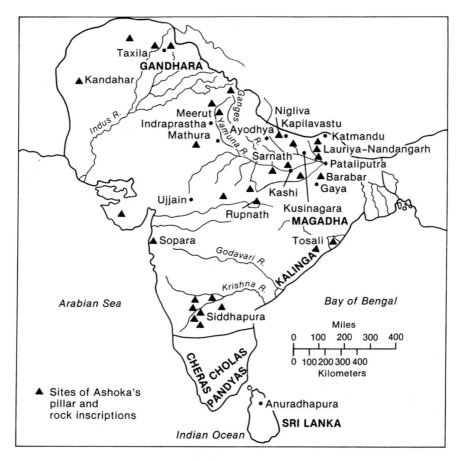

The Mauryan Empire at Its Greatest Extent, c. 250 B.C.

respect and tolerate one another's religious beliefs. "Harmony is best," he explained, "with each hearing and respecting the other's teachings." In other edicts, Ashoka mentioned two more rules; namely, telling the truth and respecting the authority of elders such as parents, teachers, and priests.

In his own actions, too, Ashoka strived to uphold the law of dharma—especially nonviolence. After Kalinga, he probably did not disband his army, but neither did he attempt any more conquests. Also, he renounced hunting—usually the favorite sport of kings—and became a vegetarian. One of his edicts announced the steps he had taken in this direction:

Formerly in the Beloved of the God's kitchen several hundred thousand animals were killed daily for food; but now at the time of writing only three are killed—two peacocks and a deer, though the deer not always. Even these three animals will not be killed in future.

To help his subjects live in harmony with one another, Ashoka dispatched a group of officials known as "dharma ministers" to explain to them the teachings of his edicts. He himself provided an example of tolerance by generously endowing the temples of Hindus, Jains, and other sects.

But of course, Ashoka reserved his greatest enthusiasm for the Buddhist religion. According to legend, he built a total of 84,000 stupas to house the relics of the Buddha.[7] And in the Ganges valley, he built thousands of rock-cut caves called *viharas* to serve as monasteries for Buddhist monks. Ashoka also convened a great conference of monks to compile the authentic teachings of the Buddha. (These teachings became the core of Theraveda Buddhism.) After the conference, groups of missionaries were sent to Kashmir, Afghanistan, Nepal, Burma, Sri Lanka, and even Greece and Egypt to spread the Buddhist religion among other peoples.

From the evidence gathered by archeologists and other scholars, Asoka was a highly effective king. His edicts and other artifacts indicate that his empire was larger than any other in the history of India, including the British Empire. Also, the fine workmanship of his pillars and rock carvings demonstrate his ability to organize large projects and to enforce high standards. Some of Ashoka's columns weigh as much as 50 tons and are so highly polished that Europeans at first believed they were made of metal.

Buddhist Views of Ashoka

Most Buddhist stories describe Ashoka as a monster of cruelty and egoism until, one day, he met a holy monk named Upagupta and was converted to Buddhism. It is likely that such portraits of Ashoka were greatly exaggerated in order to illustrate certain morals. Nevertheless, the real-life Ashoka probably encountered much skepticism from the monks of his time. In his later years, he found a way to reassure them that he had not become corrupted by the wealth and power he commanded.

---

7. The number 84,000 indicated "totality," or "completeness," in Indian thought. For example, there were said to be 84,000 atoms in the body, 84,000 Buddhist teachings, and 84,000 kingdoms in India.

Ashoka's *viharas* were a model for hundreds of later rock-cut temples and monasteries. The columns, doorway, and inside furnishings of this Buddhist temple were carved into the sheer granite of a mountain: no additional materials were brought in.

In recognition of the fact that Ashoka had governed his empire by dharma alone, Buddhist monks accorded him the coveted title of *Chakravartin*. However, they qualified this title with the words *Armed*, or *Iron-wheeled*. Unlike the "Golden-wheeled" Chakravartin of legend, Ashoka had once resorted to violence. And, of course, he had ruled only one "continent."

The Downfall of the Mauryan Empire. After Ashoka's death, his descendants ruled his empire for nearly 50 years. Then, a Hindu general named Pusyamitra seized the throne. Pusyamitra was not able to hold the empire together, however. By 180 B.C., the Mauryan Empire had once again split into hundreds of competing kingdoms.

Buddhist stories contain many obvious exaggerations concerning the destructiveness of Pusyamitra, the last king of the Mauryan Empire. But even without such exaggerations, the downfall of Ashoka's empire did illustrate one of the Buddha's most basic teachings; namely, the impermanence of all things.

APPROXIMATE DATES OF THE MAURYAN KINGS

Chandragupta	334–301 B.C.
Bindusara	301–269 B.C.
Ashoka	269–232 B.C.
Other Mauryas	232–184 B.C.

INDIA BETWEEN THE EMPIRES (180 B.C.–A.D. 320)

As the Mauryan Empire declined, a succession of foreign kings built a prosperous trading kingdom in Gandhara, which included parts of Afghanistan and northwest India. Soon, the kingdom of Gandhara was expanded into northern India and became an important link between India, central Asia, and the West. Sea routes between South India and the West also became the avenues of a thriving trade.

The Kingdom of Gandhara

The Indo-Greeks. The first kings of Gandhara were Greeks and Persians. They are known as the *Indo-Greeks* because they adopted Indian customs and eventually lost track of their original kingdoms. One of the most famous of these kings was Menander—known in India as Milinda—who ruled Gandhara from 155 to 130 B.C. According to legend, Milinda was converted to Buddhism by a monk named Nagasena in an argument that was attended by 80,000 people. The historical accuracy of the story is supported by the fact that some of Milinda's coins are stamped with the Buddhist wheel of dharma.

The Shakas and Kushans. Milinda's dynasty was displaced by the Scythians, known in India as the *Shakas*. One notable event of this era was the arrival of Saint Thomas ("Doubting Thomas"), one of the Christian apostles. According to legend, Thomas was received in Taxila by a Shaka king in A.D. 50. Soon afterward, however, Gandhara was invaded by the Kushans. Thomas then fled to a Roman trading colony on the Malabar coast. Here, he founded a church and later continued his missionary activities on the Coromandel coast. When the Portuguese arrived in Malabar in 1498, they found a sizable colony of "Saint Thomas Christians," still practicing an early form of Christianity.

The Shakas were pushed out of Gandhara by the Kushans, another tribe of horsemen from central Asia. Many of the Shakas moved south and settled in the region of Malwa. (There, they became integrated into Hindu society as *kshatriyas*, or warriors.) Meanwhile, the Kushans proceeded to expand their kingdom eastward. Based on images shown on their coins and statues, the Kushan kings were tall, rugged men who wore oversized clothes and long beards. But they were apparently more "civilized" than they appeared. Under their rule, Gandhara continued to be a major cosmopolitan center and hub of trade.

The most famous of the Kushan kings is Kanishka, who may have ruled from about 78 to 120. Kanishka's kingdom extended from Afghanistan to the city of Benares on the Ganges and also included part of central Asia.

The Spread of Mahayana Buddhism

Like Milinda, Kanishka was converted to Buddhism and enthusiastically supported his new religion. The Mahayana sect, now just beginning to separate from the Theraveda sect, especially benefited from the king's support. As Ashoka had done, Kanishka convened an assembly of monks to consolidate Buddhist scriptures. After the meeting, Mahayana teachings were carried to central Asia and to China.

In Ashoka's time, the Buddha had been represented in art by symbols such as a dharma wheel, a throne, a pair of footprints, or a bodhi tree. But as the Mahayana religion developed, artists began to create images of the Buddha and of bodhisattvas in human form. The first images of Buddha often had a "worldly" and individualistic air, as if modeled upon real persons. But in time, the Gandhara artists developed a new artistic style to illustrate the Buddha's life and message. Hallmarks of later Buddhist images include an expression of serenity and compassion, large ear lobes (a sign of beauty), and *chakra* (wheel) marks on the hands and feet. In addition, a great variety of hand gestures were created to illustrate aspects of the Buddha's life. For instance, a hand held upright signified the Buddha's "forget fear" message, and a hand pointed downward portrayed his "calling the earth to witness" as he achieved enlightenment. (The "forget fear" gesture, and certain other symbols, were soon adopted by Hindu artists as well.)

Land and Sea Trade with the West

The expanded kingdom of Gandhara served as a hub of commerce between India, central Asia, and the West. The main overland trade route went across the Hindu Kush into Afghanistan. From there, a trade caravan could either travel to Persia and western Asia or take the Silk Road to China.

Buddhist Art of the Kushan Period

The first Buddhist images often resembled princes or warriors. But in time, the animation of these early portraits gave way to an air of serenity and calm authority. In the photo at bottom left, the Buddha's pose signifies meditation. In the photo at bottom right, the "forget fear" gesture is shown.

107

After the rise of the Roman Empire, in the first century B.C., the pace of India's trade with the West accelerated.[8] Land and sea routes became much safer, and India found a large market for its products in the Mediterranean.

The sea route between South India and the Mediterranean became one of the main avenues of commerce between India and the Roman world. The trip was made easier when a merchant from Alexandria discovered how to use the seasonal monsoon winds to sail directly across the Arabian Sea to India. (This meant that ships no longer had to hug the coasts, as Alexander's fleet had done.) With the help of the monsoon winds, the trip from India to Aden took just 40 days, and Alexandria could be reached in about two months. From Alexandria, Indian luxury goods such as ivory, spices, diamonds, pearls, sandalwood, and textiles were delivered to wealthy Romans. On the return trip, Indian traders sometimes carried Roman products such as wine but often preferred to receive their payment in gold. In South India, large hoards of Roman gold coins have been found, indicating that India's merchants maintained a very favorable balance of trade with the West.

Decline of International Trade

Around the year 200, India's trade with the West came to an end as the Roman Empire was overwhelmed by invasions and other troubles. For more than a thousand years, Europe remained isolated from the East. The peoples of Europe did not forget about India, however. The accounts of Alexander's historians and of later travelers became a permanent part of Western literature. These accounts included factual details about India's peoples and riches and also many fabulous tales—thrown in for entertainment—about mythical beings. Such mythical beings were described even by reliable reporters such as Megasthenes. He wrote of a people who had ears so long that they could curl up and sleep in them, and of others who had no mouths but lived by inhaling the odors of flowers. Other favorite stories about India concerned a dog-headed people and a lion-sized animal with a triple row of teeth and trumpetlike call.

In the 15th century, these accounts of India's riches and mythical beings were studied by Columbus and other explorers and helped to inspire their voyages of discovery.

---

8. By the year 44 B.C., Julius Caesar and other generals had incorporated all of the lands bordering on the Mediterranean into the Roman Empire. Subsequently, a large part of western Asia (now the Middle East) came under Rome's rule.

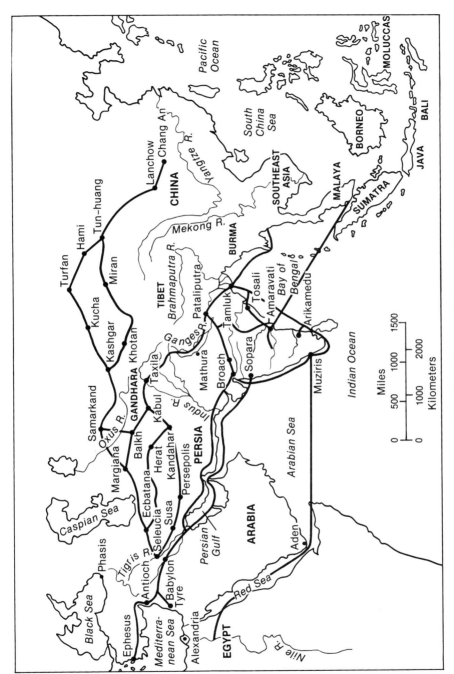

East–West Trade Routes, c. 200 B.C.–A.D. 200

109

DEVELOPMENTS IN HINDU CULTURE (200 B.C.–A.D. 300)

The centuries of busy trade with Asia and the West brought much prosperity to India's merchants and artisans. Inscriptions dating from between 200 B.C. and A.D. 300 show that most of the wealthy merchant and craft guilds of this era supported the Buddhist and Jain religions. However, Hinduism continued to have a powerful appeal to those who preferred a settled, traditional society. And soon, with the rise of the Gupta Empire, the Hindu religion recaptured its former prestige.

Several important texts of the Hindu religion were composed in the period between 200 B.C. and A.D. 300. The *Lawbook of Manu*, one of the most sacred of these, may have been composed around A.D. 200. Manu's laws reaffirm the traditional laws of caste society, and include many rules intended to uphold the purity and authority of the brahmans. For instance, one rule decrees severe punishments for a sudra who overhears a Veda being recited. Because of the strictness of such caste rules, Manu's laws are considered to be a reaction against the social upheavals that had occurred during the age of trade. Though it is unlikely that Manu's penalties were ever carried out in practice, they undoubtedly reminded Hindus to be vigilant in preserving the values and order of their society.

At the same time as Manu was composing his lawbooks, Hindus were also demonstrating their ability to absorb new currents of thought. Acknowledging the powerful appeal of the Mahayana religion, brahman authorities incorporated the Buddha into the Hindu pantheon as one of the nine *avatars*, or incarnations, of the god Vishnu. Also, Hindu artists began to portray Vishnu and Shiva in human form as *bhakti*, or devotional, sects became increasingly popular.

THE CLASSICAL AGE OF HINDUISM: THE GUPTA EMPIRE (A.D. 320–550)

Five centuries after the fall of the Mauryan Empire, much of northern India was again united under the rule of one king. This empire builder, who called himself Chandra Gupta,[9] acquired much of his kingdom by marrying the daughter of a powerful king. From the Ganges valley, he then expanded his territory west to the Punjab. The second and third Gupta kings, Samudra and Chandra II, continued to expand the empire.

---

9. Chandra Gupta was no relation to Chandragupta Maurya but may have adopted this name to invoke the earlier emperor's prestige. (The Guptas also chose to rule their empire from Pataliputra, which had been the Mauryas' capital city.)

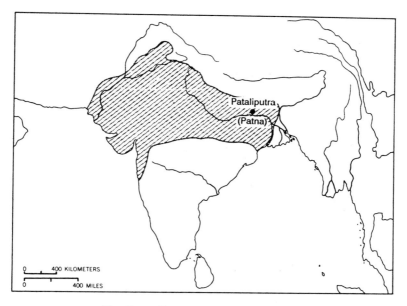

The Gupta Empire at Its Height, A.D. 400

Chandra II's reign is known as the most brilliant period of the Gupta Empire. Much of the literature and art of his day is still a central part of Hindu culture today. After the 40-year reign of Chandra II ended, in 415, the Gupta Empire continued for about a century. Then, the empire began to collapse as tides of invaders from central Asia—the Huns and the Gujaras—overran northern India.

The Gupta era is often referred to as the *classical age* of India's history. It was an age in which Hindu culture flourished and new heights were attained in arts such as temple building, painting, sculpture, and literature. The generous patronage of the Gupta kings also extended to non-Hindu sects. Thus, Buddhist and Jainist arts, too, developed and flourished.

Guptan Society and Government

The government of the Gupta kings was smaller and less intrusive than that of the Mauryas had been. Fa-Hsien, a Buddhist pilgrim who visited northern India during the reign of Chandra Gupta II, wrote that the king governed without harsh punishments and without meddlesome bureaucrats.

The people are numerous and happy; they have not to register their households, or attend to any magistrates and their rules. If they want to go, they go; if they want to stay on, they stay. The king governs without capital punishments. Criminals are simply fined, lightly or heavily, according to the circumstances.

Fa-Hsien also indicated that Manu's strict rules about brahman purity were observed in Guptan society. The untouchables, he noted, were required to announce their presence by beating a gong so that others could "avoid them, and not come into contact with them."

Wealthy city dwellers enjoyed the arts of poetry, courtship, painting, and music. In the poems and plays of the Guptan era, the pursuit of *kama*, or pleasure, is often praised as the highest goal of life. But Fa-Hsien noted that people also engaged in charitable activities: "The nobles and householders have founded hospitals within the city, to which the poor of all countries, the destitute, crippled and diseased, may repair. They receive every kind of help without charge."

The Revival of Sanskrit

The Gupta era marked the revival of Sanskrit, the language of Vedic times. (This trend had begun in Kanishka's time.) In the Gupta age, educated people spoke the language among themselves and used it to compose their poetry and plays. Also, new versions of the *Mahabharata* and the *Ramayana* were written and dramatized in polished Sanskrit.

Sanskrit is a complex, highly developed language that is difficult to translate into English. A translator has noted that while English is usually considered to have a rich vocabulary, "in comparison with Sanskrit, it is poor in the extreme."[10] Also, the translator notes, Sanskrit poets liked to use long compound adjectives which are elegant in the original but difficult to render in English. (For instance, one Sanskrit poet describes a cat as having "a-somewhat-made-into-a-hump back" and a dog as having a "saliva-smeared-open-mouth-corners-expanding-teeth-fearsomely gaping face.") In addition to the issues of vocabulary and long compounds, Sanskrit has stresses, or accents, that cannot be reproduced in other languages. The accent and meter of verses are highly important in conveying the *rasa*, or mood, of a poem.

The poet Kalidasa, who lived in the time of Chandra Gupta II, is considered to be the greatest master of the Sanskrit language. Like Shakespeare, to whom he is often compared, Kalidasa wrote plays as well as poems. Unfortunately, however, many of the subtleties of his work cannot be conveyed in translations. (A portion of his poem on the Four Seasons is quoted in Chapter 1.)

---

10. John Brough, *Poems from the Sanskrit* (New York: Viking Penguin, 1968), p. 31.

A Gupta-era portrait, representing Shiva, gives an indication of the life style enjoyed in this pleasant and cultivated age.

Advances in the Sciences

During the Gupta age, Indian mathematicians devised the use of a ten-digit (decimal) system. In this system, the concept of *zero* was introduced, making calculations much easier. The decimal system was carried to the West by Arab traders and became known as the Arabic numeral system. It has been described as India's greatest legacy to the world in the sphere of practical knowledge.

From the earliest times, India's thinkers had had an accurate idea concerning the extent of the universe and knew that the planets and stars were spherical in shape. From the Greek astronomers of Alexandria, India's mathematicians learned about the rotation of planets and how to calculate the length of the solar year. India soon adopted the Greek-Roman system of a 365-day year divided into twelve months. Aryabhata (c. 500), one of the first Indians to specialize in the science of astronomy, acknowledged his debt to the Greeks: "The Greeks are barbarians," he remarked, "but the science of astronomy originated with them, and for this they must be reverenced like gods."

APPROXIMATE DATES OF THE GUPTA KINGS

Chandra Gupta I	320–335
Samudra Gupta	335–375
Chandra Gupta II	375–415
Other Guptas	415–550
Huna invasions	450–550

Decline of the Gupta Empire

While India was enjoying an age of peace, prosperity, and creative achievement in the Gupta age, the societies of Europe and Asia were being overwhelmed by nomadic tribes from the north. Finally, India too was visited by the marauders. Beginning about 450, tribes of Huns—known in India as *Hunas*—and Gujaras began to threaten the northwestern frontier. At first, the Gupta kings were successful in repelling them, but repeated onslaughts eventually brought about the collapse of their empire.

After about 550, the main body of Huns moved on to Europe, and India began to rebuild itself into smaller kingdoms. But a number of Hunas and Gujaras, like the Shakas before them, decided to stay in India. Many of them settled in western India (present-day Malwa and Gujarat) and were certified as members of the kshatriya caste of Hindu society. In later centuries, these new kshatriyas called themselves the *Rajputs* ("Sons of Princes"). As we will see in Chapter 7, the Rajputs became famous for their spirited resistance to other invaders.

SUMMARY

The Mauryas' unification of India into one empire was a unique event in Indian history. Yet while no one managed to duplicate their achievement, many aspects of Mauryan government became a pattern for future kings. Later maharajas imitated the magnificent court life of the Mauryas and their generous patronage of the arts. Also, the king's right to collect taxes continued to be recognized. Villagers became accustomed to giving a portion of their crops to a central government, and this produce was the main source of revenue for the Guptas and most later kings.

After a few centuries, the Mauryan kings were forgotten. (It was only after some of Ashoka's pillar writings were deciphered, in the 19th century, that their memory was revived.) Nevertheless, many of the patterns they had established survived into modern times.

During the centuries of international trade, westerners became fascinated with India, and India became rich from the sale of its crafts and other products. Also, the Mahayana religion grew immensely popular in northern India and began to spread throughout Asia.

During the Gupta age, the Hindu religion again demonstrated its ability to assimilate new ideas. With the encouragement of the Gupta kings, who worshiped the god Vishnu, all Hindu sects experienced a revival. The most important Hindu gods, both in the Gupta age and today, are the triad of Brahma, Vishnu, and Shiva.

DISCUSSION AND ESSAY QUESTIONS

1. Kautilya's philosophy has often been summarized as "the ends justify the means." Is this a fair summary of his advice? Explain why or why not.

2. How did the Mauryan Empire change under Ashoka? Compare his method of governing to that of his ancestors.

3. Both Hindus and Buddhists believed that a leader's character sets the tone, or spirit, of his age. To what extent do people share this idea today? Are today's leaders expected to set a moral example?

4. Why did Buddhists believe that it is dangerous for a leader to have too much wealth and power? What modern institutions address this concern?

5. What kind of interactions took place between India, Asia, and the West during the age of trade (c. 200 B.C.–A.D 200)? What developments can be traced to these interactions?

6. Why is the Gupta age called the classical age of India? How did the Gupta kings contribute to the achievements of this era?

ADDITIONAL READINGS

A. L. Basham, *The Wonder That Was India*, 3d ed. (London: Sidgwick & Jackson, 1967). A standard reference work, with detailed discussion of the Gupta era and other periods of Indian history.

J. W. McCrindle, ed., *Ancient India as Described by Megasthenes and Arrian* (Delhi: Today and Tomorrow, 1972). In this book, as in others by the same author, descriptions of India are collected from various works by ancient Greek historians.

John S. Strong, *The Legend of King Asoka* (Princeton, N.J.: Princeton University Press, 1983). This popular book explores Buddhist ideals of kingship, with particular emphasis on those concerning Ashoka. Difficult reading in parts.

THE LAWS OF MANU

Manu's laws were probably an attempt to reestablish strict rules for Hindu society at a time when people were following a more relaxed standard of behavior. These laws were believed to have sacred authority and had a great influence on future generations.

Women's Status in Society

A girl, a young woman, and even an aged woman should do nothing independently, even in her own house. In childhood a woman must be subject to her father, in youth to her husband, and when her lord is dead to her sons. A woman must never be independent.

Even if a husband is devoid of good qualities, or seeks pleasure elsewhere, he must be worshiped as a god by a faithful wife. If a wife obeys her husband, she will for that reason alone be exalted in heaven. Women must perform no religious ceremonies (sacrifices, vows, or fasts) on their own.

Men who seek their own welfare should honor women on holidays and festivals with gifts of ornaments, clothes, and dainty food. Where women are honored, there the gods are pleased; but where they are not honored, no sacred rite yields rewards.

The houses on which female relations, not being duly honored, pronounce a curse, perish completely, as if destroyed by magic.

In that family where the husband is pleased with his wife and the wife with her husband, happiness will assuredly be lasting.

1. What is the religious duty of a wife? Does she attain "heaven" in a different way than her husband?
2. What should a wife do if her husband fails in his duties toward her? Are husbands given any advice or warnings on this subject?

SANSKRIT POETRY OF THE GUPTA ERA

While the Gupta age is known mainly for the classical dramas of Kalidasa and other masters, poetry of a more informal type was also characteristic of the age. The poetry of this age indicates that men and women probably related to each another on easier terms than the Laws of Manu *would indicate. Many of the poets also expressed an irreverent attitude toward kings and toward brahmanic learning.*

After God made your eyes of lotus-blue, took for your teeth white jasmine,
  shaped the whole face as a better lily, chose the hue and texture of
  magnolia for your skin,
He then grew tired of soft things, and within He carved from flint the
  impenetrable soul.

She who is always in my thoughts prefers another man, and does not think of me.
Yet he seeks for another's love, not hers; and some poor girl is grieving for my sake.
Why then, the devil take both her and him, and love, and her, and me.

In former days we'd both agree that you were me, and I was you.
What has now happened to us two, that you are you, and I am me?

A use can be found for rotten wood,
And infertile gound may produce some good.
Kings, when they fall, have no uses at all.

I left a loving new-wed wife behind, and slaved at books, and slept upon the ground,
And lived on alms, and disciplined my mind, to win the wisdom waiting to be found.
Yet, with the ages' knowledge I inherit, throughout the land no patronage I find.
Why should a man for learning vex his spirit, gaining neither comfort nor religious merit?

SOURCE: John Brough, *Poems from the Sanskrit* (New York: Viking Penguin, 1968).

1. What do these verses indicate about the poets' attitudes toward the opposite sex? Are their attitudes similar or dissimilar to modern ones?

THE HISTORY OF SOUTH INDIA (250 B.C.–A.D. 1300) AND THE COMING OF ISLAM

When love is ripe beyond bearing and goes to seed,
Men will ride even palmyra stems as if they were horses;
Will wear on their heads the reeking cones of the errukkam as
*   if they were flowers;*
Will draw to themselves the laughter of the streets;
*   and will do worse.*

*   Poem of unrequited love, Sangam Age*

During the era of the Mauryan Empire (c. 280 B.C.), the Tamil peoples of South India were brought into close contact with the Hindu civilization of the north. The Tamils soon expressed a strong affinity for Hindu culture and for the teachings of Buddhist and Jainist sects as well.

After many centuries of assimilation, South India began to make its own distinctive contributions to Hindu culture. Beginning about A.D. 600, a wave of *bhakti*, or devotional, religion arose in the south. The movement drew its inspiration from the Vedas and was also shaped by the Tamils' love of dance, music, and poetry. In the next few centuries, bhakti religion swept through northern India as well. During this era, the Hindu gods—especially Vishnu and Shiva—assumed the character and form that they still have for worshipers today.

118

In the year 1000, northern India was conquered by the Turkish Muslims. Three centuries later, South India, too, was visited by these invaders. In the second half of this chapter, we will see why this new tide of invasions differed in character from all earlier conquests.

THE TAMIL PEOPLES OF SOUTH INDIA

As mentioned in Chapter 3, a group of people called the *Dravidians* are thought to have been among the founders of the Harappan civilization of the Indus valley. The exact origin of the Dravidians is still a mystery. Language studies have suggested that they once lived in the Mediterranean region and in central Asia. There is also a legend that they came to India from a continent submersed by the sea.

The Dravidians, also known as the *Tamils*, probably came to South India around 2000 B.C., traveling both by land and by sea. Most of them settled in the region known as *Tamilnad* ("Tamil country"), which included the broad Coromandel plain, the Malabar coast, and the hills and

After trade with the Roman world ended (c. 200), South Indian merchants shifted their focus to the southeast. This depiction of an Indian ship was found in Java.

mountains of the Western and Eastern Ghats. It was—and still remains—the center of Tamil civilization. For this reason, it is often considered to be a separate region from the northern Deccan.

After arriving in South India, the Tamils mingled with the original inhabitants of the area and developed a thriving civilization.[1] The mainstay of their society was the produce—grain, rice, and cotton—of the Coromandel plain. But to outsiders, the Tamils became better known for the rare and exotic products they exported. These products included spices such as pepper and cinnamon; precious gemstones and pearls; sandal, ebony, and teak woods; and crafted items such as muslin and silk, bronzeware and gold jewelry. The scope of the Tamils' trading and seafaring activities is indicated by several clues. The Old Testament, for instance, relates that King Solomon imported materials from India for the building of his temple (about 1000 B.C.). By 200 B.C., as we have seen, the riches of India's seacoast bazaars were well known throughout the ancient world. After trade with the Roman world declined, around A.D. 200, South Indian merchants shifted their focus to China and Southeast Asia.

The Sangam Era of Tamil Culture (250 B.C.–A.D. 250)

The oldest known poems and epics of the Tamils are believed to date from about 250 B.C. to A.D. 250. (They are called *Sangam* literature because they were compiled by a *sangam*, or academy, of scholars.) The Sangam poets came from all levels of Tamil society: they were court poets, wandering minstrels, mothers, brahmans, and even kings. Their poems represent their "golden age" of Tamil culture and are still widely read in South India today.

During the Sangam age, the Tamils had adopted many Hindu beliefs but seldom mentioned religion in their literature. And they took even less notice of the many foreigners—Greeks, Romans, and Arabs—who lived in their port cities. Instead, their poetry dealt with traditional themes, often summarized as "love and war."

Sangam poems of love speak of private emotions, especially the many moods of courtship. Over the centuries, the poets developed a variety of literary devices to portray these moods. They had vocabulary to describe such complex emotions as jealousy-conflicting-with-love, for instance, or even an extremely lovelorn condition in which a maiden's earrings fall off by themselves. Very often, they associated human emotions with images

---

1. Archeologists have found evidence that at least two other groups had settled in South India before the Dravidians. One group came from Africa, and the other was akin to the aborigines of Australia.

in the South Indian landscape. For example, the solitude of a blue lily by the seashore symbolized longing for an absent lover.

Sangam poems of war, by contrast, speak of more public events. They portray the lives and deeds of kings, highlighting the crises, such as war, in which their resolve and wisdom were tested.

In the Sangam age, Tamilnad was ruled by three royal dynasties: the Pandya, the Chera, and the Chola. These dynasties had existed "from time immemorial," and the rivalries among them were one of the main themes of poetry.

When a king was wise and just, people believed, his kingdom flourished: his subjects were noble, his armies triumphed over any invaders and the monsoon rains appeared in timely fashion.

If a king were irresponsible or unjust, his subjects had no recourse. In such cases, however, the court poets often played a mediating role: they reminded the king of his duty, often mixing such a reminder with lavish praise. The following verse is one of the best known of the poets' statements:

> Not rice, not water, only the king
> is the life-breath of a kingdom.
> And it is the duty of a king
> with his army of spears to know
> he's the life of the wide, blossoming kingdom.

There is evidence that the poets' words were greatly respected and feared by their royal patrons. We hear of several unjust kings, for instance, who mended their ways after listening to the criticism of a court poet. Thus, the poets—like the kings—came to have a sacred role in Tamil society.

Many Sangam poems are written in praise of kings whose "irresistable wrath" overcame their enemies in battle and saved their kingdoms from invasion. The most honored kings and warriors were those who died bravely in battle, "with a body hacked by long blades." No one doubted that these heroes ascended straight to heaven.

In times of peace, the Tamil kings resided at their royal courts, with their poets, ministers, and other advisers in attendance. Here, their main function was to dispense justice to their subjects, "to protect the innocent and punish the guilty." When the day's business was over, the king feasted and was entertained by his poets, singers, minstrels, dancers, and many wives. A king's ability to enjoy such pleasures was considered praiseworthy. A truly noble king, the poets suggested, might unleash murderous passions in war but should be convivial and generous in peacetime. Kings who lavished gifts on poets naturally received special praise, and several became legendary for their generosity and kindliness. One ruler, for instance, won lasting fame by donating his shawl to a shivering peacock.

The Sangam era came to an end around A.D. 250, when the kings of Tamilnad were displaced by a group of interlopers called the Kalabhras. (The name *Kalabhras* possibly means "robbers.") During the next 350 years, nothing is heard of the Chola, Chera, and Pandya families, but they did not disappear entirely. Later, they would reemerge as chieftains and kings in the medieval era.

Assimilation of Hindu Culture in Tamilnad

Beginning in Bindusara Maurya's reign, about 280 B.C., thousands of brahman families immigrated to South India and helped bring about a fusion of the Hindu and Tamil cultures. The first sign of this assimilation was the Tamils' attitude of reverence toward brahmans and their way of life. Several Sangam poems mention the cleanliness of brahman communities; for instance, the "sinless streets where there are no dogs in the wide doorways." The brahmans' reputation for learning and honesty also won them the favor of Sangam kings: brahmans were often employed as royal ministers and were endowed with large, tax-free estates to secure their livelihood. Soon, the Coromandel coast was dotted with brahman settlements. By the early medieval era (beginning about A.D. 600), brahmans had achieved the highest status in peasant communities and played a central role in village governments.

The Caste System in Tamilnad. The caste system in South India did not follow exactly the same pattern as in the north. After the brahmans, the most respected class in Tamil society were the landowning peasants. These prosperous peasants and their chieftains were the mainstay of the army and of the economy. Thus, there was no need for a separate warrior (kshatriya) caste.

Wealthy merchants, textile weavers, and other artisans also had a respected place in society, and there were no rules to determine their exact rank in relation to others. Yet the Tamils considered it important to marry within one's own social rank. Partly for this reason, perhaps, the custom of marrying first cousins developed. This practice, still prevalent in South India today, ensures that marriage partners are of equal status. Another way of creating exclusive groups was the division of occupations into "right-hand" and "left-hand" castes. (Jobs associated with farming are called *right-hand*, while those associated with city artisans and foreign trade are called *left-hand* castes.) These labels do not necessarily imply that one group is superior to the other; they simply give each group a more clear-cut identity.

Village Sabhas. In medieval times, brahmans or wealthy peasants held all the elective offices in most villages. They maintained the village temples and water tanks, decided judicial disputes, and collected taxes for the king. Later, other groups in the village were represented through caste *panchayats*, or councils. Thus, the villages managed their own affairs. In modern India, this tradition of local autonomy has continued.

The Rise of Bhakti Sects (Seventh to Tenth Centuries)

About A.D. 600, a new dynasty called the *Pallavas* became the most powerful force in Tamilnad. The 300-year reign of the Pallavas coincided with a great wave of bhakti religion that soon spread throughout Tamilnad. Mahendra Varman I, the first Pallava king, reflected this change: originally a Jainist, he became a devotee of Shiva. At the seacoast town of Mahabalipuram, near modern Madras, the Pallavas built the first monumental temple to this god. It became the model and inspiration for many other splendid temples built in South India during the medieval period.

The bhakti movement was spread by a group of poet-singers, both men and women, who sang hymns in praise of Vishnu or Shiva. In their hymns, they told of their spiritual awakening through divine grace and were soon recognized as saints. The poet-saints who devoted themselves to Vishnu were called *Alvars*, and the Shiva devotees were known as *Nayanars*. Each group concentrated their devotions on one god alone and ascribed all the qualities of Brahman to that deity.

The message of the Alvars and Nayanars was presented in terms that everyone could understand. The human soul, they said, aspired for union with God but was unable to achieve this union on its own. Thus, there was nothing a person could do but to wait and hope for divine grace. Like the distraught lovers depicted in Sangam poems, the bhakti saints often forgot all normal cares and activities. (One ninth-century king, for instance, became so carried away by devotion that he tried to raise an army to rescue Sita, the mythological heroine of the *Ramayana*.)

The Alvars and Nayanars rejected caste distinctions and preached that all men and women are equally eligible for salvation. They had little regard for the learning of brahmans and the austerities practiced by ascetics. Such efforts are useless, they said: people must simply realize their helplessness and wait for divine grace. The following verses by Appar, one of the earliest bhakti saints, express this attitude. Like most of the saints, Appar was of low caste.

> Why chant the Vedas, hear the Shastras' lore?
> Why daily teach the books of righteousness? . . .
> Release is theirs and theirs alone, whose heart
> From thinking of its Lord shall ne'er depart. . . .

Why fast and starve, why suffer pains austere?
Why climb the mountains doing penance harsh?
Why go to bathe in waters far and near?
Release is theirs, and theirs alone, who call
At every time upon the Lord of all.

The Chola Era

In 871, the Pallava dynasty collapsed. The Chola family, who had been chieftains under the Pallavas, then became the new rulers of Tamilnad. From their capital at Tanjore, the Cholas proceeded to build the most powerful kingdom ever known in South India. During their reign, the bhakti sects flowered, and the arts of temple building, painting, and religious sculpture reached new heights. As the Cholas expanded into Sri Lanka and Southeast Asia, the revitalized Hindu religion also began to spread its influence in these areas.

During the Chola era, the life stories and mythological feats of the Hindu gods were a favorite theme of literature and art. Shiva, the god of the Chola kings, was honored more than any other. In time, artists found a way to portray all of the forces Shiva employs to keep the universe in balance. (See photo on page 28, *bottom left*.) His ability to create and to

During the medieval age and later, each major dynasty in South India developed its own style of temple building. This temple at Madurai is one of many monuments of the period.

destroy are shown in the freeze-frame of a dance; one foot crushing the dwarf of ignorance and one upraised to symbolize the liberation of souls. In addition, his many arms—representing his ability to be everywhere at once—are poised to unleash either blessing or destruction. The Chola artists' rendering of Shiva's cosmic dance is still one of the most famous of Indian images. One critic termed it "the clearest image of the *activity* of God which any art or religion can boast of."[2]

After two centuries, the Chola Empire began to decline. By 1293, when Marco Polo passed through Malabar on his way back from China, South India had become a patchwork of many small kingdoms. Yet Polo was still able to glimpse the dazzling luxury of the Tamil kings of old. He reported that one minor Pandya king was wearing enough precious stones to ransom a city: the king's adornments included 104 great pearls as well as rubies, emeralds, and other precious gems.

CHRONOLOGY OF SOUTH INDIA, 250 B.C.–A.D. 1311

250 B.C.–A.D. 250	Sangam era of Tamilnad—reign of the Pandyas, Cheras, and Cholas
250–600	Reign of the Kalabhras; Buddhist and Jainist sects become popular
600–871	Reign of the Pallavas; growth of bhakti sects and decline of Buddhist and Jainist influence
871–1071	Rule of the imperial Cholas; expansion of Tamil culture into Sri Lanka and Southeast Asia; height of medieval temple building and religious art
1071–1310	Chola kingdom decreases; other dynasties gain territory
1206	First Muslim sultanate established at Delhi
1293	Marco Polo visits Malabar coast and meets Pandya king
1311	A Muslim general pillages South India

THE MUSLIM INVASIONS OF NORTHERN INDIA

Beginning about 997, a Muslim chieftain known as Mahmud of Ghazni began to make annual conquests in northern India. He described his motives as follows:

> The entire country of India is full of gold and jewels, and of plants fit for making apparel, and aromatic plants and sugar cane. The whole aspect of

---

2. Ananda K. Coomaraswamy, *The Dance of Siva* (New York: Dover, 1985), p. 56.

the country is pleasant and delightful. Now, since the inhabitants are chiefly infidels and idolators, by the order of God and his Prophet it is right for us to conquer them.[3]

Mahmud's campaigns of terror lasted about 20 years and caused large-scale destruction and bloodshed: in one raid alone, on the temple city of Somnath, his army was reported to have killed 50,000 citizens. He also removed vast treasures of gold and jewels to his capital city of Ghazni in Afghanistan. Mahmud justified his campaigns of terror by the fact that Hindu temples contained "idols," or statues of gods. *Idolatry*, the worship of such images, was expressly prohibited in Islam.

Mahmud, the "Sword of Islam" of his day, was followed by a long succession of Muslim invaders, mostly of Afghan and Turkish descent. These warriors were excellent horsemen and made use of the iron stirrup, a new invention, to brace themselves as they fired their crossbows at a gallop. Soon, they had penetrated the entire Ganges region, slaughtering or driving into exile the religious communities they encountered.

---

3. Quoted in Francis Watson, *A Concise History of India* (New York: Thames & Hudson, 1979), p. 88.

The 240-foot Qutab Minar tower at Delhi was the first major monument built by the Muslims on Indian soil. Constructed on the site of a Hindu temple around 1200, it proclaims the victory of Islam over Hinduism.

In 1206, the Muslims established a *sultanate*, or Muslim kingdom, at Delhi and proceeded to expand to the south. At first, they met with determined resistance from the Rajput dynasties of the northern Deccan. (Many of these Rajput warriors were the descendants of earlier invaders from central Asia.) In the end, the Rajputs could not prevent the Muslim conquerors from passing to the south, and they withdrew to their mountain fortresses to await another opportunity.

The End of South India's Independence

In 1311, a Muslim general named Kafur led an army from Delhi into South India. The South Indian kings, busy with a feud among themselves, were not even able to defend major cities such as Madurai from the Muslims. After pillaging the region, Kafur retreated to the north with thousands of tons of gold, jewels, and pearls, as well as 20,000 horses and 600 elephants. Kafur's exploit is considered to mark the end of South India's independence.

THE ISLAMIC RELIGION

At first, the Muslims seemed no different from many other "hit-and-run" conquerors who had descended upon India in the past. Earlier invaders had also caused massive destruction when they first arrived, yet had eventually been absorbed into Indian society. But the Muslims' conquests in India set in motion a series of violent struggles that have continued to the present day. These continuing conflicts have much to do with the basic attitudes and beliefs of the Hindu and Islamic faiths.

As we have seen, the Hindu religion drew its inspiration from many sources and came to regard all types of religious experience as true and valid. In contrast, Islam is a *messianic* religion: that is, it is based on the teachings of one messiah, or prophet. Devout Muslims believe that this messiah, Mohammed, received and transmitted to them the direct word of God. Thus it follows that Islam is the only valid religion in the world. Moreover, Mohammed conveyed a highly detailed vision of how human society should be ordered. As the Muslim armies advanced across western Asia, this vision dramatically changed the lives of all the peoples they encountered.

The Teachings of the Koran

The Islamic religion originated in A.D. 610, in the deserts of Arabia (now Saudi Arabia). In that year, Mohammed, a merchant of the city of Mecca, announced that God had chosen him as his final Prophet, or Messenger.

As he was meditating in the desert, Mohammed reported, a great figure in the heavens commanded him to "recite." And, he said, he was able to do so under divine guidance. The revelations continued throughout Mohammed's life and were later written down in the *Koran,* or "Recitation." The Koran reveals that there is but one God—known in Arabic as *Allah*—and that people can achieve salvation only through *Islam,* or submission to Allah.

Though Mohammed was persecuted at first, his powerful message eventually gained him a community of faithful disciples. Using military means, Mohammed then expanded his influence. By the year 630—two decades after his first vision—Mohammed had conquered all of Arabia in the name of Islam. After his death in 632, his followers, the *Muslims,* continued his work. Within a few years, they had conquered northern Africa and much of western Asia (Jordan, Syria, Iraq, and Iran). A century after Mohammed's death, the Islamic empire extended from the Atlantic seaboard to the Himalayas.

In the Koran, many of the central teachings of Judaism and Christianity are confirmed as true. The authority of the Old Testament prophets—notably Abraham and Moses—is affirmed, and Jesus, too, is recognized as a true prophet. Mohammed taught his followers to respect both Jews and Christians as "People of the Book," since they had accepted the teachings of the Old and New Testaments. But Mohammed believed that many errors had crept into both the Jewish and Christian religions and that it was his role to correct them. Thus, while he preached tolerance toward Jews and Christians, Mohammed also announced that those who had heard the message of Islam and failed to heed it were condemned to damnation.

To attain salvation, the Koran teaches, people must realize that life on earth is just "a sport and a pastime," a preparation for the true life to come. When Judgment Day comes, sinners will find no escape from Allah's wrath, and the righteous will enter into the bliss of paradise. But even those who know this, Mohammed said, are constantly prey to temptations. For instance, people who achieve material wealth often feel proud and self-sufficient and so forget that Allah alone is the source of their blessings. (Reverence for material wealth or any other "false god" falls into the category of *idolatry,* the sin most often denounced in the Koran.) Thus, people must wage a constant *jihad,* or struggle, against their own evil tendencies. Mohammed described this personal struggle as the "greater *jihad,*" while the military struggle against unbelievers was termed the "lesser *jihad.*"

Mohammed taught his followers that to live a life of true *Islam,* or submission to Allah, it is not enough to have correct beliefs: a person must act out these beliefs in everyday life. In creating his *umma,* or community of the faithful, Mohammed established the laws known as the Five Pillars of Islam. To join the *umma*, a person first confesses faith in Islam by saying, "There is no God but Allah, and Mohammed is his prophet." This statement, usually repeated many times thoughout life, is the first pillar of Islam. The remaining four pillars of the faith are intended to renew this commitment. The Second Pillar specifies the five times of the day Muslims must pray to Allah, either at a mosque or at their workplaces. Third, Muslims must donate a portion of their property to the community, to be used in helping the needy and in spreading the cause of Islam. Fourth, during the month of *Ramadan* (the ninth lunar month), Muslims go without food and drink each day from dawn to sundown. (This fasting marks the period when Mohammed received the revelations of the Koran and is intended as a time of spiritual reflection.) Finally, if they are able, Muslims make at least once in their lifetime a pilgrimage to Mecca, the city Mohammed established as the center of Islam.

For the Muslim *umma*, there is no such thing as secular law, or law apart from religion: all human affairs are governed by Allah's law. When the answer to a particular question cannot be found in the Koran, Muslims turn to the traditions known as the *Sunna*. The *Sunna* are the laws and customs that Mohammed provided for his followers, either by the example of his own life or in sermons to his community. The total body of Islamic law—the Koran, the Sunna, and other oral traditions about Mohammed's life—is known as the *Sharia*, or Islamic way. The rules outlined in the Sharia extend to every aspect of life: social relations, rituals of worship, financial and legal affairs, and even styles of clothing.

To Muslims, any departure from the strict laws of the Sharia represents a threat to salvation. Yet, in each generation since Mohammed's time, new ideas and situations have arisen that are not directly addressed in the Sharia. Mohammed put great faith in the ability of his community to resolve all such questions, reportedly saying, "My *umma* will never agree together upon an error." Thus, Mohammed established the principle that decisions would be made by consensus in the Muslim community. The principle of consensus, or majority rule, gives Islam a strong democratic quality. However, there is no provision in Islam for minority rights or freedom of expression, since dissenters are considered a threat to the community.

In practice, the Muslim community is often guided in its decisions by *mullahs*, or religious scholars learned in the law. In times of turmoil or doubt, the policy of religious leaders—and the community as a whole—often has been to return to the literal teachings of the Koran, rejecting all social, political, and technological innovations that have taken place since Mohammed's day. (In modern times, this conservative approach has been labeled *fundamentalism*.)

Leadership in the Islamic World

After Mohammed's death in 632, Abu Bakr, a man who had been one of his first disciples, was chosen *caliph*, or leader, of the Muslim community. Abu Bakr was succeeded in turn by three other men who had been closely associated with Mohammed. These four came to be known as the "rightly guided" caliphs because they remained true to Mohammed's example. During the 30 years of their leadership, from 632 to 661, Islamic armies conquered Syria, Palestine, Egypt, and much of Persia. Yet, for this time, the desert town of Medina in Arabia remained the headquarters of the Muslim world, and the caliphs continued to follow the same simple, devout life style as they had in Mohammed's day. Moreover, they cautioned their generals to attribute their victories to Allah alone and to retain an attitude of piety and humility.

As the Muslim generals conquered vast territories in Asia, their new-found wealth and power created new stresses among the leaders of the community. In the power struggles that ensued, three of the four "rightly guided" caliphs were assassinated by their own followers. These episodes of Muslim-on-Muslim violence established a pattern for the next thousand years of Islamic history. Since there is no provision, in the Koran, for the election or removal of political leaders, assassination continued to mark the majority of successions.

Shiite and Sunni Sects. The murder of Ali, the last of the four "rightly guided" caliphs, was viewed as an especially tragic event in the Muslim community. Ali had been married to Mohammed's daughter Fatima and hence was the father of the Prophet's direct descendants. Later, some Muslims began to believe that a strong, charismatic leader—especially one descended from Ali—could be the instrument by which Allah makes his will known. These Muslims became known as the *Shiites*, or "Party of Ali." They believed that a great *imam*, or leader, should use his own initiative in making decisions rather than being confined by tradition. The majority of Muslims, known as the *Sunnis,* continued to believe that a political leader is merely the "first among equals" and does not have special sacred authority. Instead, they considered the *Sunna,* or traditions, to be the only legitimate source of knowledge.

The Influence of Persian Culture. During the next few centuries, many changes occurred in the Muslim world. The center of Islam moved from Arabia to Damascus and then to Baghdad, a city of legendary opulence. Under the Abbasid caliphs, who ruled the Muslim world from 750 to 1258, the art and architecture of ancient Persia came to be closely identified with Islam. The Abbasids' style of leadership, too, followed Persian models.

Although they were technically Sunni Muslims, they ruled as despots, or absolute rulers, and the more democratic traditions of earlier caliphs were forgotten. The story of the *1001 Arabian Nights* portrays the almost unimaginable luxury of the Abbasid court, where the caliph's every wish was carried out without question.

The Muslim Sultanate in India

By the 13th century, the power of the Abbasids was in decline, and several independent kingdoms had grown up around the edges of the Islamic empire. The Muslim sultanate in India was one of these. Although the leadership of the Indian sultanate rapidly passed from one dynasty to another, it was soon recognized as the most powerful kingdom in India. For the next few centuries, there were only rare interludes of peace in northern India, as the sultans struggled to subdue their Muslim rivals and quell the rebellions of Hindu princes.

Beginning in 1526, a dynasty known as the *Moghuls* took control of the Delhi sultanate and eventually extended their government through much of India. During most of the Moghul era, the Islamic religion was favored and promoted by the central government. As a result, millions of Hindus converted to Islam, either out of religious conviction or to avoid persecution. Thus, while the vast majority of Indians remained Hindus, the Islamic religion established a permanent presence in Indian society.[4]

SUMMARY

During the third century B.C., South India was brought into close contact with the civilization of northern India. The Tamil peoples found Hindu culture to be quite compatable with their own beliefs and ideas, and soon began to contribute their own ideas to it.

In the medieval age of South India (c. 600–1300), Hindu culture flourished in the bhakti movement of devotional worship. During this era, the traditional arts of South India—especially poetry, dancing, and music—were integrated into religious worship.

The arrival of Islamic armies in India set in motion a series of violent struggles that continued for centuries and created lasting enmities between Hindus and Muslims. For most Muslim rulers, piety took the form of

---

4. Before the partition of India and Pakistan, some 20 to 25 percent of India's citizens were Muslims. As of 1990, about 11 percent of India's citizens, or 92 million people, were Muslims.

waging war on unbelievers, as Mohammed had done in the early days of Islam. A few rulers, however, tried to spread the faith through acts of charity and mercy, an approach which is also sanctioned in the Koran. In the end, the campaign to extend Islam across all of Asia failed, but it left an indelible stamp on the Indian landscape.

DISCUSSION AND ESSAY QUESTIONS

1. During the Sangam age, the role of poets—like that of kings—was considered sacred. Explain why the poets' role was so important. Compare the role of a Sangam poet to that of a White House press correspondent in modern times.
2. In what ways was the bhakti movement influenced by the ancient culture of Tamilnad?
3. Describe the bhakti aspects of your own religion or of another religion you are familiar with.
4. It has been said that Islam is "both worldly and otherworldly; a complete way of life." Compose a short argument to defend or to refute this statement.
5. Throughout much of its history, the Islamic community has been known for its opposition to new ideas and other innovations. Give reasons to explain this conservative outlook.

ADDITIONAL READINGS

A. K. Ramanujan, *Poems of Love and War* (New York: Columbia University Press, 1985). This book contains eloquent translations of some of the major poetry of the Sangam age.

Frederick M. Denny, *Islam* (New York: Harper Collins, 1987). A compact and yet comprehensive outline of Islamic history and beliefs.

POETRY OF THE SANGAM AGE

The following verses fall into the category of Sangam war poems, since they concern public events. However, they also evoke the delights of peacetime and the emotions of friendship. In this respect, they draw on the tradition of Sangam love poems.

The subject of these poems is the tragic story of Pari, a popular chieftain under the Pandyas. Pari's troubles began when he refused offers from all three kings of Tamilnad to take his daughters in marriage. Angered, the three kings combined their armies and launched an attack.

Kapilar, the author of these verses, was Pari's court poet and friend. The first poem is addressed to the kings after their failure to take Pari's hill, known as Parampu. The second and third poems were composed after Pari was treacherously killed in a peace conference.

Pari's Hill

The hill is wide as the sky, the pools flash like stars.
Even if you have elephants tied to every tree there,
and chariots standing in every field, you will never take the hill.
He will not give in to the sword.

But I know a way to take it: pick carefully your lute-strings,
string little lutes, and with your dancing women with dense fragrant hair
    behind you,
go singing and dancing to Pari, and he'll give you both hill and country.

Pari's Green Land Remembered

Even when black Saturn smouldered in the sky,
even when comets smoked and the silver star ran to the south,
his crops would still come to harvest, the bushes would flower,
large-eyed rows of wild cows would calve in the yard and crop the grass.

Because his scepter was just, the green land knew no lack of rains,
there were many noble men, green-leaved jasmine flowered like the thorn
    teeth of young wildcats
in the country of Pari, father of those artfully bangled daughters.

Farewell to Pari's Hill

Now Pari is dead,
our hearts are muddy, our eyes are streaming;
we'll pray and bless and take your leave,
Parampu, hill of fame.

And we'll go our ways in search of men
who are fit to touch the dark fragrant hair
of Pari's daughters,
with many small bangles on their wrists.

SOURCE: A. K. Ramanujan, *Poems of Love and War* (New York: Columbia University Press, 1985), pp. 142–149.

1. In the Sangam age, kings and chieftains often employed their poets as ambassadors. In the first poem quoted here, the poet Kapilar was serving in this role. Was his diplomacy effective? Or might he have found a better way to appease the kings?
2. What kind of man was Pari, based on Kapilar's portrait?
3. How does the poet account for the prosperity of Pari's kingdom?

BHAKTI POEMS

The primary gods of the Hindus soon became popular in South India, for the Tamils could readily identify them with their own ancient deities. For instance, Vishnu was associated with the Tamil god Tiru-mal, who roamed the hills of Tamilnad, and Shiva was identified with the warlike Murugan.

In their hymns to Vishnu and Shiva, the bhakti poets often drew upon the traditions of Tamil love poetry to express their religious devotion.

Hymn to Tirumal (Vishnu)

In fire, you are the heat. In flowers, you are the scent.
Among stones, you are the diamond.
In words, you are truth. Among virtues, you are love.
In a warrior's wrath, you are the strength.

In the Vedas, you are the secret. Of the elements, you are the first.
In the scorching sun, you are the light. In moonlight, you are the softness.
Everything, you are everything, the sense, the substance, of everything.

Hymn to Shiva

Like treasure hidden in the ground, taste in the fruit,
gold in the rock, oil in the seed,
the Absolute hidden away in the heart,
no one can know the ways of our lord white as jasmine.

You are the forest, you are all the great trees in the forest.
You are bird and beast playing in and out of all the trees.
O lord white as jasmine, filling and filled by all,
Why don't you show me your face? . . .

Four parts of the day I grieve for you. Four parts of the night I'm mad
  for you.
I lie lost, sick for you, night and day,
O lord white as jasmine.
Since your love was planted, I've forgotten hunger, thirst, and sleep.

SOURCE: R. K. Ramanujan, *Poems of Love and War* (New York: Columbia University
Press, 1985), p. 218.

1. What qualities does the first poet ascribe to the god Tirumal (Vishnu)?
2. What emotions does the second poet feel while waiting for divine grace?

KRISHNA'S LIFE ON EARTH

*As the bhakti sects developed, the god Krishna became a special
focus of devotion. The story of Krishna's life on earth, written in the
eighth century, is one of the most beloved scriptures of the Hindu
religion. It tells of Krishna's childhood pranks, his escapades as a
youth, and his qualities of savior as an adult. Thus, worshipers are
able to relate to many different facets of the god. Today, ceremonies*

Krishna's relationship with the gopis symbolized the devotion celebrated in the
bhakti movement. Here, Krishna and the gopis bring the cows home from pasture.

in honor of Krishna range from festivals of great merriment and humor to solemn readings of his spiritual advice to Arjuna in the Mahabharata.

The following episode describes Krishna's relationship with the Gopis, the women of a small village on the Yamuna River. The Gopis do not know at first about Krishna's divinity; they believe he is a simple cowherd of the village.

It was autumn, and the nights were delicious with flowering jasmine when, as he had promised, Krishna resolved to play with the Gopis through his yogic powers. So sweetly did he play on his flute in the moonlit forest as to enslave the Gopis' hearts to him. As soon as they heard its melody, the maids of Vraja hastened to where their beloved Lord was. . . . They made their way as if in a trance, for their hearts had been stolen away by Krishna and could not turn back to their homes.

At times the Gopis sang his glory, at times he sang of them; and so they roamed about, adding grace to Brindavan's lovely woods. Coming to the cool river sands, they met the gentle breezes wafted from the waves of the Yamuna, carrying the fragrance of the lilies; and there he spent his time in loving play with the Gopis, awakened love in them, and with his looks of love gave them all delight. But when they received attentions in this way from the almighty and gracious Lord, they grew proud and thought themselves better than all else upon earth. Seeing how they were elated with pride because of their good fortune, Krishna suddenly disappeared from there, in order to humble them and give them his Grace.

Finding him no longer there, the maids of Vraja were distracted, their hearts began to burn. Singing of Krishna in loud chorus, they went about from grove to grove as if mad, seeking after him. . . . Their minds were filled with Krishna, they talked of him alone; they thought no more of themselves as apart from him, nor could they think of their homes.

Just then Krishna appeared in their midst with a smile on his flower face, clad in yellow silk and garlanded with wreaths of forest flowers. Thus seeing the Beloved, all the Gopis arose simultaneously, with eyes that beamed in delight: they were freed from their grief which was due to separation from him. They prepared a seat for their dearest Friend, and on the garments they had worn seated the Lord who is throned in the inmost heart of mighty yogis. Radiantly beautiful was he, shining amid the band of Gopis as in him they worshiped the Form that enshrines all the loveliness of the three worlds.

SOURCE: *The Gospel of Sri Krishna*, trans. Duncan Greenlees (Madras: Theosophical Publishing, 1962), pp. 76–80.

1. In what way did the Gopis change after Krishna disappeared?
2. According to the lesson of this story, how should a worshiper behave in order to achieve salvation?

VILLAGE INDEPENDENCE

South Indian villages have had a long tradition of self-government. The following document, dating from the tenth century, describes who is eligible to serve in the sabha, *or assembly, of a village called Uttaramerur. (This village was one of many that were owned and governed by brahmans.) The document also details the election procedures to be used.*

In these 30 wards those that live in each ward shall assemble and shall select each person possessing the following qualifications for inclusion in the selection by lot:

He must own [at least one-eighth] of the tax-paying land.

He must live in a house built on his own site.

His age must be below 70 and above 35.

He must know the *mantras* and *Brahamanas*. . . .

Among those possessing these qualifications only such as are well conversant with business and are virtuous shall be taken, and one who possesses honest earnings whose mind is pure and who has not been on any of the committees for the last three years shall also be chosen. . . .

[The nomination tickets for each ward shall be bundled into a separate packet.] When the tickets have to be drawn a full meeting of the great assembly including the young and old members shall be convened. . . . In the midst of the temple priests, one of them who happens to be the eldest shall stand up and lift that pot, looking upwards so as to be seen by all people. One ward shall be taken out by any young boy standing close who does not know what is inside and shall be transferred to another empty pot and shaken loose. From this pot one ticket shall be drawn and made the arbitrator. While taking charge of the ticket thus given to him, the arbitrator shall receive it on the palm of his hand with the five fingers open. He shall read out the ticket thus received. The ticket shall be read by all the priests present in the inner hall. The name thus read shall be put down and accepted. . . .

Of the 30 men thus chosen those who had previously been on the Garden Committee, and on the Tank Committee, those who are advanced in learning and those who are advanced in age shall be chosen for the Annual Committee. Of the rest, 12 shall be taken for the Garden Committee and the remaining six shall form the Tank Committee. The great men of these three committees shall hold office for full 360 days and then retire. Anyone on a Committee found guilty of an offence shall be removed at once.

SOURCE: Romila Thapar, *A History of India*, vol. 1 (Harmondsworth, England: Penguin, 1966), pp. 202–204.

1. What qualifications did a public official in Uttaramerur have to have? Give likely reasons for these qualifications.
2. What precautions did the villagers take to ensure that their elections and officials were honest?

C H A P T E R
S E V E N

THE ARRIVAL OF EUROPEANS AND RISE OF THE MOGHUL EMPIRE

Trading in merchandise is so necessary that without it the world could not go on. It is this that ennobles kingdoms and makes their people great, that ennobles cities, that brings war and peace.

Tome Pires, Portuguese official

Wars by sea are merchants' affairs, and of no concern to the prestige of kings.

A sultan of Gujarat

Around the turn of the 16th century, two groups of newcomers made their way to India. The first group, the Portuguese, came by sea, in 1498. The second group, the *Moghuls,*[1] descended into India through the mountain passes of the north 28 years later. Each of these adventurers intended to make their fortunes in India and to exert a permanent control over its vast resources. However, their spheres of activity were entirely different. The Portuguese aimed to create a seaborne empire so that they could monopolize India's trade with Asia and the West. The Moghuls, by contrast, wanted to build a land empire and had little knowledge of the sea or of international trade.

---

1. *Moghuls* is an Indian word for "Mongols." These invaders from central Asia did not consider themselves to be Mongols, however; most of their ancestors were Turkish.

Because of their differing aims, the Europeans and the Moghuls had little contact with one another. And, at first, neither had a sizable impact upon India. The Portuguese introduced the new concept of *monopoly* to the Indian Ocean but were not able to enforce their exclusive "rights" to India's trade for long. The Moghuls, though they arrived later than the Europeans, created a more lasting empire.

Sixteenth-century India was an attractive target for foreign adventurers. Even the Christians of Europe, who had been isolated from the East for more than a thousand years, knew that India was the source of the most coveted—and expensive—luxury products in the world. And the Moghuls had a much closer view of India's riches. Babur, the first Moghul emperor, first glimpsed the rich agricultural plains of northern India from the highlands of the Hindu Kush. (It was this sight, he later said, that spurred his career as a conqueror.) Moreover, it was easy for a foreigner to gain a foothold, since India had no strong central government.

THE STATE OF INDIA IN 1500

In 1500, India was emerging from five centuries of religious wars and dynastic struggles. The sultanate at Delhi had lost much of its territory to a host of challengers, so that India was now a patchwork of Muslim- and Hindu-ruled domains.

The bustling port cities of India's western seacoast were among the most cosmopolitan in the world. The largest group of traders on the coast were the Arab Muslims, who had begun to migrate to India in the seventh century. The region around Bombay was the home of the Zoroastrian *Parsis* (Persians), who had first migrated to India in the eighth century. In Malabar, the community of Christians established by Saint Thomas about A.D. 52 still flourished. And, centered in Cochin, there was a sizable Jewish community.[2]

The small kingdoms of the seacoast were the territory of the *zamorins*, or "seacost rajas." The zamorins of the western coast were either Hindu or Muslim, and their subjects worshiped in a variety of mosques, temples, and churches. Yet differences of belief seldom interfered with the harmonious—and profitable—commerce of the region. In many inland kingdoms, too, the same atmosphere of peaceful coexistence prevailed.

---

2. According to legend, the first Jewish settlers had come to India either in King Solomon's time, around 1000 B.C., or to escape the Babylonian Captivity (sixth century B.C.). Then a second group had arrived about the same time as Saint Thomas, having fled from persecutions in the Roman Empire.

Synthesizing Religious Movements

Following the Muslim invasions of northern India, many religious leaders attempted to bring about a synthesis between Islam and Hinduism. Though it proved to be impossible to reconcile the two faiths, several new sects resulted from these efforts. One of the most influential of these is the religion known as *Sikhism*.

The Sikhs. The saint known as Nanak (1469–1538) was a *Guru,* or revered teacher, from the Punjab. Nanak taught his followers that there was no difference between the God of Hinduism and of Islam; it was the forms of organized religion that created apparent differences.

In later times, Nanak's disciples came to be known as the *Sikhs,* and they have maintained their separate identity to the present day. Nanak's teaching that divine revelation comes through private meditation, and especially by invoking the name of God, has remained central to Sikhism. Also, the tradition of appointing a Guru to head the community was continued long after Nanak's time. The nine Gurus who succeeded Nanak helped to keep alive his original teachings and organized the defense of the community in increasingly troubled times. (Later in this chapter, we will see how the Sikh religion was shaped by the persecutions it suffered under Aurangzeb, the sixth Moghul emperor.)

The Sufis. In parts of northern India, the mystical *Sufi* sect of Islam found great popularity among Hindus and Muslims alike. The Sufis often lived in voluntary poverty and preached a doctrine of toleration and universal love. Like the bhakti saints of Hinduism, their goal was to reach an individual union with God. Also like the bhakti saints, the Sufis often used music, dance, and poetry as a means to attain religious ecstasy. The dances performed by "whirling dervishes" are one of the best known aspects of Sufism. The Spanish dance music called *bolero* was also inspired by Sufi meditational music.

THE PORTUGUESE QUEST TO REACH INDIA

The voyage of Vasco da Gama to India in 1498 was the culmination of a long and difficult quest. Today, Gama's voyage is seen as one of the greatest events of the European Age of Exploration, an era that brought the medieval age to a close and ushered in the modern age. But in 16th-century Portugal, Gama's feat—like most other events—was seen as an episode in the ongoing struggle between Christianity and Islam. In this context, Gama's voyage was a rare Christian victory in a bitter contest that had lasted nearly 800 years.

During the great Muslim conquests of the seventh and eighth centuries, most of the lands bordering on the Mediterranean Sea—the commercial center of Europe—had been incorporated into the Islamic world. For the next thousand years, the Mediterranean region was a militarized zone between the Christians and the Muslims. Holy wars and bitter polemical campaigns were waged throughout the region—in Jerusalem and Syria, Constantinople, northern Africa, and in Spain and Portugal.

But even while the Muslim *jihads* and Christian crusades were being carried on, Turkish caravans and Arab trading ships continued to bring their rich cargoes of Eastern spices and silks to the Mediterranean. In medieval Europe, spices such as pepper, mace, cinnamon, and nutmeg were highly valued because they were useful in "preserving"—or masking the taste of—the poor-quality foods that people depended on in winter. Certain spices were also considered to be drugs: cinnamon, for example, was thought to be a remedy for heart and kidney problems. The fact that the Muslims gained the main benefit from this trade aroused the ire of devout Christians.

The "Heroic Age" of Portugal

Though Portugal was one of the smallest and poorest states in Europe, it had long been in the forefront of the Christian-Muslim struggle. The long quest that culminated in Gama's voyage to India was set in motion by Prince Henry of Portugal (1394–1460), a leader of the crusading Order of Christ. From 1418 to his death in 1460, Prince Henry, "the Navigator," sponsored the first voyages of discovery into the stormy, uncharted seas of the Atlantic. As the voyages proceeded, the possibility of a sea route to the East became increasingly apparent. After a ship had rounded the great western bulge of the African continent, Henry's cartographers began to realize that Africa might be a peninsula. Soon, the map that had served orthodox Christians for 550 years—a flat earth with small seas—was replaced by new charts showing a curved earth with great oceans. In 1488, Bartholomeu Dias sailed around the Cape of Good Hope, thus paving the way for Vasco da Gama's voyage.

In the fall of 1497, Gama sailed into the stormy seas surrounding the Cape of Good Hope and, a few weeks later, landed on Africa's eastern coast. At Malindi (in present-day Kenya), he found a skilled Arab navigator who showed him how to sail across the Indian Ocean. On 22 May 1498, Gama sailed into the port of Calicut on the Malabar coast of India. Though Gama's appearance caused little stir in India, it was a landmark event in Europe. The discovery of an all-sea route to India meant that the Europeans' long centuries of isolation were at an end. Moreover, Gama confirmed the stories of India's legendary riches: the cargo of spices and luxuries he brought back proved to be worth 3000 times the cost of his voyage.

The Portuguese in India

When Vasco da Gama and his men arrived at Calicut, they were hailed in their own Castilian language by two Muslim merchants from North Africa. "May the Devil take thee! What brought you hither?" the merchants shouted. Gama did not record his reaction to this surprising coincidence. But Alvaro Velho, one of the crewmen, remarked in his diary, "We were greatly astonished to hear this talk, for we never expected to hear our language spoken so far away from Portugal."[3]

Soon after their arrival, the Portuguese attended a service at a Hindu temple. During the ceremony, the priests "threw holy water upon the captain-major and gave him some [white earth]." From this experience, the Portuguese concluded that the Hindus were Christians. (This mistake was only cleared up during the next Portuguese voyage, that of Pedro Cabral in 1500.) Then Gama and his men trooped to the palace of the zamorin to arrange a trade agreement.

Though the zamorin of Calicut received Gama hospitably, he expressed disappointment at the poor quality of the goods that the Portuguese wished to exchange for spices. Nevertheless, Gama and his men were allowed to depart with a precious cargo of pepper, gems, and other products.

Soon after Gama's triumphant return to Lisbon, the king of Portugal took the title "Lord of the Conquest, Navigation, and Commerce of Ethiopia, Arabia, Persia, and of India." At this time, the Portuguese did not have a single ship in the Indian Ocean, and the Turks and Arabs were firmly in control of the "navigation and commerce" of all the regions mentioned. But by the rules of European statecraft at the time, Portugal's king had a clear title to the region—if only he could enforce it.[4]

On his next voyage to India, in 1502, Gama's mission was to seize the city of Calicut and establish Portugal's monopoly on India's trade. This time, he brought with him a squadron of ships mounted with powerful cannons, the one technology in which 16th-century Europe could claim superiority over Asia.[5]

---

3. Alvaro Velho, *Roteiro: A Journal of the First Voyage of Vasco da Gama*, vol. 99 (London: Hakluyt Society, 1898), p. 49.
4. Portugal based its claim to the Indian Ocean on its "rights of discovery," which were confirmed by the pope. In the Europeans' view, Hindus and Muslims had no right to free passage in the ocean because they had not explicitly claimed it as their property.
5. Unlike Indian-made ships, which were designed for peaceful trade, Portugal's oceangoing carracks were strong enough to carry cannons on their decks. Cannons had been known in India but were used mostly for ceremonial purposes.

Before reaching Calicut, Gama's fleet encountered a Muslim pilgrim ship returning to India from Mecca. One of Gama's men matter-of-factly described the scene of horror that ensued:

> We took a Mecca ship on board of which were 380 men and many women and children, and we took from it fully 12,000 ducats, and goods worth at least another 10,000. And we burned the ship and all the people on board with gunpowder, on the first day of October.

Gama then demanded that the zamorin of Calicut expel all the Muslims from his city and turn it over to the Portuguese. But the zamorin replied that the 4000 Muslims in Calicut were his valued subjects and refused to surrender the city. Before departing, Gama massacred several hundred fishermen in the harbor, but the zamorin did not change his mind.

Though the Portuguese never conquered Calicut, they were able to establish bases in the nearby ports of Cranganore, Cochin, and Quilon. But Affonso Albuquerque, Portugal's viceroy in India from 1509 to 1515, soon realized that Malabar was only a small part of the Muslim-dominated trade empire; the larger network of routes extended all the way from East Africa and the Mediterranean to China and Japan. The key port of Malacca, in

The Portuguese colony at Cochin was established one mile south of the main city, a safe distance (the zamorin hoped) from the Muslims, Hindus, Jews, and Saint Thomas Christians living there.

Southeast Asia, supplied some of the richest wares of all. There, merchants traded their Indian rice, pepper, and cotton textiles for exotic spices such as cloves, mace, and nutmeg from the Moluccas ("Spice Islands")—or even for silks and porcelain from China.

In 1510, Albuquerque conquered Goa, a city well situated to command the trade of India's western coast. With Goa as their capital, the Portuguese then built a network of 50 settlements and forts extending all the way to Macao, in Southeast China. Their bases in Malabar, Sri Lanka, and Malacca gave them domination of the spice trade at its sources, and other forts enabled them to bar Muslim ships from strategic waterways. For several decades, from 1515 to 1560, the Portuguese replaced the Muslims as the preeminent power in the Indian Ocean.

In each major Portuguese settlement, the Roman Catholic Church —represented by Jesuit priests and educators—was soon established, and Hindu temples were destroyed or converted to forts. At first, the Jesuits' efforts were focused on the Saint Thomas Christians. But in the 1540s, a more ambitious program of conversions began when Francis Xavier arrived in Malabar. In mass ceremonies, the future saint baptized thousands of Hindus as Christians.

During the 16th century, the Portuguese earned more income by looting Muslim traders than by carrying spices via the hazardous Cape route. But around midcentury, the Portuguese began to lose their crusading fervor. By this time, many of the Portuguese soldiers of Goa had married local women and wished to settle down to a life of trading or farming. In any case, Portugal was too small a country to defend its far-flung empire for long. In all, there were only about one million people in 16th-century Portugal, and a historian has calculated their military strength as follows:

> There were never as many as 10,000 able-bodied men in the whole of "Asia Portuguese" between the Cape of Good Hope and Japan; and the largest force that they ever put in the field . . . did not exceed 2000 men.[6]

Decline of the Portuguese Empire

The heyday of the Portuguese Empire in India ended about 1600. Soon afterward, the Dutch and other Europeans began to make regular voyages by the Cape route and even conquered many of Portugal's settlements and forts. (Goa, however, remained a Portuguese possession until 1961, when it was incorporated into the modern nation of India.)

---

6. C. R. Boxer, *Portuguese Conquest and Commerce in Southern Asia, 1500–1750* (London: Variorum reprints, 1985), p. 156.

The downfall of the Portuguese was hastened by the same overconfidence and defiance of the odds that had brought them their astonishing successes. For instance, even after it became clear that their resources were overextended, Portuguese governors did not attempt to consolidate their gains. Instead they continued to view all of their conquests as sacred and waged many costly battles to retain them.

Another cause of Portugal's problems was the competition it received from Holland and England. These emerging states had embraced such novel ideas as free enterprise and representative government, and had gained renewed vigor and strength as a result. But Portugal was still a medieval society in its outlook and way of life. All enterprises were directed by the king and his bureaucrats in Lisbon, who often had little knowledge of conditions overseas. One viceroy's complaint illustrates a typical misunderstanding. "They never seemed to learn," he said, "that any ship which left Lisbon after the first day of April could only reach Goa in the same year by a miracle."[7]

In Portugal, merit played little part in the promotion of officials: the *fidalgos*, or noblemen of the royal court, held all important offices. In Dutch society, by contrast, the sons of blacksmiths and bakers were able to earn high positions through merit, and individual initiative was given freer rein. One commentator has compared the two nationalities as follows:

> Where the empires of the old Catholic powers were on tight leash from Madrid and Lisbon . . . the new joint-stock imperialists of Amsterdam roamed the globe like half-trained hounds, and it took more than a command to call them from the chase.[8]

During the 17th century, the Dutch did not win any more friends in India than the Portuguese, but they had a much greater impact on the region's trade and commerce.

The Portuguese Legacy. Though the Portuguese became known mainly for their intolerance and terrorist acts, they did leave a lasting imprint of their culture in India. From their widespread trading empire, they introduced several new crops to the subcontinent, such as pineapples and papayas from the Americas and peanuts from Africa. They also introduced European styles of painting and church architecture to Goa, giving that state the distinctive character it has today. And in their efforts to spread Christianity, Jesuit missionaries created grammar books of local languages that are still highly valued by Indian and European scholars.

---

7. Diogo do Couto, quoted in Winius, *Fatal History,* p. 98.
8. Winius, *Fatal History*, p. 61.

THE MOGHUL EMPIRE

The Moghul Empire marked an important era in Indian history: it provided the foundation for British rule in India and eventually for the modern state of India. But the era is chiefly remembered for its imperial splendor and larger-than-life personalities, which had no parallel in later times. The English-language term *mogul* (a person with superlative wealth and power) is one legacy of the period.

The six kings who reigned during the height of the Moghul Empire (1526–1707) are still remembered by name and are often referred to as the Great Moghuls. The life stories of these six kings—their romances, battles, and family tragedies—were well documented in literature and art and are still a favorite topic of discussion. And the great palaces and mosques they built are among the world's most popular tourist attractions. The Taj Mahal at Agra, built by Shah Jahan in memory of his favorite wife, is one of the most famous legacies of the era.

In accordance with the Muslim custom of *purdah*, the wives and daughters of the Great Moghuls were shielded from public view. They lived in a well-guarded palace—the *zenana*, or harem—and wore veils when they appeared outside so that no one might see their faces. But despite their seclusion, several women of the *zenana* achieved independent fame during the Moghul era. Chief among them were Nur Jahan, the power behind the throne in Jahangir's reign; Mumtaz Mahal, the "Lady of the Taj"; and Princess Jahanara, who tried to prevent a tragic civil war between her brothers.

Babur

Babur, the founder of the Moghul dynasty in India, was a prince from central Asia. On his father's side, he was descended from Timur the Lame (Tamerlane); and on his mother's side, from Genghis Khan.[9] But by Babur's lifetime, the family domain had shrunk to a small mountainous kingdom in what is now southern Russia. Babur inherited this kingdom, called Ferghana, at the age of 11. Against all odds, he was able to defend his inheritance from the many nomadic groups who tried to seize it from him.

At the age of 15, Babur decided to enlarge his kingdom. With a small band of horsemen, he captured Samarkand, which had been Timur's capital city. Babur was well pleased with this conquest: in his memoirs, he remarked on the beauty of Samarkand's gardens, paintings, and great

---

9. Timur (c. 1336–1405) and Genghis Khan (c. 1162–1227) were two of the most successful conquerors in central Asian history.

REIGNS OF THE MOGHUL KINGS

Babur	1526–1530
Humayun	1530–1540
Sher Shah and son	1540–1555
Humayun	1555–1556
Regency	1556–1560
Akbar	1560–1605
Jahangir	1605–1637
Shah Jahan	1638–1658
Aurangzeb	1659–1707

public buildings. But the Uzbeks of the region rose in rebellion, and Babur was forced to withdraw. Ferghana, too, was lost. After several years of wandering, Babur captured Kabul, in what is now Afghanistan. At Kabul, Babur abandoned his plans for a northern kingdom and began to think about India.

After making several forays into the Indus valley, Babur realized that Ibrahim Lodi, the sultan of Delhi, was an unpopular sovereign. Though the sultan had 100,000 troops and Babur only about 12,000, Babur resolved to challenge the imperial forces. In his words, "I placed my foot in the stirrup of resolution and my hand on the reins of confidence in God, and marched against Sultan Ibrahim." In April 1526, Babur met and defeated Ibrahim's army at Panipat, near Delhi. The battle lasted just half a day, for the sultan's massive army was soon outmaneuvered by Babur's experienced Afghan cavalry.

After the battle, Babur marched to Delhi and then to Agra, which he established as his main capital. One of his first acts was to lay out a Persian-style pleasure garden at Agra, and he also built several mosques and baths. (In return for Babur's moderation, the nobles of Agra gave him the famous Koh-i-noor diamond, then appraised at "half the daily expense of the whole world.")

The Rajput Challenge. In the spring of 1527, Babur faced his first major crisis as emperor of India: a great Rajput army was marching north to expel him. Because of their proud military traditions, the Rajputs were a more formidable enemy than Ibriham's army had been.

The greatest of the Rajput clans claimed divine descent, and all Rajput warriors upheld a code of chivalry in which death was considered preferable to defeat or submission to a foreign power. One of their favorite readings was a passage from the Bhagavad Gita in which Krishna tells Arjuna, "Soldier, engage in such a battle as this; if thou art slain, thou wilt obtain heaven; if victorious, thou wilt enjoy a world!'' Rajput women played no small role in supporting the warriors' resolve. When a chieftain was killed in battle, his wives customarily committed *jaupur,* or suicide by fire, rather than submit to an invading army.

The Rajputs were led by Rana Sanga of Mewar, whose first ancestor was said to be the Sun. Sanga was marked by 80 wounds from previous battles—he lacked an eye and an arm, and one leg had been crushed by a cannonball—but his determination was undiminished.

Rana Sanga's army quickly surrounded Babur's much smaller force near Agra, and it appeared that the Moghul era would soon be over. But at this juncture, Babur related, he found a way to inspire his troops: he shattered his golden drinking cups and vowed that he would never again violate Muslim law by drinking wine. After this dramatic announcement, the Moghul army rallied and finally defeated the Rajputs.

Legend of Babur's Death. By 1530, Babur's conquest of northern India was at last secure. But in that year, Humayun, his eldest son and heir, fell ill and nearly died. According to legend, Babur vowed to give his own life in exchange for that of his son, and soon afterward was heard to say: ''I have borne it away!'' At that moment, it was said, Humayun's recovery began, while Babur slowly fell ill and died.

Up to the time of Babur's death, the unity of his empire had depended entirely on his own forceful personality; he did not have time to establish the legitimacy of his dynasty or to organize a new form of government. Thus, the empire he had built was on precarious ground.

Humayun and Sher Shah

Several years after Humayun ascended the throne, it became apparent that his dependence on alcohol and drugs—a family failing—was draining his resolve and energy. Although he won several major battles, there were also times when he was indecisive and careless. In 1540, Humayun lost his empire to Sher Shah, one of his father's most capable generals. For the next 15 years, Humayun and his family lived as refugees in Kabul, while Sher Shah set about reorganizing the Moghul Empire.

In 1555, after the deaths of Sher Shah and his son, Humayun made his way back to Delhi. Once again, he established himself as king, putting an end to the regional wars that had broken out. But just a year later, Humayun was fatally injured when he tripped and fell down the marble steps of his observatory. Akbar, his 13-year-old son, was now crowned emperor.

Akbar the Great

As a child, Akbar had shown little interest in preparing himself to be emperor. Though he had a quick mind, he was an unwilling student and never even learned to read: instead, he spent most of his time outdoors, riding horses and chasing wild game. After his coronation, Akbar continued his strenuous outdoor sports while his regent wielded the real power of the throne. Akbar's former nurse and her family were also powerful influences at the court.

In one of the major shifts that marked his career, Akbar suddenly dismissed his regent in 1560 and announced that he would act as king himself. But Adham Khan, the son of his nurse, continued to wield power and one day brazenly assassinated the man whom Akbar had appointed as prime minister. When Akbar realized what had occurred, he knocked Adham unconscious and had him thrown to his death from a balcony of the palace. Now, in 1562, there was no longer any doubt that Akbar intended to be king.

The next challenge to Akbar came from the Rajputs. As in Babur's time, the Rajputs were a force that could not be ignored. From their castle-fortresses in Mewar and Marwar they controlled the land routes to the western coast and often exacted high tolls from caravans and pilgrims

The first 12 years of Akbar's reign were marked by conquests and other forceful actions to consolidate his rule. This page from a Moghul scrapbook shows Akbar (on second elephant) chasing a rebel prince across the Ganges.

traveling to Surat. Thus, their activities could seriously disrupt the business of the empire.

Akbar's first overture to the Rajputs was to take a Rajput princess as his wife. By this act, Akbar brought an important Rajput clan into his empire, and demonstrated his respect and tolerance for his non-Muslim subjects. Other Rajput clans did not accept Moghul rule until Akbar had defeated them in battle. But in the treaties that followed, Akbar showed himself willing to accommodate their fierce pride. They were allowed to enter the Moghul palace without surrendering their arms and were excused from making the deep salaam, or prostration, usually performed in the emperor's presence. Moreover, they could sound their kettledrums up to the gate of Akbar's palace. In the centuries that followed, Rajput warriors came to be considered the most important allies of Moghul kings and princes. (One clan, however—the descendants of Ranga Sanga—never submitted to Moghul rule.)

Administration of the Empire. By 1576, Akbar had completed his military campaigns: Rajputana, Bengal, and Gujarat had submitted to Moghul rule, and the empire extended across all of northern India. Akbar now turned his attention to administrative affairs. Up to this time, the Moghul empire had been organized as a system of armed camps. A military base was established in each conquered province, and a trusted noble appointed to rule each fief. But there was no common law or administrative policy to bind the provinces together. Moreover, the governors often became corrupt or oppressive and sometimes even declared their independence from Delhi. To discourage this tendency, Sher Shah had transferred his governors every two years. Akbar now added several new reforms.

Under Akbar's system of government, several officials shared the responsibility for each province. Thus, the various officials were forced to collaborate and to oversee one other's work. All ministers reported directly to their superiors at the Moghul court. When instances of corruption or mismanagement came to light, the offenders were promptly punished.

A central feature of Akbar's government was the *mansabdari* system. In return for maintaining a force of cavalry, a *mansabdar,* or commander, received a salary that far exceeded his costs. Princes of the royal family, governors, diwans, and other high officials were given *mansabs* ranging from 12,000 to 2,000 horses. But even a *mansab* of 1,000 was enough to sustain a lavish life style, with a well-appointed palace, large harem, and sizable treasuries of gold and jewels.

The *mansabdars'* salaries were paid in cash and were given on the basis of merit alone, so that no hereditary nobility was created. When a *mansabdar* died, his property was seized by the royal treasury.

Agricultural Reforms. Many of Akbar's reforms were carried out under the able leadership of Todar Mal, a Hindu raja who served as *diwan* (finance minister) and *wazir* (prime minister) of the empire. Todar Mal is best remembered for his sympathetic treatment of the peasants, who had been grievously exploited by most previous regimes. Under Todar Mal's administration, farm lands throughout the empire were carefully surveyed so that officials could assess a fair tax for each plot. The emperor's share of farmers' crops was then set at an average of one-third, a lower figure than previously collected. Also, any officials found to be extorting additional payment were severely punished. Due to Todar Mal's reforms, India's farmers became more prosperous and productive than ever before.

Akbar's Theory of Kingship. Prior to Akbar's reign, all Muslim sultans had discriminated against non-Muslims. This policy was firmly rooted in Islamic tradition, which held that non-Muslims could not long be tolerated in a Muslim state. Muslim authorities disagreed as to whether Hindus—who were termed "idolators"—should be put to the sword or simply made to pay a special tax. In practice, most sultans had found the latter policy to be more feasible. But their religious advisers (the *ulema*) often encouraged additional persecutions, and Islamic law was clear on this point: it was a ruler's duty to spread the faith and to make life difficult for those who refused to convert.

Early in his reign, Akbar took several measures that were intensely displeasing to the *ulema.* He forbade the enslavement and forcible conversion of Hindu prisoners of war, and took as his chief wife a Hindu Rajput princess. In 1564, two years after this marriage, he abolished the *jizya,* or poll tax, that Hindus paid in lieu of conversion or death. By this extraordinary act, Akbar announced that he was no longer the defender of Islam but would extend equal protection to all subjects. Abul Fazl, Akbar's close adviser and biographer, recorded Akbar's new definition of his role. A true king, he said, must not be "mother to some and stepmother to others." Rather, he should "regard all classes of men and all sects of religion with the single eye of favor."

Though Akbar did not use the word *dharma* in defining his role, his description of a king had a strong resemblance to the *Chakravartin* described by the ancient Hindu and Buddhist philosophers:

> Race and wealth and the assembling of a mob are not enough for this great position. It is clear to the wise that a few among the holy qualities are magnanimity, lofty benevolence, wide capacity, abundant tolerance, exalted understanding, innate graciousness, natural courage, justice, rectitude, strenuous labor, proper conduct, profound thoughtfulness and laudable overlooking of offences. And . . . so long as [a king] has not wisdom sufficient to overpower improper desires and unbecoming anger, he cannot be fit for this lofty office.

Only such a person, Akbar said, could fulfill the primary duty of a king—namely, to "inaugurate universal peace."

A New Religion. In 1578, Akbar experienced a spiritual crisis one day while hunting. Just as the royal party was to begin shooting, Akbar suddenly gave orders that the hunt was to cease and "not the feather of a finch was to be touched." For several nights, the emperor meditated alone in a stone cell near his palace. Then he began to summon members of the *ulema* for weekly discussions on religion. Soon, the discussion sessions were expanded to include scholars of the Hindu, Jain, Zoroastrian, and Christian faiths. The progress of Akbar's thinking was described by Abul Fazl:

> There gradually grew in his mind the conviction that there were sensible men in all religions, and austere thinkers and men with miraculous gifts in all nations. If some truth were thus found everywhere, why should Truth be restricted to one religion or to a comparatively new creed like Islam, scarcely a thousand years old?

Akbar grew increasingly impatient of the conflicts among religious sects and began to search for new ways to bring an atmosphere of harmony to his empire. In 1581, he announced the foundation of a new religion, which he called the *Divine Faith.* Akbar himself was the center of this new faith, which combined elements of Sufism, Hinduism, and other sects. Converts to the Divine Faith were taught to regard Akbar as a "most wise, just, and God-fearing king" whose decisions could be trusted even if they were not completely approved by the *ulema.* Followers of the emperor's cult worshiped the sun and became vegetarians. In deference to his own cult and to Hinduism, Akbar also issued a decree making it a capital offense to slaughter a cow.

Although the Divine Faith disbanded at Akbar's death, the Moghul emperor continued to be regarded as a semidivine being long afterward. The ceremony and daily public audiences that Akbar established at his court also contributed to this legacy.

The Royal Court. For the first few years of his reign, Akbar did not have any surviving children. Desperate to have an heir, Akbar visited a Sufi holy man for advice and reassurance. The next year, the first of Akbar's three sons was born. In gratitude, Akbar named the baby *Salim,* after the saint, and decided to build a new palace near the hermit's cell at Sikri. Soon, the entire court had moved to the village, and the palaces at Delhi and Agra were abandoned. Akbar's elaborate new palace—known as Fatehpur Sikri, or "City of Victory"—was begun about 1569 and served as capital of the empire for two decades. (Then, Akbar suddenly abandoned the site and moved his court to Lahore.)

In the design of Fatehpur Sikri, Akbar created a harmonious synthesis of Muslim and Hindu architectural styles. The work of reconciliation and synthesis also continued within the court. Hindu officials became the equals of Muslims in top levels of the administration, and several Hindu artists were among the "nine jewels" of Akbar's court. One result of Akbar's patronage was a new, distinctively "Moghul" style of art in which the abstract designs of Persian art were combined with the realism and "action" of Hindu painting.[10] This new style was employed to illustrate scenes from the most popular works of Hindu literature—the *Mahabharata,* the *Ramayana,* and the life of Krishna.

The Royal Routine. Akbar conducted his affairs according to a fixed routine which was carried out, as far as possible, in full public view. The beginning of his day was announced by the playing of music. After spending about two hours in prayers and meditation, Akbar made a public appearance at his balcony as the sun rose. (This appearance was the revival of an ancient Hindu custom.) Next, Akbar proceeded to his public audience hall. Here, the princes of the royal family and high officials of the empire assembled near his throne, while lower officials and petitioners gathered in a separate enclosure. One visitor noted that the court was "always thronged with multitudes of men of every type" and that even the poorest petitioners were admitted. At this public *darbar,* or audience, Akbar usually heard petitions and made administrative decisions. On Thursdays, however, he devoted himself to the administration of justice. He soon became renowned for the impartiality of his decisions and for the strict accountability to which he held his officials and friends.

In the afternoon, Akbar mounted the lotus throne in his private audience hall to conduct affairs of state. Radiating from the throne were four

---

10. In Islam, realism in art is prohibited; only abstract designs are allowed. But Akbar believed that artists who portrayed nature realistically had more, not less, respect for Allah's creation.

catwalks that permitted Akbar's highest ministers to approach him from their separate stations. Below, advisers, officials, ambassadors, and other guests gathered to offer their opinions. At times—especially when the discussion turned to religion—Akbar abandoned his throne and restlessly paced the catwalks. One of the Jesuit priests who took part in these sessions remarked:

> Whilst one of his questions was being answered, he would suddenly ask another. He had not the patience to hear one explanation at a time; but in his eagerness for knowledge, tried to learn everything at once, like a hungry man trying to swallow his food at a single gulp.[11]

After the business of the day and a period of recreation, Akbar often continued his work far into the night. Visitors to the court often remarked on the remarkable energy he brought to each activity in his daily schedule:

> At one time he would be deeply immersed in state affairs, or giving audience to his subjects, and the next moment he would be seen shearing camels, hewing stones, cutting wood, or hammering iron, and doing it all with as much diligence as though engaged in his own particular vocation.[12]

After Akbar's death, his successors maintained his schedule of official duties to the extent they were capable. One commentator has credited this daily routine for giving a momentum to the empire that earlier Muslim dynasties had lacked.

> The king's appearance before the general public at sunrise was instrumental in stirring up the imagination of the masses and it made profound appeal to their loyalty. His transaction of business in an open darbar also reduced the chances of domination by any particular minister, officer or clique at the court. And above all, the system thus established by Akbar became a tradition and was followed by his successors until the last days of the Moghul empire.[13]

Akbar's last years were marred by a revolt led by Salim, his eldest son and heir, and by troubles in the Deccan. In 1605, Akbar died at the age of 63, after a reign of 45 years.

---

11. Father Pierre du Jarric, *Akbar and the Jesuits*, trans. C. H. Payne (New Delhi: Tulsi Publishing House, 1979), p. 30.
12. Ibid., p. 206.
13. Ashirbadi Lal Srivastava, *Akbar the Great*, vol. 2 (Agra: Shiva Lal Agarwala, 1967), p. 40.

Jahangir

At his coronation, Salim took the name *Jahangir*, or "World-Seizer." But he showed little interest in conquest and instead devoted himself to the pleasures of the royal court. In his memoirs, Jahangir candidly described his addiction to alcohol and opium, even bragging that he was more alcoholic than his ancestor, Babur.

In Jahangir's daily schedule, periods of rest and recreation increasingly filled the time allotted for state affairs. William Hawkins, an English sea captain who came to know Jahangir well, described his routine. About 45 minutes after sunrise, Jahangir appeared at his window for the benefit of the crowd assembled below. Then he went back to sleep and reappeared at noon, to view an elephant fight or other "sport." In midafternoon, he sat in state at open darbar, attended by a multitude of nobles, and heard petitions from subjects. The rest of the day was occupied by feasting, drinking, and other entertainments. By late evening, Hawkins said, the emperor had reached such a state that "he is not able to feed himself, but it is thrust into his mouth by others."

A portrait of Jahangir on an hourglass throne (*left*) seems to suggest that time is running out for the Great Moghul. But the emperor's present glory is indicated by the great personages paying him homage (even James I of England is included among these). The capable and enterprising Nur Jahan (*right*) was the "power behind the throne" during Jahangir's reign. She was one of the few *zenana* members to have her portrait painted.

Jahangir's life lasted far longer than anyone expected, but his poor health was a constant cause of concern. Thomas Roe, an ambassador from England to the Moghul court, remarked that the emperor's morning appearance was crucial to the stability of the empire: "If he were unseen one day and no sufficient reason rendered, the people would mutiny; two days no reason can excuse."

During Jahangir's reign, all observers agreed, the real power of the throne was wielded by his capable wife, whom he called *Nur Jahan* ("Light of the World"). Assisted by her father and brother, Nur Jahan made the major decisions necessary to keep the empire together. She chose Shah Jahan, Jahangir's most capable son, as the heir apparent, and arranged for him to marry her niece, Mumtaz Mahal ("Exalted of the Palace"). But Shah Jahan proved to be too independent, and she shifted her support to a younger prince. Shah Jahan then mounted a rebellion against his father. In one episode of this succession struggle, Jahangir was captured by a Rajput army, and Nur Jahan rode to his rescue on an elephant.

In October 1627, Jahangir died of natural causes. Shah Jahan, who was in the Deccan, quickly advanced toward Agra to claim the throne. But soon, his journey through Gujarat and Rajputana took on the character of a triumphal procession, for Nur Jahan had run out of credible pawns to set upon the throne. When he reached Agra, Shah Jahan ordered the murders of his surviving brother and all of his nephews and male cousins. After this bloodbath, Shah Jahan was crowned in an elaborate celebration. Nur Jahan, who no longer had the power to cause trouble, was retired with a sizable pension.

Shah Jahan

Shah Jahan made it his life's work to restore the prestige of the Moghul Empire, which had been much diminished during the succession struggle. During his reign, the material splendor of the Moghul court reached unprecedented heights, and several ambitious campaigns were waged to expand the empire. But Shah Jahan's reign was not a golden age for the peasants of India, whose labor paid for his vast armies and monumental building projects. François Bernier, a Frenchman who came to India at the end of his reign, remarked, "No adequate idea can be conveyed of the sufferings of that people. . . . Their revolt or their flight is only prevented by the presence of a military force."

The Taj Mahal, Shah Jahan's most famous monument, was dedicated to the memory of his beloved empress Mumtaz Mahal, who died in 1631 while bearing their 14th child. The Taj was built of pure white marble quarried in the Deccan, and its design reflected Shah Jahan's passion for

The pages of Shah Jahan's scrapbook portray an ever serene monarch enjoying the quiet delights of court life. This portrait, taken at the time of his accession, gives no hint of the succession battles that have just ended.

Persian art and architecture. A visiting Portuguese friar noted that the blocks of marble were "of such unusual size and length that they drew the sweat of many powerful teams of oxen and of fierce-looking, big-horned buffaloes."

When work on the Taj was well under way, Shah Jahan started construction of a new palace at Delhi. This palace complex—known as the Red Fort because of its massive red stone retaining wall—covers 124 acres and housed many thousands of retainers and courtiers. Many of the larger buildings were lavishly decorated with silk carpets, gold brocaded fabrics, and colorful silk canopies, and one palace—the harem—featured interior fountains and streams. (The harem palace alone housed 5000 people, for some of the royal princesses had as many as 100 servants apiece.)

One of the central symbols of Shah Jahan's reign was the famous Peacock Throne, which graced his private audience hall at Delhi. The

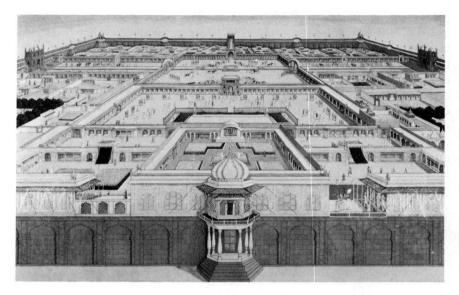

A bird's eye view of Shah Jahan's Red Fort reveals the expanse of marble within the 75-foot-high sandstone walls.

peacocks decorating the throne were outlined in diamonds, emeralds, pearls, and rubies, and its pillars and base were made of solid gold. Emblazoned on the walls of the audience hall, in golden letters, was the verse:

> If on earth there be a Paradise of bliss,
> It is this, it is this, it is this!

During Shah Jahan's public audiences, a great crowd of nobles and ambassadors thronged the hall, and a group of armed hangmen guarded the throne. Far above the crowd, a visitor reported, "glittered the dazzling figure of the Grand Moghul, a figure to strike terror, for a frown meant death."

The Succession Wars. Shah Jahan's actions upon ascending the throne—especially the murders of his male relatives—set a regrettable precedent. Subsequently, all future princes, including his own sons, knew that their probable destiny was "crown or coffin." There would be almost no exceptions.

Late in Shah Jahan's reign, a deadly war of succession broke out among his four sons. The central players were Dara Shikoh, the eldest prince, and Aurangzeb, the third son. Foreigners described Dara Shikoh as a courteous, intelligent prince with mystical leanings. He was fascinated by the teachings of holy men, both Sufis and Hindus, and wrote a book (*The Mingling of the Two Oceans*) in which he tried to reconcile the beliefs of Islam and Hinduism. Like most Moghul princes, he had to struggle to control his temper, and it was said that he "entertained too exalted an opinion of himself." But he was by far the most popular of Shah Jahan's sons.

Aurangzeb was strikingly different in character. He was less sociable and disapproved of Dara's liberal views. From an early age, he lived the strict religious life of an orthodox Muslim and won the wholehearted support of the *ulema*. Dara referred to him as "the bigot" and "the prayer-monger."

Two other siblings, Shuja and Murad, lacked the intensity of their feuding brothers. They were both fond of wine, women, and song and tended to shirk responsibility. Jahanara, the eldest daughter, was known for her intellect and charitable works and was also a great beauty. Though she and Dara were close friends, Aurangzeb also trusted her. Jahanara devoted herself to the futile effort of making peace among her brothers.

A portrait of Aurangzeb as a youth emphasizes the crusading mission of the future emperor. Aurangzeb was portrayed with a halo above his head, like the saints of Buddhist and Christian art.

In keeping with Moghul tradition, Shah Jahan had given all of his sons important military commands. All of them had tried, but failed, to expand their father's empire into Persia. Later, each became viceroy of a large province. Dara Shikoh, his father's favorite, was named heir apparent in 1655.

In 1657, Shah Jahan became seriously ill. Immediately, Aurangzeb began to plan a rebellion, and won Shuja and Murad to his side with flattery and promises. He also had the support of the empire's orthodox Muslims, who agreed that Dara Shikoh was a dangerous "infidel." In May 1658, Aurangzeb and Dara Shikoh met on a battlefield near Agra. At first, Dara Shikoh and his Rajput troops gained the upper hand. But at a crucial moment, Dara was persuaded to dismount from his elephant and lead a charge on horseback. When his troops saw his elephant without a rider, they assumed he had been killed and began to flee. Thus, the battle was lost.

Soon after the battle, Aurangzeb ordered the murder of Murad and imprisoned Shah Jahan in his Red Fort at Agra. There, the former emperor spent the rest of his days in captivity, gazing at the tomb he had built for his empress. Jahanara voluntarily shared her father's imprisonment until his death in 1666. Shuja was pursued to the jungles beyond Bengal and was never heard from again. Dara Shikoh was eventually captured and brought back to Delhi, where Aurangzeb paraded him through the streets in disgrace. Bernier described the scene:

> Dara was seated on a miserable and worn out elephant; he no longer wore the necklace of large pearls which distinguished the princes of Hindustan, nor the rich turban and embroidered coat; he and his son were now habited in dirty cloth of the coarsest texture. . . . The crowd assembled upon this disgraceful occasion was immense; and everywhere I observed the people weeping and lamenting the fate of Dara in the most touching language.

Soon after this outpouring of popular sympathy, Aurangzeb had Dara decapitated. According to one story, he then delivered the severed head to his imprisoned father.

Aurangzeb (Alamgir)

At his coronation, in 1659, Aurangzeb took the name *Alamgir*, or "Holder of the Universe." During his long reign, he waged war on all "unbelievers" and, at the same time, greatly enlarged the Moghul Empire. But the price of his conquests was economic ruin and the overwhelming unpopularity of his government. By the end of his life, Aurangzeb had

Like many earlier Muslim conquerors, Aurangzeb launched a campaign to destroy Hindu temples and build mosques in their place. In this 19th-century view, his mosque at Benares towers over the Hindu holy city.

become a bitter old man who regretted the immense destruction he had caused.

Aurangzeb's reign became notable for the "nationalist" independence movements that arose in response to his persecutions. Nearly every ethnic and religious group in India—Hindus, Sufis, Sikhs, Rajputs, and Jats—were the targets of his wrath, and millions of them were killed by his armies and executioners. But Aurangzeb's stern and bloodthirsty policies had an unexpected result: the people he martyred were soon immortalized in legends and songs, and thus inspired others to even greater feats of rebellion.

Among the many rebels who rose against the Moghuls, two of the most notable were the *Marathas* and the *Sikhs*. Both groups continued to serve as symbols of resistance from "foreign" domination long after Aurangzeb's death.

The Marathas. The Marathas were a devoutly Hindu people who lived in the countryside called *Maharashtra,* in the northern Deccan. Like the Rajputs, they had learned to thrive in a harsh, barren terrain and had a proud military tradition. But whereas the Rajputs lived by an elaborate code of chivalry and ancestral pride, the Marathas' way of life was more democratic and practical. Mountstuart Elphinstone, a British governor who later had much experience with both groups, compared them as follows:

> A Rajput warrior, so long as he does not dishonor his race, seems almost indifferent to the result of any contest he is engaged in. A Maratha thinks of nothing *but* the result, and cares little for the means.

Shivaji, the most famous leader of the Marathas, led his people's rebellion from 1647 until his death in 1680. After establishing the Marathas' independence from the Muslim sultan of Bijapur, Shivaji took on the entire Moghul Empire. Aurangzeb later admitted that his long campaign against Shivaji, whom he called the "Mountain Rat," had failed. "My armies have been employed against him for 19 years," he said, "and nevertheless his state has always been increasing."

Shivaji was a pioneer in the art now known as guerrilla warfare. He and his warriors had 25 hill forts—some of them built into the sheer faces of the Western Ghats—to resort to in times of need. Thus, they were an elusive enemy and became renowned for their ability to launch surprise attacks and escape with impunity.

The Marathas often relied on daring acts of subterfuge to accomplish their goals. One of the most celebrated feats of Shivaji's career occurred in 1659, after he was pursued to one of his mountain fortresses by a bold Muslim general. Feigning defeat, Shivaji agreed to meet his adversary on a clearing below the fort. Wearing a long, flowing robe, he advanced toward the burly general with arms outstretched. But when the general yielded to his embrace, Shivaji stabbed him with the steel "tiger's claws" attached to his fingers. As the general died, a concealed band of Marathas sprang from their hiding places and routed his army.

Though the Marathas never succeeded in building an India-wide empire, their daring exploits have continued to be a central symbol of Hindu nationalism to the present day.

The Sikhs. Between the time of Akbar and Aurangzeb, the Sikhs evolved from a private, peace-loving sect to a militant brotherhood. They are thus one of the foremost examples of the changes wrought by Aurangzeb's persecutions.

During Akbar's reign, the Sikhs benefited from the emperor's policy of tolerance. Akbar granted to the sect's fourth Guru a sacred site known as Amritsar, in the Punjab. (The temple later built on this ground is still the Sikhs' holiest shrine.) But Arjun, the fifth Guru, incurred Jahangir's displeasure when he supported a rebellion; as a result, he was tortured and beheaded. In 1675, Teg Bahadur, the ninth Guru, was similarly martyred by Aurangzeb when he refused to become a Muslim. After Teg Bahadur's horrible death, his son Gobind vowed revenge. As the tenth Guru, Gobind organized the Sikhs into a militant fraternity known as the *Khalsa,* or "Elect." To enter the Khalsa, a novice drank water stirred by a sword, shared a sacramental meal with other members, and renounced all caste distinctions. Members also adopted a distinctive dress code that featured five objects beginning with the letter *k*: long hair, short pants, a comb, a dagger, and an iron disk. Today, the Sikhs still bear these distinguishing marks and also take the surname *Singh* ("Lion").

The Decline of the Empire. In 1679, Aurangzeb reimposed on Hindus the *jizya,* or poll tax, which Akbar had revoked more than a century before. His sister Jahanara tried to prevent this rash action, asking him to see the Hindus as an ocean and himself as a ship that needed the support of the ocean. But Aurangzeb refused to relent. When a great crowd of people thronged the streets to protest the burdensome tax, he had them trampled by elephants.

At the time the *jizya* was reimposed, a Rajput prince wrote to the emperor as follows:

> Your subjects are trampled underfoot; every province of your Empire is impoverished; depopulation spreads, and difficulties accumulate. . . . If your Majesty places any faith in those books by distinction called divine, you will be there instructed God is the God of all mankind, not the God of Muslims alone.

Yet Aurangzeb was soon to embark on a 25-year military campaign to quell the rebels in the Deccan. During all these years, he and his half million soldiers and camp followers lived in a mobile tent city, their unprofitable activities draining the royal treasuries and devastating the countryside. By the time of Aurangzeb's death, in 1707, the vast wealth and imperial prestige of the Moghuls had been exhausted beyond hope of recovery.

The End of the Moghul Empire

In 1739, the weakness of the Moghul Empire was exposed when a Persian army swept through northern India, looted the Moghul palaces of their gold and jewels, and even carted off the Peacock Throne. After this debacle, the Moghul kings still continued to serve as a symbol of unity and of bygone glory, but had little real authority. In 1862, the last Moghul king died in a British prison.

SUMMARY

At the beginning of the 16th century, two determined groups of conquerors, the Portuguese and the Moghuls, arrived in India. The Portuguese intended to bring India's peoples and riches into their own cultural orbit, thus strengthening the Roman Catholic empire and striking a blow at Islam. The first Moghul kings were more interested in governing India than in spreading their Islamic faith. Akbar, the third Great Moghul, found a way to win the loyalty of India's diverse peoples and to create a respected central government. But while Akbar's ideas were popular among the majority of his subjects, they aroused the wrath of orthodox Muslims. In Akbar's great-grandson, Aurangzeb, the Muslims at last found a champion who would dismantle the many reforms that Akbar had set in motion. As a result, the empire entered a period of precipitous decline.

Once the Moghuls had established the idea of unity and imperial power, it became possible for another group of outsiders, the British, to seize control of the system. In the next chapter, we will see how the British became the new rulers of India.

DISCUSSION AND ESSAY QUESTIONS

1. In 1500, the Portuguese could have chosen to establish themselves in India as peaceful traders. Why did they not choose this option?

2. Define the word *ethnocentric*. Would it be fair to describe the 16th-century Portuguese as ethnocentric? Explain why or why not.

3. Describe the duties of a king as defined in Muslim theology. In what ways did Akbar's view of his job differ from the traditional one?

4. Compare Akbar's reign to that of Ashoka 18 centuries before. What did each ruler see as his main duty? Why did each achieve great popularity? What new problems did Akbar face?

5. What gave the Moghul Empire strength enough to endure through the reigns of Jahangir, Shah Jahan, and Aurangzeb?

SUGGESTED READINGS

William Wilson Hunter, *A History of British India*, vol. 1 (London: 1899). The first chapters of this classic work describe Portugal's role in the age of exploration.

Waldemar Hansen, *The Peacock Throne* (New York: Holt, Rinehart, 1972). A colorful and detailed account of the Moghul Empire.

THE SIKHS

The word Sikh *means "disciple." Nanak, the founder of the sect, taught that people must find God within their own hearts, rather than through the teachings of organized religions. In this undertaking, the aid of a Guru, or teacher, was considered indispensible. Nanak and the nine Gurus who succeeded him provided leadership for the community during its formative period.*

At first, the Sikhs abhorred religious factionalism and violence. ("There is no Hindu and no Muslim," Nanak said.) But by the late 17th century—after suffering martyrdom and persecutions under two Moghul kings—the Sikhs had become a military brotherhood.

The first selection quoted here is typical of Nanak's poetry: it refers to the practices of contemporary religious sects and outlines the virtues Nanak believed were necessary to salvation.

The second passage is by Gobind Singh (1666–1708), the tenth and final Sikh Guru. It is addressed to Alamgir (Aurangzeb) and mentions the violent deaths of four of the emperor's sons. (Several of Alamgir's favorite children sided with his Hindu enemies and were exiled, imprisoned, or killed in punishment.)

Advice to a Muslim Governor
Nanak

Make love thy mosque; sincerity thy prayer-carpet; justice thy Koran.
Modesty thy circumcision; courtesy thy Kaaba; truth thy Guru; charity thy
    creed and prayer;
The will of God thy rosary, and God will preserve thine honor, O Nanak.

Message to Alamgir
Gobind Singh

When all other resources are rendered unavailing,
It is justified then to unsheathe the sword.
Strange the way you keep your promises—
One should consider it evil to swerve from the truth.
Do not wield the sword in ruthless bloodshed;
Heaven's sword shall one day strike you too.
Man, do not be unmindful of the terrible retribution of the Lord.

Creator of the universe and all that is in it.
He has created the little ant as well as the mighty elephant.
He cherishes the humble and destroys oppressors.
He bears the name—Cherisher of the Humble;
He does not need man's gratitude or his offerings.

What though my four children have been killed—
Living still is the coiled serpent.
What bravery is this that you extinguish sparks of fire,
But raise a vast conflagration!

SOURCES: H. G. Rawlinson, *India: A Short Cultural History* (New York: Praeger, 1952), p. 378. Ainslee T. Embree, ed. *Sources of Indian Tradition,* 2d ed., vol. 1 (New York: Columbia University Press, 1988), p. 509.

1. Describe the arguments used by Nanak and Gobind Singh in addressing a Muslim ruler. What goal were they trying to accomplish? What similarities and differences were there in their methods of persuasion?

C H A P T E R
E I G H T

THE RISE OF THE BRITISH EMPIRE (1600–1877)

On a small island in another quarter of the globe, in a narrow street . . . a company of peaceable merchants meet. These are the conquerors of India; these are the absolute sovereigns of this splendid empire.

A Swedish traveler, 1840

The British empire in India was a classic example of *imperialism*—the conquest and rule of a foreign land for the benefit of a home country. The guiding principle of Britain's empire—as of the empires built by Portugal, Spain, and other European powers after 1500—was the well-being of the ruling country, not of the conquered lands.

Imperialism grew out of *nationalism,* the force that was reshaping Europe during the Age of Exploration. After establishing their identities as separate states, the European nations had begun to vie with one another for wealth and influence. Their competition at first centered on trade, then escalated into a battle for political influence and direct control of foreign lands. In the course of this vigorous contest, Britain, France, Holland, Portugal, and Spain each carved out major empires in Asia and the New World. Their successes in these conquests seemed to confirm the feelings of national pride that had inspired them in the first place.

Nationalism, the exuberant force that brought about imperialism, has also been the downfall of most imperialists. In the first years of their rule, British governors could claim that India had no independent identity as a nation—its many religious and ethnic groups, castes and classes were only held together by the British-imposed government. But India, too, was to have a nationalist movement. In the early 20th century, under the leadership of Mahatma Gandhi and others, the Indian peoples demonstrated that they had a vision of unity that transcended the many divisions apparent in everyday life. In Chapter 9, we will see how the Indian nationalist movement grew and finally succeeded in overthrowing the British *raj*.

THE EUROPEAN COMPETITION TO REACH INDIA

In a series of edicts issued around the turn of the 16th century, the pope of the Roman Catholic Church granted to Spain and Portugal the exclusive right to travel by the southwest and southeast sea routes to India. For a time, the pope's decrees were regarded as valid international law even by non-Catholic nations. Thus, the buccaneering sea captains of England and Holland were forced to begin their quest for India in the stormy seas to the north. In more than a dozen major voyages, they searched for a passage through the ice floes of eastern Canada and western Russia, and even attempted to sail straight over the North Pole. But no northwest or northeast passage to India was discovered. Finally, Elizabeth I of England decided to disregard the papal edicts. "The use of the sea and air is common to all," she declared. In 1588, England forcibly asserted this claim by defeating the combined Armada of Spain and Portugal. By the end of the century, both English and Dutch ships were making regular voyages to India via the Cape route.

The British East India Company

On the last day of the year 1600, Elizabeth I granted a license to the newly formed East India Company to carry on England's trade with India. Like a medieval guild, the company was given a monopoly, or exclusive right, to its trade. The company was expected to be self-supporting, however; its funding came from private stockholders rather than from the government. And since the stockholders expected each venture to return a profit, the English company soon found it could not afford the type of "armed commerce" practiced by the Portuguese and the Dutch. After failing to dislodge the Dutch from the Moluccas ("Spice Islands"), the English company decided to concentrate its trade in India's coastal cities.

Sir Thomas Roe, an ambassador from the English court, tried to convince the Great Moghul Jahangir to grant the company favorable trading concessions in India. But Jahangir could not see why he, an all-powerful monarch whose every wish was law, should bind himself with written treaties. Nevertheless, Roe concluded that it would be futile to resort to stronger measures. The company must content itself with "quiet trade," he advised, "for without controversy it is an error to affect garrisons and land wars in India."

Up to the mid-18th century, the company seldom departed from this principle of "quiet trade."[1] But within one short period (1757–1818), the East India Company suddenly grew to be the greatest political and military force on the subcontinent. This rapid transformation has been described as an "involuntary" and even "unconscious" process, for no one had planned or intended it. The company's only motive had been commercial profit. Yet as its employees pursued the goal of "quiet trade," the company acquired garrisons, armies, vast tracts of territory, and finally dominion over a large part of India. With hindsight, the reason became apparent: the goal of "quiet trade" had been an impossibility in 18th-century India.

The State of India in the 18th Century

In the declining years of Moghul power, most provincial governors of the empire had established independent, hereditary dynasties. Like the Moghul kings of old, these princes lived a life of elaborate luxury and wielded absolute power over their subjects. But none was powerful enough to establish peace over a wider area. At times, an uneasy peace was maintained through alliances and treaties among the rival princes. But these compacts were constantly being undermined by intrigues, disputes, and open warfare.

Of the major powers within India, the Marathas should have had the best hope to establish an India-wide government. Their stout defense of "brahmans and cows" against Aurangzeb's armies had given them wide appeal among the majority of India's peoples. But since Sivaji's time, the Marathas had taken many bandits and outlaws into their ranks. They now made their living by plundering and had become highly unpopular in most regions.

Many foreign observers noted the extremes of wealth and poverty that existed in India. Villagers were subject to the arbitrary tolls exacted by powerful officials and marauding robbers, and enjoyed little security of life or property.

---

1. One exception, a disastrous land war against Aurangzeb, only confirmed the accuracy of Roe's judgment.

HIERARCHY OF MOGHUL RULERS IN 18TH-CENTURY INDIA

Great Moghul	The Moghul emperor in Delhi commanded little real power in the 18th century, yet still had a measure of prestige and authority. An official *firman,* or decree, from the emperor often gave an air of legitimacy to a conquest or law.
Subahdar	Ruler of one of the large provinces (*subahs*) of the Moghul Empire. In theory, a *subahdar* (''viceroy'') was appointed by the Moghul emperor at Delhi. In practice, however, they usually gained their offices by force and afterward obtained a decree from the Moghul emperor.
Diwan	Revenue-collector and civil judge of a province.
Nizam	Military commander of a province.
Nawab	Ruler of a smaller province within a *subah.* (In British slang, the nawabs came to be known as *nabobs.*)

EUROPEAN TRADE IN INDIA

By 1700, the English company had established three regional headquarters for its trading activities in India. Calcutta, on the Hoogly River in the Ganges delta, was the most recent of the company's settlements. It was fast becoming a thriving center for the trade of Bengal, one of India's wealthiest provinces. On the Coromandel coast—at that time called the *Carnatic*—the company had established its main settlement and fort at Madras. Bombay, on India's western coast, was the third major center of the company's trade.

Each of the company's settlements had been constructed on land leased from local rulers. In an attempt to avoid exorbitant tolls and taxes, the company had chosen to build most of its forts and towns on undeveloped tracts or wastelands. Other European traders had followed much the same policy. None of the Europeans had been able to gain dominance over the others or to establish a monopoly on any part of India's trade.

Dupleix and Clive

By 1740, the English company considered the French East India Company to be its ''most dangerous rival'' in India. Joseph Dupleix, governor of the French settlements from 1741 to 1754, felt an even more forceful hostility toward the English. Pondicherry, the French capital in the Carnatic, was only 75 miles from Madras.

Joseph Dupleix aimed his first effective blow at the English company in 1746. At this time, England and France were at war in Europe, and

Dupleix was able to obtain a French squadron with which to seize Madras. Until a European peace treaty was concluded, in 1748, Madras and its treasures remained in French hands.

After the return of peace, Dupleix could no longer obtain military aid to harass the English. In fact, his superiors in Paris admonished him to avoid any conflicts with other traders. "Nothing is more opposed to commerce than war," they wrote. However, Dupleix soon found an opportunity to carry on what has been called his "private war" against the British.

In 1748, the royal dynasties of the Deccan became embroiled in a succession dispute. The outcome of this struggle was of great interest to European traders, for the victors would gain the two most powerful offices in South India: one would be crowned *subahdar* (viceroy) of the Deccan, and the other would become *nawab* (deputy viceroy) of the Carnatic. In the past, the French and English companies had remained "neutral" in such struggles—they had sent gifts and flattering messages to the various contenders, yet had remained on the sidelines while battles were fought. But now Dupleix decided to take a more active role.

In several local skirmishes, Dupleix had discovered that a small regiment of European-trained Indian soldiers, called *sepoys,* could overcome the much larger armies of local princes.[2] Accordingly, he decided to use his French–Indian troops to support a pretender to the throne. After a year of intrigues, military marches, and battles, Dupleix's plan succeeded: the nawab of the Carnatic was slain and Dupleix's candidate installed in his place (July 1749). In 1751, another of Dupleix's candidates was crowned as subah of the Deccan. The new nawab and subahdar expressed their gratitude to Dupleix by presenting him with extravagant gifts. Among other favors, he received a rich treasury, a force of 7000 cavalry, and a vast tract of land extending from the Krishna River to Cape Comorin. To celebrate his success, Dupleix constructed a new city ("The City of Dupleix's Victory") and erected a commemorative pillar.

The new subahdar and nawab were not Dupleix's "puppets," or figureheads; the day had not yet come when Europeans would directly rule an Indian kingdom. Yet the two princes were required to support Dupleix's anti-English policies, for they depended on his troops to retain their power. For the most part, they did not mind their continuing association with the Frenchman. In India, Dupleix now commanded the greatest admiration and respect, for his enterprises always seemed to be attended by good fortune.

---

2. Under European generals, the sepoys learned how to maintain discipline under fire and also had the advantage of more accurate firearms—a recent development in Europe.

As Dupleix's successes mounted, the situation of the English became increasing desperate. Their candidate as nawab of the Carnatic—a son of the previous nawab—was being besieged at Trichinopoly, and the company could not spare enough soldiers to rescue him. Moreover, Dupleix controlled all of the land surrounding English settlements, so that traders now needed French permission to travel inland. Thus, it seemed that Dupleix's dream of expelling the English from India was close at hand.

When the fortunes of the English company were at their most desperate, a young employee named Robert Clive came up with a plan of action. Clive had come to India at the age of 18, entering the company's service as a clerical employee. In 1746, two years after his arrival, he had been obliged to flee Madras when the city was captured by the French. Now, in 1751, Clive had seen action in several military skirmishes and had shown an ability to make clearheaded decisions under fire.

Clive's plan of action was a bold one: English troops should attempt to seize Arcot, he suggested. Since Arcot was the nawab's capital city, the English, if successful, could at one stroke regain their reputation as a military power. Though this course of action entailed many obvious risks, Clive was given a force of 500 soldiers—the majority of them sepoys—to make the attempt.

The Siege of Arcot. Clive executed the first part of his plan with little trouble; within days, his troops had captured Arcot. But then the nawab sent an army of 10,000 troops to besiege the city. After several weeks, the city's ramparts had begun to crumble, and the occupiers were running desperately short of supplies. Yet Clive and his 240 remaining soldiers continued to defend the mile-long perimeter of the fort, refusing all offers of surrender. By the 50th day of the siege, their heroic defense had aroused the admiration of a large Maratha army that had been plundering the countryside nearby. The Marathas moved to join with Clive, and the nawab's army withdrew.

After joining with the Marathas, Clive's army marched to Fort St. David, destroying Dupleix's City of Victory along the way. At Madras, Clive met with Stringer Lawrence, a military officer who had just arrived from England. For the next two years, Lawrence and Clive continued the task of undoing Dupleix's work and restoring the reputation of the English. In June 1752, they rescued the English-supported pretender from Trichinopoly and defeated the Indian and French armies that had been besieging him. Dupleix's nawab was captured and killed, and the English candidate installed in his place.

Despite many setbacks, Dupleix remained unflagging in his efforts to undermine the English. Several of his intrigues, in fact, nearly succeeded. But Dupleix could not find capable generals to carry out his plans, and

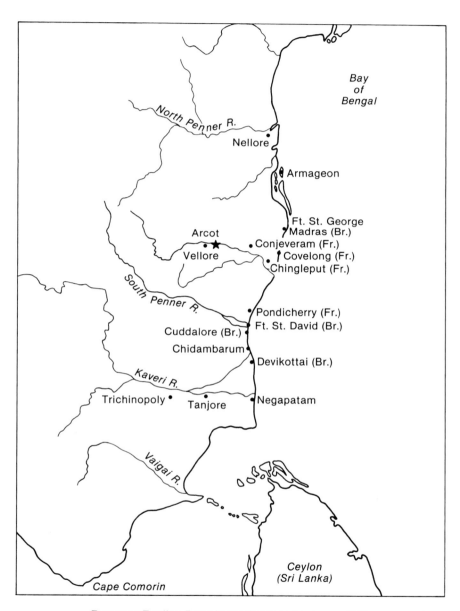

European Trading Posts in the Carnatic Region, c. 1745

he did not have a talent for military leadership himself. He also lacked Clive's ability to work effectively with his peers. By 1754, the French company had suffered so many reverses that its directors decided to recall Dupleix.

Events in Bengal

In 1756, the English company received news of a new crisis that overshadowed the continuing turmoil in the Deccan. Calcutta, in Bengal, had long been the most peaceful and prosperous of the company's settlements. But a transition of rulers suddenly set in motion a train of unexpected events. The elderly nawab of Bengal died, leaving the throne to his volatile young grandson. Siraj-ud-daula, the new nawab, had often expressed a lively hostility for the English and apparently decided to expel them before their power grew any greater. After issuing several ultimatums, which the English traders did not take seriously enough, Siraj marched on Calcutta with a large army. At his approach, most of the English inhabitants of the city escaped down the river by boat. The city's governor and military commander also fled, leaving less than 200 men to defend the fort. Within hours, the small regiment surrendered. Siraj ordered his officers to imprison the remaining soldiers and retired for the night.

The Black Hole Incident. Lacking precise instructions, Siraj's officers decided to lock the English prisoners in the fort's small dungeon. This dark, airless dungeon was known to the English garrison as the "Black Hole." According to a survivor's report, 146 men and one woman were imprisoned in the Black Hole that night, and only 20 came out alive the next morning; the rest had died of suffocation, thirst, and shock.[3] When news of this tragedy reached England, it aroused great indignation. In some published versions of the story, Siraj himself was portrayed as the prisoners' torturer, actively enjoying their pleas for water and air. Thus, the episode created a popular image of Indian rulers as unprincipled and cruel and of English traders as their hapless victims. In England, the Black Hole retained its hold on the public imagination for more than a century.

In August 1756, the company's employees at Madras learned of what had happened in Calcutta on 20 June. In December, Clive arrived in Bengal with a force of 2300 men and retook Calcutta the next month. But England's reputation could not be redeemed until Siraj made repara-

---

3. According to a 20th-century study, there may have been only 64 prisoners, of whom 21 came out alive.

tions for the injuries he had caused. This seemed unlikely, for Siraj had been boasting that the English could be governed "with a pair of slippers." Moreover, Siraj's army of 50,000 might at any moment be reinforced with French troops, for France and England were again at war. Faced with this military impass, Clive resorted to diplomacy. He soon discovered that Siraj—like most Indian princes—had many dangerous rivals and enemies. Among these were some of the highest officials of the court, including his great-uncle and chief general, Mir Jaffir. Needless to say, Clive cultivated the goodwill of all potential conspirators. In June 1757, he arranged a secret treaty between the East India Company and Mir Jaffir, spelling out the exact terms of the general's treachery. Two days later, Clive led an army toward Siraj's capital of Murshidabad to do battle.

The Battle of Plassey. At Plassey, a small village midway between Calcutta and Murshidabad, Clive's army of 3000 men made their camp within sight of Siraj's army. Siraj's army now numbered 40,000 infantry and 15,000 calvalry. Of this, a sizable portion was commanded by Mir Jaffir, who had agreed to defect to the English. Nevertheless, the English troops spent a nervous, sleepless night on the eve of battle.

The Battle of Plassey, celebrated in legend as Clive's greatest victory, was actually less eventful than many of his other adventures. When English artillery fire began to strike Siraj's camp, one of his high officials advised him to flee the field. Siraj acted on this treacherous advice, and the bulk of his army dispersed soon afterward. Later, Siraj was captured and killed by a son of Mir Jaffir.

In accordance with the terms of the secret treaty, Mir Jaffir was crowned as nawab of Bengal and afterward distributed a large part of Siraj's treasury to the company. Although the treasury proved to be less than expected, Calcutta was substantially compensated for its losses. Clive and several other company employees also received large private fortunes for their part in the affair.

THE BIRTH OF AN EMPIRE

At Plassey, Clive had established the East India Company as a territorial power in India, a role that promised far greater riches than commercial trade. But the company's trading concerns were not ignored. Under a series of decrees issued by Mir Jaffir, English goods were allowed to travel duty-free throughout Bengal while the trade of Indian merchants was taxed and restricted.

In 1765, the Moghul emperor at Delhi recognized the East India Company as the official diwan, or revenue-collector, for Bengal. Here, Clive receives the decree from the emperor's hands.

The Exploitation of Bengal. After Clive's return to England, in 1760, the activities of the company's employees in Bengal began to take on the dimensions of a major scandal. First, they had found a way to collect enormous bribes by dispensing political favors. Also, they had enriched themselves—but not the Company—through their tariff-free private trade. In Bengal, such behavior was not considered unusual. As one historian has explained it: "To have political power and not to use it for making money was inconceivable in India."[4] But in 18th-century England, the customary procedure was just the reverse: wealth was used to gain political office, not the other way around. Thus, the traders' extravagant plundering was viewed as a national disgrace.

In 1765, the company's directors appointed Clive as governor of Bengal so that he might "save the empire he had founded." During the two years he stayed in Bengal as governor-general, Clive took energetic measures to establish the company on more solid footing. From the Moghul emperor, he obtained a decree recognizing the East India Company as the official diwan, or revenue-collector, for Bengal. And to improve the company's reputation at home, Clive rooted out corrupt officials and restored a

---

4. Nirad C. Chaudhuri, *Clive of India* (Bombay: Jaico Press, 1978), p. 140.

sense of discipline among the ranks. But after Clive's departure, corruption again began to flourish. And as a new generation of wealthy "nabobs" returned to England, the people of Bengal were reduced to a state of abject poverty. In 1770, the British people were shocked to hear of a massive famine that claimed the lives of an estimated one-third of Bengal's people. The company's employees, it was rumored, had profited from the disaster by speculating in rice.

The Question of Government

A commercial enterprise such as the East India Company was obviously ill-suited for the task of governing. It seemed logical, therefore, that the British government should take control of the company's territories. But legally, the company did not have an empire, or even an acre of land; it only collected tax revenue on behalf of the Moghul emperor. As a result of this and other dilemmas, the company was allowed to retain its empire until 1858. But meanwhile, the government took an increasingly close interest in the company's affairs and especially in the appointment of the governors who would rule in Calcutta.

An Experiment in Governing: Warren Hastings (1772–1785)

The appointment of Warren Hastings was seen as a hopeful solution to the company's problems. Having joined the company at the age of 18, Hastings knew India and its people well. Also, he had earned a reputation for personal integrity and was thought to have a determined and resolute character.

In later times, Hastings was judged by his admirers to have been "the savior of the empire" and "the greatest of all the British governors." But to his enemies, Hastings was "a captain-general of iniquity" and "the greatest delinquent that India ever saw." Given the tasks that Hastings was asked to perform, it is not surprising that his critics contradicted one another. On the one hand, he was to provide a "good government" for Bengal, a province that was much larger than England. On the other, he was to siphon off enough revenue from Bengal to enrich both the company's shareholders and the British government. In the end, Hastings was far more successful in the second goal than in the first.

Unfortunately for Hastings, his superiors had greatly overestimated Bengal's wealth. By 1772, the once prosperous province of Bengal was in ruins, and the company on the verge of bankrupcy. Nevertheless, by taking direct control of the tax-collecting operation, Hastings found enough revenue to offset much of the company's deficit. But even this turnaround was not enough. To make matters worse, Hastings had to deal with two unexpected emergencies that greatly increased his expenses.

During Hastings' tenure in office, British armies in North America were fighting, and losing, the American War of Independence. In 1778, news of a major British defeat at Saratoga reached Calcutta. At the same time, Hastings learned that the company's governor in Bombay had entered into a disastrous war against the Marathas. Hastings would have been justified in ignoring this crisis. However, he believed that the catastrophe in America made it imperative to save the reputation of British arms in India. Without delay, he sent a rescuing army to Bombay. But while the first army was engaged 2000 miles to the west, an even more serious crisis erupted in Madras—a formidable coalition of Muslim princes and Maratha chieftains had decided to eliminate the British power from the Carnatic. In the fall of 1780, their army of 40,000 men swept across the peninsula and descended on Madras. Hastings now sent his best remaining general to save the city. At the same time, through skillful diplomacy, he enticed some of the Marathas into an English alliance. By the summer of 1782, the two crises were resolved: the status quo had been restored in Bombay, and Madras had been saved from extinction.

Ironically, Hastings had rescued Britain's empire in India just as the empire in America—which had been built intentionally—was lost. But in his own lifetime, Hastings received little praise for this feat. Instead, a growing chorus of public opinion was beginning to view him as the instrument of British "misrule" and interference in India. As a result of public pressure, Hastings resigned his office in 1785. After his return to England, he was impeached before Parliament on 20 charges involving his actions as governor.

The Attacks on Hastings. The attacks against Hastings were led by Edmund Burke, one of Britain's most respected elder statesmen. In a fiery speech delivered to the House of Commons (in December 1783), Burke described Hastings' government in Bengal as "one of the most corrupt and destructive tyrannies that probably ever existed in the world." All of India's earlier conquerors, Burke noted, had at least left behind them "some monument, either of royal splendor or of useful beneficence." But the company had returned nothing to India in Hastings' long term as governor:

> If tomorrow we were expelled from Hindostan, nothing would remain to indicate that it had been possessed during the inglorious period of our dominion by any better tenants than the orang-outang or the tiger.

Burke's speech reflected what has been termed ''the rising humanitarian feeling of the age'' and focused intense public scrutiny on the issue of British rule in India. While the idea of undoing Clive's work found little support, many people expressed a sense of shame at the way India's ancient and venerable culture had been exploited. William Cowper, the most popular author of the day, summarized the public debate in these three lines of verse:

> Is India free? And does she wear her plum'd
> And jewell'd turban with a smile of peace?
> Or do we grind her still?[5]

In the course of a lengthy trial, it was shown that Hastings had resorted to many tyrannical and oppressive acts in his efforts to raise revenue.[6] Yet it was also clear that his activities had not been prompted by self-interest. After seven years, Hastings was finally acquitted of all the charges against him.

Although the trial of Hastings was inconclusive, it did help to define the behavior expected of a governor. Moreover, the drama of a public trial had demonstrated the workings of the *rule of law*, in which magistrates were bound by the same standards of conduct as all other citizens.

A New Type of Government

In its East India Act of 1784, the British Parliament outlined new rules for the company's administration. From now on, the company was to provide a government that acted in the public interest. Moreover, the British-controlled empire was to be a good neighbor to other powers within India. In the words of the act, ''To pursue schemes of conquest and extension of dominion in India are measures repugnant to the wish, the honor and policy of this nation.''

Lord Cornwallis (1786–1793). Charles Cornwallis, the man who succeeded Hastings as governor, was the type of ruler who would henceforth be sent to India. A member of England's landed aristocracy, Cornwallis

---

5. William Cowper, *The Task* (1784), bk. 4.
6. Hastings had resorted to several extraordinary methods of raising revenue that even Clive had not considered. For instance, he had rented a British army to a despotic ruler so that the latter might conquer a neighboring province. He had also extorted vast sums of money from the popular raja of Benares, nearly provoking a widespread rebellion in northern India.

had no previous connection with India or with the company. (In fact, just five years before, he had surrendered to General Washington at Yorktown, thus ending the American Revolutionary War.) In England, Cornwallis was known as a man of rigid integrity and competence, with standards of personal conduct that far exceeded the normal practices of the day.

Cornwallis' first concern was to create a system of government that was as efficient and incorruptible as possible. He demanded from employees a commitment to public service and paid them respectable wages (a measure the company had always resisted). By so doing, Cornwallis completely altered the conditions under which young men joined the company. The dedicated civil service he brought into being later came to be known as the "steel frame" of the British Empire.

Another cornerstone of good government, Cornwallis believed, was the separation of powers and functions. Of the three branches he established in the company—revenue-collecting, commercial, and judicial—the judicial branch was assigned the highest authority. This meant that the Supreme Court (established in Calcutta in 1773) could overrule the governor himself. The supreme authority and independence of judges was an entirely new concept in India, where the ruler had always been considered the highest "court of appeal" for his subjects. Although it was to be many years before a workable system of justice could be realized, the courts eventually did have the independent role that Cornwallis had intended.

EXPANSION OF THE EMPIRE

In foreign affairs, it was Cornwallis' policy to avoid interference in other states and to promote a stable "balance of power" among them. However, this policy ran into difficulty when Tipu Sultan, ruler of Mysore, launched a major war of expansion in South India. Tipu's aggressions soon began to take on the character of religious warfare, for he was a militant soldier of Islam. In the summer of 1790, Cornwallis deemed it necessary to enter the fray. After several hard-fought campaigns in which he himself took the field as commander, Cornwallis finally forced Tipu to surrender. By the terms of the peace treaty (signed in March 1792), Tipu was allowed to keep half of his kingdom. The other half was distributed among the remaining great powers of South India (the British, the Marathas, and the nizam of Hyderabad).

Within several years, the undaunted Tipu was again making trouble. To some British observers, it seemed that Cornwallis' moderate treaty terms had been dangerously naive. Indian rulers did not appreciate the "balance of power" concept, they argued; the permanent goal of a Muslim ruler or Hindu raja was to expand his territory at the expense of others. Thus, to ensure peace in India, the British would have to assert their power forcefully in every region where disturbances arose.

The Age of Expansion

In 1798, Richard Wellesley arrived in Calcutta as governor-general. Like Cornwallis, Lord Wellesley was a titled aristocrat who had been trained for the role of command. Soon after his arrival, the British "age of expansion" began.

Wellesley's first priority was to put an end to "Tipu the Tiger," for Tipu was now receiving French support for his anti-British schemes. After a difficult yearlong campaign, Tipu was defeated and killed (in May 1799). In his palace, British soldiers discovered an ingenious mechanical toy that depicted the late ruler's lifelong dream: a British soldier being noisily devoured by a tiger.

After the defeat of Tipu, Wellesley installed a Hindu raja upon his throne. The bulk of the Mysore kingdom, however, was annexed by the company. In acquiring other territories, Wellesley developed the system of Residency, or *subsidiary alliances*. When a prince was threatened by a rival power, the governor offered to station a British army in his capital. In payment for the army's upkeep, the ruler ceded to the company a portion of his kingdom. Moreover, he agreed that a British Resident (adviser) would dictate his foreign policy. Thus, the company gained territory and influence, and the prince was assured of security. Of course, the prince

A mechanical toy found in Tipu's palace fancifully depicts the fate he wished on all red-coated soldiers.

This splendid Residency at Hyderabad proclaimed the paramountcy of British influence in the region. Wellesley's system of subsidiary alliances was later extended to many other Indian kingdoms.

would soon find that he had lost his independence. But given the alternative, many rulers were satisfied with the bargain.

The nizam of Hyderabad became the first great prince to accept a British subsidiary force. As a result of this treaty and the conquest of Tipu, the company now controlled, either directly or indirectly, most of southern and central India. The Maratha confederacy was the only major power still opposing British rule.

Continuing Expansion

The "Sacred Trust." During Wellesley's tenure in office (1798–1805), the mission of the East India Company underwent drastic change. Dismayed by the "anarchy" and "misrule" that prevailed in the princely states, Wellesley was determined to bring as large a territory as possible under British rule. He did not pretend that this would be a profit-making enterprise. Rather, he said, the empire in India was a "sacred trust" that had been given to the British nation. Though Wellesley was recalled, his successors shared his vision of a well-ordered empire under British protection. Moreover, they were highly connected aristocrats who had the personal prestige needed to enforce their views. Thus, the wars of expansion continued.

By 1818, when the final war against the Marathas was concluded, it was possible to speak of a British empire in India. British paramountcy was now undisputed throughout the length of the Ganges valley, in most of the Deccan, and in the South. In the 1820s, the eastern and northern borders of the empire were established through wars with the Gurkhas of Nepal and the Burmese.

The Northwest Frontier. To ensure the security of the Ganges valley, British governors concluded, it would be necessary to establish a "buffer zone" to the west. However, practical limits were encountered when the

The British Empire in India, c. 1900

Attempts to expand the British Empire into Afghanistan resulted in massive tragedies. Shown is a British encampment at the Khyber Pass during the Second Afghan War.

British tried to establish a client kingdom in Afghanistan. In the First Afghan War (1838–1842), an entire British army of 16,000 men perished in the Hindu Kush. The Second Afghan War (1878–1880) ended nearly as tragically as the first, with devastating loss of life and no gain in territory.

Failure to create a buffer zone in Afghanistan left the Northwest Frontier—the northern Indus valley—as the final boundary of the British empire in India. In the Frontier provinces, the British encountered the Pathans, or Afghans—the same fiercely independent people who had repelled their invasions of Afghanistan. Farther east, in the Punjab, Muslims of Indian descent were in the majority. The Sikh nation was also centered here, and there was a sizable minority of Hindus. The task of keeping the peace among all of these diverse groups taxed the ingenuity of many British administrators and is still a major problem for the governments of Pakistan and India.

UNIFYING AND GOVERNING

Once an empire had been assembled, there remained the even greater task of governing it. But first, it would be necessary to decide what the basic mission of government should be. Should the British government impose

Western-style institutions and laws in India, as Cornwallis had outlined? Or should the government modify its approach to suit existing traditions, acting more as a guardian or caretaker?

A System of Justice

In Indian tradition as in the West, one of the first duties of government was to provide justice. But what brand of justice should the British government dispense in India? According to Western ideas, a government should ensure that all citizens were treated equally under the law, regardless of religion, race, caste, or social status. But Indian systems of law had always accorded different rights and privileges to these various classes.

In upholding the "rule of law" as they knew it, British judges had often defied sacred traditions and outraged public opinion. One of the most infamous incidents of this type occurred in Hastings' day, when a Supreme Court judge decreed the death penalty for a brahman convicted of forgery. This decision was completely contrary to Hindu law, which protected brahmans from capital punishment even for such crimes as murder. The controversy aroused by this and other incidents made it apparent that judges would have to be more flexible in their approach. Yet, at the same time, they were expected to administer a uniform brand of justice throughout the empire.

The complex procedures of English justice also presented a problem. In traditional India, justice was often administered by a village *panchayat*, or council. Because the council members knew the disputants personally, they were able to evaluate their testimony and make a decision on the spot. But British justice was administered in an impersonal way, by a judge who knew none of the parties. Moreover, the many tedious procedures involved in court proceedings had become an object of satire even in England. In the words of Thomas B. Macaulay, a leading expert, English justice was "neither so cheap nor so speedy as might be wished."

Macaulay believed that a legal system should accomplish two objectives: it should "suppress crime with the smallest possible infliction of suffering" and "ascertain truth at the smallest possible cost of time and money." In 1834, Macaulay was given the task of compiling a law code for India. His code of criminal law eventually won wide acceptance among both Hindus and Muslims—a feat that even the great Akbar had been unable to achieve. The "universal principles" of justice it sets forth are still the foundation of penal law in modern India.

In the field of civil law—such matters as land rights, family law, and religious practices—the British were less successful in finding "universal principles" upon which all could agree. But as increasing numbers of Indian judges and lawyers participated in the system, the central principles of Western law came to be more widely accepted. As one historian remarked, law was "the first official sphere in which Indians won distinction, and perhaps for that reason is especially cherished."[7]

Education and Language

In 1835, it was decided that English would be the official language of the empire and that new universities would offer only English-language studies. This step was a victory for the "Westernizers," who believed that English institutions, ideas, and technology were the "key to all improvements" in India. Rammohun Roy, a prominent Hindu reformer, agreed. Rather than encouraging Sanskrit studies and other learning that was "already current in India," he said, the government should offer English-language instruction "embracing mathematics, natural philosophy, chemistry and anatomy, with other useful sciences."

Those who advocated the English-language policy realized that it might hasten the day when India could become an independent, self-governing nation. However, they had no qualms about such an event. A prosperous, self-sufficient India, they argued, would be "the proudest monument of British benevolence." Moveover, this unselfish work would be rewarded by vast new opportunities for commerce:

> It would be, on the most selfish view of the case, far better for us that the people of India were well-governed and independent of us, than ill-governed and subject to us; that they were ruled by their own kings, but wearing our broadcloth, and working with our cutlery. . . .[8]

Modernization and Unification

In the 1840s, the technology and material improvements of Britain's industrial revolution were rapidly introduced to India. Irrigation projects, schools, and public health facilities provided the "monuments" to British rule that Burke had hoped to see. Highways, railroads, and telegraph lines also made their mark on the landscape, linking widely separated regions of India for the first time. Perhaps most significant of all was a new, India-wide postal service, inaugurated in 1854. By linking even the remotest villages to the larger communications network, the "penny post" mails—together with the rapidly expanding railroads—helped to create a new sense of a unified state.

---

7. Percival Spear, "The Mughals and the British," in A. L. Basham, *A Cultural History of India* (London: Oxford University Press, 1975), p. 359.
8. Thomas B. Macaulay, charter speech, 10 July 1833.

Carried away by visions of modernization and improved efficiency, the government began to annex princely states at an accelerated rate. But then, in 1857, this energetic program suddenly came to an end. A violent reaction showed that the government had long since lost contact with its subjects.

THE REBELLION OF 1857–1858

In May 1857, the peace of northern India was shattered by an army rebellion. Following the initial revolt, warfare between rebellious sepoys, village peasants, and British armies continued for more than a year. The meaning of this violence is still debated. In the view of most Indian nationalists, it was the first battle in the movement that eventually led to India's independence from British rule. But many British historians have viewed the incident as a "mutiny" that was motivated by personal grievances rather than nationalist feelings.

The troubles began when the army issued a new type of gun, the Enfield rifle, which required soldiers to bite the ends of greased cartridges before loading them. A rumor spread that the cartridges had been dipped in cow lard and pig lard, substances repugnant to both Muslim and Hindu sepoys. The army first denied, then admitted, the truth of the rumors, and finally issued new cartridges that could be lubricated with vegetable oil. But by now it was too late: the sepoys were outraged by the affront and believed it had been part of a deliberate plot to impose the Christian religion on them.

On 10 May 1857, the sepoys of Meerut rose in rebellion after suffering harsh disciplinary measures for their initial protests. After murdering two of their officers, the sepoys made the 30-mile march to Delhi and "liberated" the city from British rule with the help of Delhi's Indian troops. They then met with the aged Moghul emperor and proclaimed him their leader. During the summer, there were incidents in widely separated regions as news of the rebellion spread. With the aid of loyal Sikh regiments from the Punjab, the British finally recaptured Delhi in September. But the war continued for nearly another year. Major massacres of British civilians occurred at Lucknow and Cawnpore, and murderous reprisals were carried out in much of the surrounding countryside.

After the British regained control of the Ganges valley, the Moghul emperor—who had served as a rallying point for the rebels—was exiled to Burma. A British captain took it upon himself to murder the emperor's sons. Thus, the venerable dynasty founded by Babur came to an end.

British policymakers realized that there had been more at stake in the rebellion than the matter of the cartridges: the rebels had been fighting to

A memorial to the British who perished at Cawnpore gives an indication of the emotionality surrounding this episode. Many years later, the British community recognized that the Mutiny had been a tragic episode for Indians too.

defend a whole way of life against a government that they still viewed as foreign. Steps were immediately taken to conciliate those who had been offended. In August 1858, the company's rule officially ended, and the British government assumed direct control of the empire. (The governors of India now assumed the title of *viceroy* to indicate their direct link to the crown.) A proclamation issued by Queen Victoria assured the Indian people that the government would never again annex princely kingdoms upon slight pretexts and would respect the religious beliefs of all subjects. And in 1877, the queen was officially proclaimed as empress of India. This gesture proved to be popular in India, for the semisacred royal office at least provided an emotional and ceremonial center for the empire—a quality that had been lacking in the company's government.

The rebellion of 1857 marked a sharp dividing point in the history of the British empire in India. The government ceased to be complacent about its policies and scrupulously observed the religious liberties that Victoria had proclaimed. Yet, at the same time, the style of British rule became more remote, authoritarian, and impersonal. It became fashionable once again—as it had been in the ancient and medieval worlds—to regard India as mysterious and unknowable.

By 1878, India was the "jewel in the crown," or the centerpiece, of an empire that included Canada, Australia, Burma, large parts of Africa, and many other outposts extending from the Caribbean Islands to China. Around this time, the doctrine of "sacred trust" was elaborated. The civilizing mission that Britain had undertaken, it now appeared, was "in obedience to a higher law and a nobler aim." In his poem "White Man's Burden" (among other works), Rudyard Kipling portrayed the rigid sense of duty and self-sacrifice with which Victorian imperialists carried out their thankless task:

> Take up the White Man's burden—
> No tawdry rule of kings,
> But toil of serf and sweeper—
> The tale of common things. . . .
>
> Take up the White Man's burden—
> And reap his old reward:
> The blame of those ye better,
> The hate of those ye guard.

In 1877 and later, royal ceremonies—often with a military character—were a hall-mark of the British empire in India. Shown is one such event: a march-past of the camel corps in honor of a visit by the Prince of Wales.

SUMMARY

The way in which a small group of English traders built an empire in India has been described as a "series of improvizations under pressure." The most important advantage the traders had was their sense of national purpose and destiny. Their group discipline gave them a confidence and unity that other powers lacked. Moreover, it enabled them to exploit the many divisions that existed in India.

The expansion of the empire was justified by the need to provide peace and security for British-controlled domains. Later, the list of benefits to be provided by British rule was expanded. As social and economic reforms occurred in England, British statesmen found new ways in which the government of India might promote the "greatest happiness of the greatest number of people." However, the momentum of reform was checked in 1857, when a rebellion demonstrated that the government had not won the hearts and minds of its subjects.

Though British rule brought undeniable benefits to India, there was less altruism in its operation than at first appeared. Indian nationalists were able to offer convincing proof that Britain's economic interests, not India's, had mainly benefited. After making a careful study of the matter in the late 19th century, Romesh Chunder Dutt, a prominent economist, concluded: "History does not record a single instance of one people ruling another in the interests of the subject nation."

DISCUSSION AND ESSAY QUESTIONS

1. Imagine that you are an English newspaper reporter stationed in 18th-century Madras. Describe the exploits of the British East India Company during the years 1751 to 1757.

2. What image of the British nation did Clive's exploits produce? How did this image change after Plassey?

3. Describe the rights and duties of a ruler in India. What new ideas on this subject did the British introduce?

4. What were some of the main differences between Moghul and British rule? Consider such factors as assimilation into Indian life, ties with the original homeland, and ideas about government.

5. How did British rule help to lay the foundation for an independent Indian nation?

ADDITIONAL READINGS

Nirad C. Chaudhuri, *Clive of India* (Bombay: Jaico Press, 1978). An admiring biography of the British hero who founded an empire in India. In recounting the events of Clive's career, the author draws many comparisons between British and Indian cultures.

E. M. Forster, *A Passage to India* (many editions available). In this famous novel, Forster illustrates the breakdown in communications between the British and Indian communities in the early 20th century. Several of the characters try to bridge the gap between the two cultures, but are not successful.

BRITISH RULE AND TRADITIONAL INDIA

During the 19th century, direct British rule brought peace, security, and an efficient administration to a large area of India. But there remained hundreds of "subsidiary states" in which older traditions and ceremonies were observed. British administrators were dismayed by the "chaos" and "lawlessness" of the princely states. Yet this very disorder seemed to provide something that the British territories lacked. A historian with experience in India explains.

Tax Collecting Styles, Old and New

As soon as they had forgotten the bad old days when a man could not step out of his house with any expectation of finding the thatch still on the roof when he came back, men in the British districts began to look regretfully across the border at the turbulence, the confusion and the excitement of the state. They found life dull in British India, where the Company provided no fireworks and no sanguinary contests between wild beasts when anyone married or came of age, where the business of collecting revenue was a dull monotonous grind, with nothing to alleviate the misery of parting with hard-won cash. In a State, now, revenue collection combined the excitement of a sweepstake in reverse, a militiaman's field-day, the Eatonswill election and a bull-fight in a small Spanish town. An officer traveling in Oudh one day found some villagers busily repairing the parapet of a small fort. They expected a visit from the revenue collector, they explained.

"And you will resist?"

"Of course. We will offer him 1000 rupees and he will demand 10,000. Then we shall go into the fort and he will fire his guns and we shall fire our muskets. Then we shall parley and then there will be more firing. In the end, after two or three days, we shall give him 3000, which is what we always do give."

"But would it not be quicker to give him 3000 in the first place?"

"Quicker, yes, but that is not how we do it." — And the implication is clear that it would be much less fun.

This is the reverse to the well-known story from the Governor-General's camp on the borders of Oudh. Hearing a heavy cannonading from across the river, Lord Hardinge made inquiries from the district officer and was told: "Oh, that is only our neighbors in Oudh collecting their revenue."

SOURCE: Philip Woodruff, *The Men Who Ruled India,* vol. 2 (London: Jonathan Cape, 1954), pp. 321–322.

1. How did British rule affect the traditional life style of Oudh?

LIBERAL OPINION IN BRITAIN

*The British East India Company was one of the first instances of a
modern corporation. It was different from earlier types of enterprises
in that it was not owned or managed by particular individuals. Instead, ownership was shared by a large number of shareholders, and
management duties were carried out by commmittee. According to
some critics, the company's corporate structure enabled it to evade
responsibility for its actions. As the British Parliament debated
whether or not the company's rule in India should continue (in 1858),
one pamphlet writer offered the following reflections.*

The Company—the Directors! Who are they? What are they? Have they
any responsible name—any fixed residence? Have they any individuality such
as may enable those whom they have wronged or injured, to bring home to
them the punishment due to their misdeeds and their crimes? Nobody knows
who they are. Their names are constantly changing. They have neither a
responsible name, nor a fixed residence. They have no individuality which
may be held responsible; and nobody in the flesh who may be subjected to
punishment. They are a *corporation* which, according to the law, has no soul,
and yet, according to the same authority, can never die. . . .

The dominion of the Company's Government, acquired in India, has been
the simple growth of a long succession of wars, quarrels, treaties, intrigues,
systematically planned and carried out by the Company's Government, and
their unscrupulous agents and representatives. . . . The whole system of the
East India Company's Government is grounded upon the broad principle of
spoilation and robbery. . . . Not content with commercial restrictions and
monopolies; with a system of the most extortionate and vexatious taxation, it
has assumed the absolute ownership of the entire land of the country.

SOURCE: *The Government of India: As It Has Been, As It Is, and As It Ought to Be*
(London, 1858).

1. Is it true that a corporate structure can help individuals to evade responsibility for their actions?
2. Does this writer give a fair picture of the company's activities in India up to
   the year 1858? Explain why or why not.

C H A P T E R

N I N E

THE INDIAN NATIONALIST MOVEMENT

Come up out of your narrow holes and look abroad. See how the nations are on their march. Do you love man? Do you love your country? Then come, let us struggle for higher and better things. Look not back—no, not even you hear the dearest and nearest cry—look not back, but forward march!

Swami Vivekananda

In 1838, several rock inscriptions in a long-forgotten Indian language were deciphered by a British official. These messages proved to be the words of Ashoka, the great Mauryan emperor who had reigned over India more than 2000 years before. The discovery that Hindu and Buddhist kings had once ruled an all-India empire stirred great excitement among European scholars. But to a small group of friends in Calcutta—India's first nationalists— the discovery had even greater meaning. These English-educated Indians were beginning to dream about a new empire in Asia, much like the one Ashoka had ruled. Like Ashoka's empire, the new Indian empire would cover all of the subcontinent. And it would be run by people who had been born and bred in the country. This time, however, there would be no king to watch over the land and settle the people's quarrels. Instead, the people themselves would be the rulers.

INDIA AND THE WESTERN WORLD

Nearly a hundred years after the Battle of Plassey, observers noted that Hindu culture was almost "immutable," its basic patterns completely untouched by Western influence. This continuity was largely due to the *brahmanical tradition*, which had kept alive such basic concepts as karma, dharma, and the sanctity of brahmans. As a result of these values—and the stable social order provided by the caste system—India's villagers had known how to preserve their society without any guidance from outside. One British official described the villages as "little republics" that had upheld their essential independence thoughout the ages:

> The Village Communities are little Republics, having nearly everything they want within themselves, and almost independent of any foreign relations. They seem to last where nothing else lasts. Dynasty after dynasty tumbles down; revolution succeeds to revolution; Hindu, Pathan, Moghul, Maratha, Sikh, English, are masters in turn; but the village communities remain the same.[1]

In the Great Rebellion of 1857–1858, the villagers of northern India had shown that they were willing to take up arms to defend their way of life. And they had won their main point: the British government had retreated from its Westernizing policies. However, in the opinion of India's first nationalists, this standoff did not resolve the problem. If India's villagers were to avoid the calamity of future invasions and conquests, there was only one solution: they must join together to create an independent, self-governing nation. And to accomplish this task, they would have to borrow some ideas and institutions from the West.

First Intellectual Contacts between India and the West

When English-language education was introduced to India (1835), British reformers predicted that this measure would create new allies—a group of Indians enthusiastic in their support of the empire. In the words of Thomas B. Macaulay, English education would create "a class of persons, Indian in blood and color, but English in taste, in opinions, in morals and in intellect." In part, this prediction came true. The first English-educated Indians felt increased respect for the British people and for the ideals they lived by at home—especially *representative government* (democracy) and individual rights. However, their knowledge of these principles also gave them a new perspective on imperialism, the government of one people by another.

Though they represented only a tiny elite in India, the middle classes of English-educated Indians proved to be the dynamic force that led

---

1. Charles Metcalfe, quoted in Percival Spear, *Twilight of the Moghals* (Karachi: Oxford University Press, 1980), p. 117.

India's peoples to nationhood. For more than a century, these influential professionals—lawyers, journalists, doctors, professors, and merchants —carried on the agitations and reforms that eventually led to independence from British rule. At the same time, they worked to transform their society so that it could take its place in the world's community of democratic nations.

In the long fight for independence, Muslims and Hindus were at first united in their goals and tactics. However, as we will see, the Muslim community ultimately decided that its interests could not be served in a Hindu-majority nation. As a result, when Independence came in 1947, the separate state of Pakistan was created to satisfy the aspirations of Indian Muslims.

Natural Rights, Nationalism, and Nation Building

By the 19th century, the concept of *self-determination* had become a central ideal of Western civilization. According to this ideal, the only legitimate government was one that ruled with the consent of its people. Moreover, each distinctive group of people had the right—and the duty—to create its own nation.

The process of nation building was inspired, in part, by the idea that all human beings have certain "natural rights"—such as the right to be free and to enjoy the fruits of their labors. As this idea spread, it inspired dramatic revolutions in England, America, and France (in 1689, 1776, and 1789). These societies went on to establish nation-states in which democratic institutions, rather than divine-right monarchs, were the basis of government.

The ideals of liberty and equality were a powerful force in nation building because they drew people together and gave them new hope for the future. And the spirit of *nationalism* was equally important.

Nationalism is often described as an "awakening" in which people realize they are part of a wider community, or nation. The exact shape that this community will take cannot always be predicted. People may feel commonality with others because they speak the same language or have the same ethnic identity. A shared religion, history, or other tradition might also be the determining factor.

In some respects, the spirit of nationalism was not a new or particularly Western development; it had existed in some form in many different societies. However, it was not until the 19th century that the word *nationalism* gained its current meaning. The idea of considering the people as the most important element of a state is one of the main characteristics of modern nationalism.

THE HINDU RENAISSANCE

When the first Indian nationalists began to dream about nation building, their thoughts naturally turned to religion. They considered the Hindu religion to be the main source of unity and continuity in the subcontinent; there was no other common tradition that could knit India's peoples together.[2] However, the nationalists were dismayed when they thought about all the various sects and forms of worship that had grown up in Hinduism. Because religion was considered to be an individual matter, Hindus followed no set rules in matters of worship and belief.

In the early 19th century, Indian nationalists began a century-long effort to define their civilization and develop a new vision of the future. Their first goal was to find a set of clear-cut doctrines that all Hindus could agree on. A new, simplified religion would be an important source of unity and strength, they believed. Equally important was the matter of social reform. All nationalists agreed that Hindu culture must be "purified" so that it better expressed the ideals of social unity and equality. A particular focus of concern was the status of women and of the "untouchables."

The reform movement was largely carried on in the Indian press, which included English-language newspapers as well as hundreds of regional-language presses. Societies and discussion groups also provided a forum where new ideas could be exchanged. Because of this open debate, the Hindu community gained a new sense of self-awareness and of progressing to "higher and better things." Modern ideas about democracy and secular institutions also became more widely known.

Rammohun Roy and the Brahmo Samaj

Rammohun Roy (1774–1833)—often called the "Father of Modern India" —was the first high-caste Hindu to make a detailed study of Western culture and Christianity. He was also a scholar of Islam, Sufism, Buddhism, and Hinduism—all of the major religions known in his native Bengal. As a result of this comparative study, Roy came to believe that the essence of religious truth is *monotheism*, or belief in one God. He also expressed admiration for the moral teachings of Jesus, which he considered an eloquent statement of universal values.

Roy decided that the pure monotheism of the *Upanishads* should be the basis of Hindu worship. For this purpose, he founded a new sect known as the *Brahmo Samaj* ("Society of the Divine"), in 1828. The samaj was devoted to worship of "the Eternal, Unsearchable, and Immutable

---

2. Nearly all of the first Indian nationalists were Hindus. Muslims did not become active in nationalist causes, in significant numbers, until later in the century (1880s).

Being, who is the Author and Preserver of the Universe." The use of images in worship was strictly forbidden, for Roy believed that this popular Hindu practice was corrupt. The samaj observed no distinctions of caste or race: it was a universal church, open to all.

After Roy's death, several notable reformers continued his work and kept alive his main principles. These included the idea that all beliefs should be examined in the light of reason and conscience; the ideal of equality and active charity toward others; and the elimination of prejudices that create divisions among people.

Dayananda Sarasvaty and the Arya Samaj

The Brahmo Samaj inspired hundreds of similar societies. One of the most notable of these was the *Arya Samaj* ("Aryan Society"), which attracted members in the hundreds of thousands. Dayananda Sarasvaty, the founder of this society, did not accept the idea that Christianity—or any other aspect of Western culture—had anything to offer India. Instead, he took his inspiration from the Vedas, the first scriptures of the Aryan invaders. The activism and military glory of these conquerors, he believed, were the true foundation of the Indian nation. Sects that preached the avoidance of harm and withdrawal from the world (especially Jainism) therefore represented corrupt views.

In Sarasvaty's opinion, the "Aryas" were not a particular caste or race. Rather, they were "all men of superior principles." The samaj observed no caste distinctions, and all members were encouraged to study the Vedas—an activity traditionally forbidden to the untouchables. The samaj also undertook active charitable work such as famine relief, homes for orphans and widows, and schools for girls as well as boys.

Ramakrishna and the "Soul of India"

The late 19th century was an exciting time in India; a time of great intellectual activity and nationalist fervor. Much of this activity took place in the cities of Calcutta, Bombay, and Madras, where the centers of communication—the universities and the presses—were located. Many of the leading Indian nationalists were professional men who spoke English, dressed in Western style, and had traveled widely in Europe. However, one of the most influential of them lived completely apart from this busy world. This was the sage known as Ramakrishna (1836–1886), who lived all his life in rural Bengal. At a critical time in the nationalist movement, this modern saint inspired new pride and self-respect in the Hindu community. He came to symbolize the "soul of India"—the tireless quest for spiritual knowledge that had shaped Hindu civilization from the beginning.

Ramakrishna's talent for spiritual pursuits became evident when he was still a child. At the age of six, it was said, he fell into a state of *samadhi*, or consciousness of the world's unity—an experience that ordinarily requires years of yogic discipline and training (see Chapter 2). When he was 20 years old, he became the temple priest at a shrine on the Ganges River. The temple was devoted to the goddess Kali (consort of Shiva), who is known for her destructive capabilities as well as her character as a "Great Mother."

At the temple of Kali, Ramakrishna made this goddess the center of his meditations. After a period of failure and desolation, he suddenly had a vision of the goddess and of the "ocean of the Spirit" known as Brahman. Following this experience, Ramakrishna felt "a burning desire" to experience other forms of religious worship. One by one, he meditated on the central figures of other faiths, including Mohammed and Jesus. Each time, the end result was the same: an individual figure appeared and then merged into the "shoreless ocean" of Brahman.

As news of Ramakrishna's visions spread, he began to receive hundreds of visitors, from all walks of Indian society. The advice he dispensed to these callers was recorded in a book called *The Gospel of Sri Ramakrishna*.

Ramakrishna's central message was that all religions are valid and true in their essence; they are simply different paths to the same end. Thus, there is no point in arguing over theology or trying to define God. Worship is an individual experience, and each person must arrive at the end in his or her own way:

> Do not argue about doctrine and religions. There is only one. All rivers flow to the Ocean. Flow and let others flow too! The great stream carves out for itself according to the slope of its journey—according to race, time and temperament—its own distinct bed. But it is all the same water. Go . . . flow on towards the Ocean!

With respect to the current controversy over "idolatry," Ramakrishna explained that the use of images often helps a worshiper to visualize the "shoreless ocean" that is God. The images are like blocks of ice that melt into the ocean when the vision is achieved.

Ramakrishna provided a new logic for the ideals of equality and charity that the nationalists had been preaching. Active service to humankind is the same as worship of the divine, he said, for all beings—especially humans—are manifestations of God. "You are seeking God? Very well, look for Him in man!"

Ramakrishna's intense visions of world harmony left him ill-equipped to deal with the turmoil and discords of everyday life. As a result, he decided that he must have a disciple to carry his message to the outside world. In the Western-educated, skeptical young man known as Vivekananda, he finally found his chosen student.

Vivekananda and the Meeting of East and West

Narendranath Dutt (1863–1902), better known as Vivekananda, was about 20 years old when he met Ramakrishna. As a student, he had become interested in Western philosophy and science, and planned to earn a law degree. Thus, he was surprised to learn that he was the chosen disciple of a Hindu saint. As to why he had accepted this mission, Vivekananda noted: "One of his glances could change a whole life."

Through his contacts with Ramakrishna, Vivekananda came to have a renewed appreciation of Hindu religion and culture. He also remained an admirer of Western ideas but came to think that neither the West nor India had fully realized itself. Each civilization had something to learn from the other, he decided.

In a four-year tour of America and Europe, Vivekananda explained the Hindu religion to Western audiences. He also offered a critique of Western culture. In the West, he thought, people had come to see technology as "progress" because it satisfies their material needs. But they had forgotten that human beings have a spiritual side as well. And though modern science has brought many benefits to humankind—especially the habit of "free and independent thought"—it tends to ignore those aspects of life that cannot be verified by observable "facts."

Vivekananda's speeches were received with great enthusiasm, and helped to revive interest in India.[3] And in India, he gave new hope and confidence to the nationalist movement. In a rousing speech delivered at Madras, for example, he convinced his audience that India had its own unique mission in the world:

> Up, India, and conquer the world with your spirituality! Aye, as has been declared on this soil first, love must conquer hatred, hatred cannot conquer itself. Materialism and all its miseries can never be conquered by materialism. . . . Spirituality must conquer the West. Slowly they are finding out that what they want is spirituality to preserve them as nations. They are waiting for it, they are eager for it. . . . Now is the time to work so that India's spiritual ideas may penetrate deep into the West. Therefore, young men of Madras, I specially ask you to remember this. We must go out, we must conquer the world through our spirituality and philosophy. There is no other alternative, we must do it or die.

---

3. Previously, interest in Indian philosophy had been kindled when 18th-century scholars first translated the ancient Hindu scriptures into English. In the West, these Sanskrit works had been valued "as gold," and had been an inspiration to several influential movements—including the Romantic movement, the American transcendentalists (Emerson and Thoreau), and several schools of German philosophy.

THE BATTLE FOR REPRESENTATION

The first goal of the Indian nationalists was to gain offices in government, especially in the Indian Civil Service (ICS) and in the viceroy's advisory councils. It was in these agencies that the vital issues of the country were decided—how tax monies would be spent, whether foreign wars would be declared, and which new laws and public works should be introduced. Until Indians could participate in these decisions, nationalists said, the policies of government would continue to be shaped by British interests.

In theory, Indians were granted an equal opportunity to hold jobs at all levels of the ICS. Applicants were to be chosen strictly on the basis of merit, according to the results of a competitive exam. But the exam was held only in England, not in India, and Indians faced many other hurdles as well. Some of India's most brilliant and determined students journeyed all the way to England to take the exam, passed it with high marks and yet failed to gain responsible office in British India.

The Indian National Congress

In December 1885, 70 nationalists from all parts of India traveled to Bombay to found a new association, the Indian National Congress. From this modest beginning, the Congress grew to be the largest and most influential of India's nationalist groups. In its yearly meetings and resolutions, the Congress demonstrated the growing unity of the nationalist movement.

In their first meeting, the Congress members called on the government to spend less of India's revenues on armaments and more on social programs such as education and famine relief. They also resolved that the people of India should have a "proper and legitimate share" in the government. These two points were to remain the center of Congress policy for the next 60 years.

The first 15 years of the Congress were marked by excitement and high hopes, yet also by increasing frustration as its demands were ignored. The government continued to spend as much as 50 percent of Indian revenues on military ventures, and another 25 percent went to Britain in payment for various charges. The result of this drain of wealth was the impoverishment of India's peoples. Beginning in 1895, periodic famines and widespread poverty began to take a toll of millions of lives in Indian villages. Despite token efforts at relief, the population of India actually began to decline.

The Partition of Bengal. During the viceroyalty of Lord Curzon (1899–1905), the power and self-confidence of the imperial government reached new heights. Due to Curzon's ability as an administrator, the bureaucracy of goverment grew more efficient than ever before. And British influence was extended even into Tibet and Afghanistan.

Curzon belonged to the school of imperialists who believed that Britain had a "sacred mission" to spread its civilization abroad. He also saw another compelling reason why British rule should continue indefinitely: "As long as we rule India we are the greatest power in the world. If we lose it, we shall drop straight-away to a third-rate power."

Because of Curzon's imperialist views, he naturally had little sympathy for Indian nationalism. In 1900, shortly after taking office, he remarked: "My own belief is that the Congress is tottering to its fall, and one of my great ambitions while in India is to assist it to a peaceful demise." In the end, however, he failed to achieve this ambition. Instead, he provided the very issue that Congress needed to mobilize mass support.

In 1905, Curzon announced that Bengal was to be divided for administrative reasons. To the leaders of Congress, the reason for partition was obvious: the government was trying to weaken the nationalist movement by dividing its oldest stronghold.[4]

Almost immediately, there was a storm of protest in the Indian press, followed by mass demonstrations in which bonfires were fed by British-made textiles. All sectors of Bengal society joined in the protests and in the boycott of British goods that followed. It was now clear that the populace at large was beginning to be aroused by nationalist sentiment.

The agitations in Bengal were met by severe reprisals from the government. Nationalist leaders were imprisoned, presses shut down, and students subjected to floggings and jail terms. Yet there were also positive results for the nationalists. The popular movement to boycott British products and buy only *svadeshi* (Indian-made) goods helped to revive traditional industries such as spinning and weaving. Newer Indian industries also flourished. In 1907, the Tata brothers from Bombay founded the Tata Iron and Steel Company, which became one of the world's largest steelworks. The money for this enterprise came from a successful cotton mill that the family had started in 1877.

Hindu-Muslim Divisions. The phrase "Mother India" was one of the most popular slogans of the Congress movement. It was meant to promote unity and pride among all of the peoples and cultures of the subcontinent. However, like many of Congress's activities, this phrase

---

4. Since East Bengal had a Muslim majority, the new province would have a separate religious identity.

had far more meaning for Hindus than for Muslims.[5] Increasingly, Indian Muslims came to think of themselves as a separate community within India. This sentiment was actively encouraged by British officials, who were happy to see divisions opening up in the nationalist movement. In 1906, the *Muslim League* was founded to provide a separate forum for Muslim nationalism. Though many Muslim leaders retained their ties to Congress, the League eventually came to be the more popular forum.

World War I (1914–1918)

In August 1914, Britain declared war on Germany, thus beginning the First World War. Immediately after this declaration, India was notified that it, too, was at war with Germany. Surprisingly, India's middle classes demonstrated overwhelming support for Britain, as did the princes of the royal states. The leaders of Congress, too, fully cooperated with the war effort, believing that their efforts would be rewarded with independence. Within 20 days, nearly 30,000 Indian soldiers had set sail for the battlefields of France.

As the war dragged on, disillusionment began to set in. Reports of casualties began to mount as more than a million Indians departed for foreign battlefields. India's economic contribution to the war effort was also enormous and was shown in the increasing poverty of the countryside. Yet the government of India made no move to reward these sacrifices with a measure of freedom. It was in these dark days that the nationalist cause suddenly had new cause for hope. A new leader, Mohandas K. Gandhi, had appeared on the Indian scene.

MAHATMA GANDHI AND THE TACTICS OF NONVIOLENCE

The history of the Indian nationalist movement after World War I is largely the biography of one man, Mohandas K. Gandhi. Gandhi had spent much of his career abroad and came back to India only in 1915, when he was 45 years old. Soon after Gandhi's return, Rabindranath Tagore, India's best-known poet, accorded him the title of *Mahatma,* or "Great Soul." To Tagore, as to most people who met him, Gandhi now had the unmistakable aura of a saint—a man who had conquered all personal desires and so had enough energy to serve "the whole of mankind."

---

5. Islam did not include any concept of the earth as Great Mother. Also, the Muslims' primary allegiance was to Turkey (then the home of the Muslim caliph, or supreme ruler) rather than to India.

Alone among nationalist leaders, Gandhi was able to reach out to Indian villagers and fashion a unique strategy attuned to their experience and values. Within a few years, it was clear that this saintly man, dressed in the simplest garb of a village peasant, was the most powerful man in India—and one of the most influential leaders in the world.

Gandhi's Early Career

In his youth, Gandhi had not been deeply religious. Instead, his main concern had been to find a respectable profession and to fulfill his family responsibilities. Married at the age of 13, as was common in Hindu society, Gandhi was the father of two sons by the age of 18. At this time (1888), it was decided that he should pursue a career of law and politics, a family tradition. Though his father had died, other relatives scraped together the money he needed to earn a law degree in London.

After being admitted to the bar in London, Gandhi returned home and tried to find work as a lawyer. But he found that he was too bashful and too principled to make his way in Indian law courts. In 1893, at the age of 24, he accepted an offer to go to Natal, South Africa, to undertake a law case. Within a short time, he had established a flourishing practice there.

Despite the wealth and respectability he achieved in South Africa, Gandhi was—like all nonwhite citizens of that country—a constant victim of racial bias. In his autobiography, Gandhi described the humiliations that he endured and his first efforts to assert his dignity as a human being. Within a short time, he had become known as a man who could organize protests and write petitions against unjust laws and practices.

The incidents of racial bias that Gandhi experienced were part of a much larger pattern in South Africa. After the British government abolished slavery in its colonies (in 1833), white plantation owners in South Africa had begun to import indentured laborers from India. Many of these laborers had stayed on in the country after earning their freedom in a five-year term of hard labor. By 1894, the black and Indian citizens of Natal outnumbered the white settlers (British and Dutch) by about three to one. But the white minority still held the reins of power and were determined to keep nonwhites "in their place."

The Evolution of Nonviolence

In the charged atmosphere of South Africa, Gandhi became increasingly committed to the cause of social justice. However, he soon realized that his reasoned arguments and appeals had little impact on the problem. He then began to develop new ideas about human conflicts and ways to resolve them.

A central influence on Gandhi's thinking was the Jainist teaching about the "relativity of truth." As we have seen in Chapter 4, this idea was expressed in the parable of the blind men and the elephant. The moral of the story is that people come to many different ideas of the "truth" because of their limited viewpoints.

In keeping with this Jainist precept, Gandhi advised his law clients to listen to their opponents' point of view and to admit any errors of their own. As a result, most of Gandhi's cases were settled through arbitration rather than law court proceedings. Gandhi believed that compromises resulted in fairer outcomes than the assumption that one party is "right" and the other "wrong." Another benefit, in his view, was that people learned to take charge of their own affairs.

The Search for Truth. Gandhi believed that every human being has an innate ability to understand the "truth"—what is right and wrong. Yet, without realizing it, people are blinded by their passions and cannot see beyond their individual interests. In his autobiography, subtitled *My Experiments with Truth,* Gandhi indicated how he had gone about the task of improving his own understanding. With rigorous honesty, he recounted the episodes in his early life that he considered most shameful. He had realized, after each act of unkindness or willfulness, that selfish impulses had overcome his better judgment. However, he had not always been successful in reforming his conduct. At the age of 37, therefore, he decided to make self-discipline the central rule of his life. Following the ancient Hindu tradition called *brahmacharya* ("realization of Brahma"), Gandhi vowed that he would henceforth live a life of poverty and chastity, and would strictly control such emotions as anger and pride. By taking this step, Gandhi believed that he could hear the "inner voice" of conscience more clearly. He was also more in tune with the suffering of others.

The Birth of Nonviolent Resistance (Satyagraha)

In the same year he became a *brahmacharyi* (1906), Gandhi launched his first major campaign of nonviolent resistance. The occasion was a new law in the Transvaal province that required all Asians to carry registration cards. The Indian community believed that this law violated their dignity by treating them as criminals. At a public meeting, Gandhi's followers resolved to stand up to the government, accepting the risk of beatings, imprisonment, and even death to assert their views. Believing that no human being can be certain that he or she is correct—and that the use of violence is always wrong—Gandhi decided that the protesters must take upon themselves all of the suffering necessary to resolve the conflict.

Gandhi explained that people should not engage in nonviolent resistance merely to make an impression on outsiders. Rather, it must be an acting-out of conscience—of the "inner voice" that should guide all actions. Gandhi invented the term *satyagraha*—meaning "soul force," or "holding fast to the truth"—to describe this approach.

In Gandhi's first *satyagraha* campaign, thousands of Indians, including Gandhi himself, were thrown into jail. Gandhi then negotiated a compromise with a government official. When the agreement fell apart soon afterward, he organized another demonstration at which more than 2000 Indians burned their registration cards. This symbolic act inspired a new spirit of unity in the community and increased the number of *satyagrahis* who joined the movement. By 1914, the year he left South Africa, Gandhi had won several concessions from the government. However, the greatest change had taken place within Gandhi himself. Having come to South Africa as a shy lawyer undertaking his first case, Gandhi was returning to India as a fearless champion of the oppressed.

Gandhi and India's Villages

When Gandhi returned to India, his friend G. K. Gokhale, a prominent member of Congress, advised him to spend a year getting to know the people of India before he involved himself in national politics. Accordingly, after establishing his ashram (communal farm) at Ahmedabad, Gandhi began his travels. Since he always traveled on foot or in the cheapest railway accommodations, Gandhi came into contact with thousands of rural people. He was dismayed by the poverty and unsanitary conditions he saw, but came to have great respect for the character of India's villagers. They seemed to "overflow with faith," and to have a "profound knowledge of dharma," he remarked.[6]

It became obvious to Gandhi that India's future would be shaped by its villagers, who represented over 80 percent of the population. It was they, and not the middle-class lawyers and teachers, who represented India's "salvation." But before they could liberate India, the villagers would have to uplift themselves from their present poverty and despair.

During the remaining war years, Gandhi busied himself with three regional campaigns on behalf of farmers and textile workers. After organizing them into cohesive groups, Gandhi demonstrated how they could stand up for their rights. In doing so, they faced the risk of starvation and

---

6. Bhikhu Parekh, *Gandhi's Political Philosophy* (Notre Dame, Ind.: University of Notre Dame Press, 1989), p. 44.

Following their return to India (1915), Gandhi and his wife, Kasturbai, established a new ashram at Ahmedabad. The ashram soon became the center of Gandhi's labor and social reform movements.

beatings. But Gandhi's own suffering for their cause, in jail terms and voluntary fasts, inspired similar courage on their part. In the end, the workers succeeded in winning improved wages and working conditions.

Gandhi's campaigns were the first labor movements and strikes that had ever been organized in India. Within a few years, millions of workers in all parts of India were resorting to these tactics to improve their lives.

Hartal against the Rowlatt Acts (1919)

When World War I ended (November 1918), it was expected that the British government would reward India for its enormous wartime sacrifices by granting a measure of self-government. But instead, in March 1919, the government enacted the repressive *Rowlatt Acts*, known in India as the "Black Acts." By the terms of the acts, Indians were deprived of most civil rights: they no longer had the privilege of free speech, for example, and could be arrested and imprisoned without warrant. The Rowlatt Acts represented a rude awakening for those who had believed in the essential good faith of the British government. When they became law, Gandhi immediately shifted his attention from social reform to nationalist politics.

Several days after the Rowlatt Acts were published, Gandhi called for a 24-hour *hartal*, a traditional day of mourning in which all activity is suspended. On 6 April, an impressive silence spread across India as stores and offices closed, and people stayed home from work to pray and fast. However, in the following days, there were scattered incidents of violence against British targets. When Gandhi heard of the violence, he called off his *satyagraha* campaign. He had made a mistake of "Himalayan proportions," he said, for people were not yet ready for the task he had assigned them. In atonement for his error, Gandhi fasted for three days.

The Massacre at Amritsar. While Gandhi was recovering from his fast, British troops carried out a massacre of unarmed civilians at Amritsar, in the Punjab. On Sunday, 13 April, a crowd of several thousand Hindus had gathered in a public square to celebrate a festival. In doing so, they were defying a new order that banned all public meetings. When the crowd gathered, General Dyer, the military commander of the region, brought a troop of riflemen up to the narrow entrance of the square and opened fire. After ten minutes, nearly 400 people lay dead and more than 1200 were wounded.

Dyer's act of terror was at first praised by his superiors. However, as public outrage over the incident mounted, an investigation was carried out. Dyer was relieved of his command, and a new package of reforms was offered to the Indian people. But by now, few Indians had any remaining faith in the British government.

The New Congress Movement

By 1920, Gandhi was recognized as the most powerful leader in India. He was known and revered by millions of villagers and was popular even in the Muslim community.[7] In Congress meetings that year, Gandhi received approval for two major new plans. First, he transformed Congress from a political club into a mass movement. Anyone could now join Congress, and the movement was represented by grass-roots committees in every district of India. Second, Gandhi launched a one-year *satyagraha* campaign of noncooperation. Reasoning that the British could not govern without the cooperation of the people, Gandhi called on everyone to give up official jobs, boycott British products, and generally say no to the government.

---

7. Gandhi had become a leading advocate of an important Muslim cause, the call for restoring the caliphate (capital) of the Ottoman Empire, which the British had dismembered after the First World War.

Noncooperation and Civil Disobedience. Thousands of young nationalists enthusiastically joined Gandhi's movement and gave up promising careers to work for *satyagraha*. Jawaharlal Nehru, who later would become the first prime minister of independent India, was one of these young disciples. But Gandhi's message of dedication and self-control did not reach all of India's citizens. The year was marked by Muslim "holy war" against Hindus in Malabar, soon retaliated by Hindu riots against Muslim targets.

In British law, the program of noncooperation was construed as sedition, or rebellion against the government. Thousands of the most dedicated *satyagrahis* (though not Gandhi himself) were thrown in jail. As a result, the movement began to lose strength, and Gandhi was urged to start a new campaign to revive morale. He was reluctant at first, fearing an outbreak of violence. But finally, in 1922, he agreed to launch a limited campaign in his home province of Gujarat. In the small district of Bardoli, he directed that noncooperation be escalated to *civil disobedience*—a more active kind of defiance in which citizens disobeyed a law for reasons of conscience. Gandhi himself watched over this transition but unfortunately was not on the scene when violence erupted. In the tiny village of Chauri Chaura, a group of demonstrators set fire to a police station, killing 22 policemen. When Gandhi heard about this incident, he called a halt to the campaign.

The news that Gandhi had called off the civil disobedience campaign came as a great shock to the members of Congress. Many of them had made enormous sacrifices for the cause, giving up careers and family life to spend months in jail. Moreover, it now seemed certain that victory was within reach, if only Gandhi would drop his objections to violence. But Gandhi was not able to do so. To say that a positive outcome could come from violence, he said, would be "the same as saying we can get a rose through planting a noxious weed." Nor could he agree that an end is more important than the means used to gain it. "Means are after all everything," he said.

In Gandhi's view, the moral authority of a leader was something that remained constant; it did not rise and fall according to circumstances. However, in the eyes of British officials, Gandhi had lost most of his authority and prestige when he halted the civil disobedience movement. Within a month, he was arrested on a charge of "promoting disaffection towards the Government." On 18 March 1922, Gandhi cheerfully admitted the truth of this charge in a British court. (His speech on this occasion was to become one of the world's most famous political documents.) He was sentenced to six years in prison, but for reasons of ill health served less than two years on this occasion.

The Spinning Wheel Movement

When he recovered his health, Gandhi "retired" from public life and devoted himself to the task of nation building from within. His three main projects were to promote Muslim-Hindu unity; to bring the "untouchables" back into the fold of Hindu society; and to introduce a spinning wheel into every household in India. The third project was never far from Gandhi's thoughts. If the spinning wheel movement were successful, he believed, the other goals would be realized as well.

In 1917, Gandhi had begun a campaign to popularize the spinning wheel and to revive the ancient crafts of home spinning and weaving. He himself had become an expert in the task of spinning yarn from raw cotton, and had even devised a portable wheel that he could carry with him wherever he went. In Gandhi's view, the spinning wheel was a central symbol of self-help. It could eliminate the "enforced idleness" that the imperial economy had imposed.[8] And rather than buying factory-produced cloth from England, villagers could become completely self-sufficient in the matter of clothing.

As part of his noncooperation campaign, Gandhi called upon nationalists to boycott foreign and factory-made textiles and wear only *khadi* (homespun) clothing. The wearing of *khadi* had obvious symbolic value. It meant that wealthy lawyers and merchants would wear the same homespun white garments as the poorest peasant: outward signs of economic status, caste, and religion would be eliminated. And, at the same time, the nation would free itself from its dependence on foreign textiles.

In 1925, at Gandhi's behest, spinning became a necessary qualification for membership in Congress: all members were required to turn in 2000 yards of cotton yarn per month as their dues. This measure was strongly protested by many Western-educated professionals. But Gandhi felt that they, most of all, would benefit from spinning. City dwellers, he believed, live a "highly artificial life" that is "totally out of harmony" with their surroundings. But by performing the same work as the villagers, at least for an hour a day, they would overcome this disharmony and learn the "dignity and strength" of manual labor. At Gandhi's suggestion, the spinning wheel was adopted as the symbol of Congress and now appears on the flag of independent India.

Many nationalists were impatient with the spinning wheel movement, for it lacked the drama and excitement of public demonstrations. But Gandhi continued to insist that spinning was an essential part of nation

---

8. The British government had discouraged Indian cottage industries such as weaving. Instead, India's raw cotton was shipped to English mills to be made into cloth. The finished cloth was then sold at a high profit in Indian markets.

building. In the two decades following the Bardoli experiment, he launched only one major campaign of civil disobedience. This was the Salt March to the sea, which—to the world at large—was to become the central symbol of the Indian nationalist movement.

The Salt March (1930)

In 1930, Gandhi decided to lead a protest against the salt tax, one of the most burdensome aspects of the British regime. The tax on salt had existed ever since Clive's day and had been controversial even then. By taxing an item that was a daily necessity, especially for laborers in a hot climate, the government was extracting large sums of money from its poorest subjects.

Gandhi's plan was to march to the ocean with 78 of his followers and collect salt that had washed up on the beach. By this simple illegal act, he would demonstrate the unfairness of taxing a substance that nature had made available to all. In the face of this defiance, the government would have two choices: it could either rethink its policy or enforce it by violent means.

In his Salt March to the sea, as in other programs, Gandhi framed the issues of the day in vivid pictorial terms.

The violent suppression of Gandhi's *satyagraha* campaign demonstrated to the world that armed force was the basis of India's government.

As usual, Gandhi notified the viceroy of what he was about to do and gave him an opportunity to negotiate a compromise. (None was forthcoming.) He also notified the international press of his impending action so that world attention was focused on the issue. One eyewitness reporter noted that the daily trek of Gandhi and his ragged band at first seemed an "anticlimax" in terms of world news. Yet it gradually became apparent that something important was happening—"something completely un-European and yet very, very moving."[9]

When he reached the sea, Gandhi stooped over and picked up a pinch of salt. His followers—by now a large throng—began to collect salt on the beach and to manufacture more. Soon, millions of people up and down the coast were doing the same. In cities all over India, there were spontaneous demonstrations in which women, for the first time, played a prominent part. At first the government did nothing. Then, after a month of suspense, the army and police suddenly swung into action. The police moved through crowds with clubs, beating the nonresisting demonstrators on their heads and bodies. More than a hundred *satyagrahis* were killed

---

9. Glorney Bolton, quoted in F. Watson and M. Brown, *Talking of Gandhiji* (London: Longmans, Green, 1957), p. 58.

Indian women played a prominent part in the nationalist movement of the 1930s and 1940s. These *satyagrahis* have chosen to stay in jail rather than pay a fine to the government.

outright; thousands more were carted off to hospitals; and 60,000 to 100,000 were thrown in jail. Among those imprisoned were Gandhi and Jawaharlal Nehru, the president of Congress that year.

The Round Table Conferences and Limited Reforms

The successful *satyagraha* campaign demonstrated to the world that British rule in India was based on armed force, not on the assent of the Indian people. To salvage its reputation and honor, the British government was now compelled to the bargaining table.

In 1931, Gandhi was released from prison to attend the first Round Table Conference in London. Gandhi appeared at the Conference, and at Buckingham Palace, in his simple homespun dhoti—an act that aroused the ire of Winston Churchill and other conservative statesmen. But while Gandhi's relations with top officials were often strained, he received a far more cordial reception from thousands of ordinary citizens. Everywhere he traveled, excited crowds lined his path.

In four years of talks and conferences, little was achieved. The main problem was that the government was determined to keep its empire. Also, there were many divisions in the nationalist ranks. Though the Congress

A group of women in Lancashire, England, were among the enthusiastic crowds who greeted Gandhi in 1931. Their cordiality was unexpected, for Gandhi's *khadi* movement had ruined the region's textile industry.

and Gandhi represented the majority of Indians, leaders from three other groups—the Muslims, the untouchables, and the royal princes—expressed separate demands.

Finally, the government published a new constitution, the Government of India Act of 1935, which granted limited autonomy in 11 of India's provinces. In 1937, popular elections were held to elect representatives for those provinces. In the elections, Congress won an overwhelming victory over all other parties. Jawaharlal Nehru and other leaders now had reason to proclaim that Congress represented all of India. However, two powerful leaders thought otherwise. They were Mohammed Ali Jinnah, of the Muslim League, and Dr. B. R. Ambedkar, leader of the untouchables.

Efforts to Build Social Unity

The outbreak of World War II (1939–1945) was a decisive event in India's struggle for independence. It was apparent to all that even if Britain won the war (as it did), it would not have enough remaining strength to keep India in subjection. Thus, it was imperative to heal India's social divisions so that the nation would be ready for independence by the war's end.

It was Gandhi's most fervent wish that all of India's peoples attain nationhood together. In the war years, as during the past quarter century, he worked to overcome the divisions that had arisen between Hindus and Muslims, and between upper-caste Hindus and the so-called untouchables.

Muslim-Hindu Divisions. Mohammed Ali Jinnah, leader of the Muslim League, was Congress's main opponent in the struggle to create a unified India. In 1920, when Gandhi had assumed leadership of Congress, Jinnah had resigned from the organization. "You will never get your independence without bloodshed," he had remarked. Jinnah's comment expressed one of the issues that divided the two communities: nonviolent resistance was based on Hindu traditions, not Muslim ones. Jinnah's opposition to the idea of "one Indian nation" did not lessen with time. In 1940, he announced that the subcontinent must be partitioned to create a separate Muslim nation. "Hindus and Muslims belong to two different religious philosophies, social customs and literatures," he said.

Gandhi strongly disagreed with the idea of two nations in India. Most Indian Muslims were Hindu converts, he pointed out, and shared the same customs and way of life as other Indians. Gandhi made many determined efforts to keep India united and to stem the *communal,* or factional, violence that broke out between Hindus and Muslims during times of crisis. But he could not put out all of the fires that Jinnah started. In August 1946, as independence drew near, Jinnah proclaimed a Direct Action Day of Muslim solidarity. In Calcutta alone, the toll of "direct action" was 5,000 dead and 100,000 homeless, and the violence spread to other cities as Hindus took revenge. This murderous rampage all but ended the ideal of one nation.

The Untouchables. Almost all Indian nationalists agreed with Gandhi's view that untouchability was the "greatest blot upon Hinduism" and was not justified in any Hindu scripture. Yet most orthodox Hindus found it difficult to set aside age-old rules concerning ritual purity and the strict separation of castes. Through his own personal example, Gandhi hoped to bring about a change of heart. As noted in Chapter 2, Gandhi referred to the untouchables as *harijans,* or "children of God." In his ashram, *harijans* lived side by side with all others, and Gandhi strongly encouraged marriages between them and other castes. (In fact, in his last years, Gandhi would not attend a wedding unless it was such a "mixed" marriage.) In 1932, Gandhi began a *fast unto death* on behalf of the *harijans.* In response, thousands of upper-caste Hindus invited *harijans* to enter their temples and homes, and so persuaded Gandhi to end his fast.

In the view of Dr. B. D. Ambedkar, eloquent champion of the untouchables, Gandhi's efforts could never be enough to raise his people to equality. As long as the caste system existed in any form, he believed, the *scheduled castes* (untouchables) would suffer discrimination. In the end, a compromise was reached. The scheduled castes would have special representation in the legislatures of independent India. In return, Ambedkar would drop his claim that they were non-Hindus.

THE COMING OF INDEPENDENCE

When World War II ended, the only question about Indian independence was how it would take place, and when. During the war, Gandhi had suggested that the British simply leave India to work out its own destiny. ("Quit India!" was his slogan for this policy.) But others feared that British withdrawal, if not carefully prepared, would leave a wake of turmoil and civil war.

In 1942, Gandhi had appointed Jawaharlal Nehru as his "political heir." This meant that Nehru would be Congress's spokesman in negotiat-

Jawaharlal Nehru, a popular leader among the socialist youth of Congress, became Gandhi's designated heir in 1942.

ing for independence and would be the first leader of the new nation. Nehru, a handsome, charismatic leader, came from a prominent brahman family and had been educated in England. (His main fields of study had been science and law.) Though his outlook was more "modern" and "Western" than that of Gandhi, he had faithfully followed Gandhi's lead throughout the *satyagraha* campaigns. By 1945, Nehru had spent nine years in jail as a result of his nationalist activities.

Lord Mountbatten: The Last Viceroy

In February 1947, the British government announced that it was sending its last viceroy to India. Lord Mountbatten, a member of the British royal family, was the man chosen for this assignment. Before he returned home, Mountbatten was to sort out the legacy of nearly 200 years of British rule and turn over his power to "Indian hands."

Mountbatten's first goal was to find a way to keep India united. In the eyes of the world, this was the one positive legacy that Britain could leave to India after its centuries of "divide and rule" policies. But after weeks of frantic negotiations with Nehru, Gandhi, and Jinnah, Mountbatten decided that unity could not be achieved. Jinnah, who commanded massive support among Muslims, simply would not budge on his demand for a separate Muslim nation.

The fate of the maharajas of India, once the favored allies of the British government, was one of the most vexing questions to be decided in the year 1947–1948.

After establishing the basic outline for a partition of India and transfer of power, Mountbatten turned his attention to the problem of the princes. There were 565 royal domains in India, ranging from states as large as Spain to small kingdoms of a few square miles. The maharajas and nawabs had long enjoyed the protection of the British government, for their loyalty had given the empire an air of legitimacy and glamour. But now they would have to accede to either India or Pakistan. Surprisingly, Mountbatten obtained the accession of nearly all of the states. One notable exception was Kashmir, a Himalayan kingdom fabled for its beauty. Though most of Kashmir's people were Muslims, its Hindu ruler did not want to accede to Pakistan. The disposition of Kashmir has remained a source of conflict between India and Pakistan to the present day.

The Tragedy of Partition

In giving in to Jinnah's demand for partition, Nehru and Mountbatten believed that they had reached the most peaceful solution possible. But Gandhi had warned that a terrible tragedy would ensue from this decision.[10] As the day of partition approached, it became clear that Gandhi's instincts had been correct.

The exact borders of Pakistan and India were not published until 15 August 1947, the day of independence. But by that time, thousands of people had already been slain in communal riots, and hundreds of thousands of families were on the march—Muslims fleeing from India, and Hindus and Sikhs from Pakistan. In a migration that may have been the largest in human history, about 15 million people fled their homes and lands to go to the country of their religion. As many as half a million—and possibly even a million—never made it to safety but died or were killed on the way.

The Death of Gandhi

Gandhi felt no joy on India's Independence Day, for the savage killings and communal hatred of partition appeared to have destroyed his life's work. In the days following independence, Gandhi became a champion of the Muslim minority who remained in India. Through prayer meetings and fasts, he had been able to stem the slaughter of Muslims in Calcutta and Delhi. When he recovered his strength, he planned to walk from Delhi to Pakistan as a gesture of brotherhood between the two Indian nations. But

---

10. To avert this tragedy, Gandhi had even suggested that Jinnah, rather than Nehru, be appointed as India's prime minister.

he never had a chance to make this last journey. On 30 January 1948, Gandhi was shot dead as he was walking to a prayer meeting. The assassin, a fanatical Hindu, had been enraged by Gandhi's overtures to the Muslim community.

The next day, as tributes to Gandhi poured in from around the world, millions of grief-stricken people silently filed into Delhi to attend the funeral services. Jawaharlal Nehru perhaps best expressed the sentiments of people throughout the world as they mourned the Mahatma's passing: "The light has gone out of our lives and there is darkness everywhere."

SUMMARY

The nationalist movement in India was launched by a small group of English-educated intellectuals in the early 19th century. In the tracts written by Western philosophers, these Indian students first learned about the concepts of *representative government* and *natural rights* (now called human rights). In light of these ideas, they began to regard the phenomenon of imperialism in an entirely new way.

Though the first nationalists were, in the words of one British official, a "microscopic minority" of India's peoples, they had an influence far beyond their numbers. And when Mahatma Gandhi returned to India, the nationalist struggle was transformed into a true mass movement.

To the world at large, the frail figure of Mahatma Gandhi came to be the central symbol of the nationalist struggle. Rejecting the traditional wisdom of revolutionaries, Gandhi announced that nonviolence is a far more powerful weapon than guns or bombs. Due to his influence, the language of political struggle was forever changed.

Martin Luther King, Jr., leader of the civil rights movement in the United States, described Gandhi's influence as follows: "Gandhi was probably the first person in history to lift the love ethic of Jesus above mere interaction between individuals to a powerful and effective social force on a large scale."

DISCUSSION AND ESSAY QUESTIONS

1. Working with a partner, list five events or circumstances that might inspire a feeling of nationalism.
2. What role do national heroes play in inspiring an independence movement? Give examples from any independence movement you are familiar with.
3. If the British wished to continue their rule in India indefinitely, was the introduction of English education a good idea or a mistake? Explain why.

4. Gandhi believed that his tactic of nonviolent resistance, or *satyagraha*, required far more courage than the use of violence in settling a conflict. Do you agree with this opinion? Explain why or why not.

5. When asked to describe Gandhi's impact upon India, some villagers gave the following response: "He taught Indians to be patriotic and self-reliant. He taught the importance of everyday concerns as well as high politics. He taught brotherhood and no class distinction. He taught that Indians must stand on their own feet and supply their own needs."[11]

Using one of Gandhi's campaigns as an example, explain how his activities helped to promote the qualities mentioned by the villagers.

ADDITIONAL READINGS

Larry Collins and Dominique Lapierre, *Freedom at Midnight* (several editions available). This popular book reconstructs the events of 1947-1948, one of the most exciting and eventful years of Indian history. The main personalities in the negotiations for independence—the Mountbattens, Nehru, Gandhi, and Jinnah, among others—are drawn in vivid detail.

Louis Fischer, *Mahatma Gandhi: His Life and Message for the World* (New York: Mentor, 1954). This is a relatively short biography; the author's longer work is entitled *The Life of Mahatma Gandhi.* Fischer's works are among the most popular biographies of Gandhi.

Mohandas K. Gandhi, *An Autobiography: The Story of My Experiments with Truth* (several editions available). Gandhi's own book offers a more critical view of his life than any other. In it, he candidly reviews his "mistakes" and weaknesses, and recounts his efforts to overcome them.

Ved Mehta, *Mahatma Gandhi and his Apostles* (New York: Viking-Penguin, 1977). This well-written book consists of 16 biographical sketches and reminiscences of Gandhi. The author has interviewed many of the people who knew Gandhi best and also provides his own insights.

---

11. Quoted in Geoffrey Ashe, *Gandhi* (New York: Stein and Day, 1968), p. 386.

GANDHI ON TRUTH, NONVIOLENCE, AND SUFFERING

While he was engaged in the struggle for Indian independence, Gandhi wrote down his thoughts almost daily. These writings have been assembled in the multivolume work entitled Collected Works of Mahatma Gandhi. *Most of the following passages originally appeared in four weekly newspapers that Gandhi published during the years 1919–1948.*

No man can claim that he is absolutely in the right or that a particular thing is wrong because he thinks so. (1909)

Truth resides in every human heart, and one has to search for it there, and to be guided by truth as one sees it. But no one has a right to coerce others to act according to his own view of truth.

Man and his deed are two distinct things. It is quite proper to resist and attack a system, but to resist and attack its author is tantamount to resisting and attacking oneself. For we are all tarred with the same brush, and are children of one and the same Creator, and as such the divine powers within us are infinite. To slight a single human being is to slight those divine powers, and thus to harm not only that being but with him the whole world. [*Autobiography*]

Of Gandhi's later disciples, one of the best known was Martin Luther King, Jr. In 1959, the Reverend King and his wife, Coretta, visited Gandhi's shrine at Delhi and met with Prime Minister Nehru.

Nonviolence in its dynamic condition means conscious suffering. It does not mean meek submission to the will of the evil-doer, but it means pitting one's whole soul against the will of the tyrant. (1925)

A man cannot do right in one department of life whilst he is occupied in doing wrong in any other department. Life is one indivisible whole.

Suffering is infinitely more powerful than the law of the jungle for converting the opponent and opening his ears, which are otherwise shut, to the voice of reason. . . . If you want something really important to be done you must not merely satisfy the reason, you must move the heart also. . . . [Suffering] opens up the inner understanding in man. Suffering is the badge of the human race, not the sword. (1931)

NONVIOLENT RESISTANCE: THE DHARASANA SALT RAID

Gandhi's nonviolent campaign against the salt tax was observed by members of the international press and focused worldwide attention on the concept of satyagraha. *The following report by a United Press reporter describes a demonstration led by one of Gandhi's followers, Mrs. Sarojini Naidu. It took place while Gandhi himself was in jail.*
Note: A lathi *is a long, heavy stick used as a club.*

Madame Naidu called for prayer before the march started and the entire assemblage knelt. She exhorted them: "Gandhi's body is in jail but his soul is with you. India's prestige is in your hands. You must not use any violence under any circumstances. You will be beaten but you must not resist; you must not even raise a hand to ward off blows." Wild, shrill cheers terminated her speech. . . .

Suddenly, at a word of command, scores of native police rushed upon the advancing marchers and rained blows on their heads with their steel-shod *lathis.* Not one of the marchers even raised an arm to fend off the blows. They went down like tenpins. From where I stood I heard the sickening whacks of the clubs on unprotected skulls. The waiting crowd of watchers groaned and sucked in their breaths in sympathetic pain at every blow.

Those struck down fell sprawling, unconscious or writhing in pain with fractured skulls or broken shoulders. In two or three minutes the ground was quilted with bodies. Great patches of blood widened on their white clothes. The survivors without breaking ranks silently and doggedly marched on until struck down. When every one of the first column had been knocked down stretcher-bearers rushed up unmolested by the police and carried off the injured to a thatched hut which had been arranged as a temporary hospital.

By eleven the heat reached 116 in the shade and activities of the Gandhi volunteers subsided.

SOURCE: Webb Miller, *I Found No Peace* (New York: Simon & Schuster, 1936), pp. 192–196.

THE VIOLENCE OF PARTITION

*The tragic events surrounding the partition of India created an endur-
ing legacy of bitterness and hatred. While violence between Muslims
and Hindus was nothing new, the migration of millions of people from
their homes caused an unprecedented escalation of this warfare. In
the article quoted here, an officer in charge of keeping the peace in
the Indian Punjab describes what he saw.*

The major problem was to guard these trains, because when they stopped at
night the local villagers used to attack them. The worst places were in Punjab.
For instance, I remember seeing a train come in from Pakistan and there
wasn't a single live person on it; there were just bodies, dead and butchered.
Now, that train entered India, and the people saw it. And the next Pakistan-
bound train that came, they set upon, and the slaughter was incredible.

And then there were huge walking convoys of people coming in across
the border, millions, wounded, without food, without clothes, carrying what
they could, just streaming across the border helter-skelter. And then inside,
where you had Muslim pockets, you had to provide protection for them,
because otherwise they would be slaughtered. And every time there was a
slaughter on the other side, or trains and vehicles came with dead bodies,
there was a reaction on this side. When there was a reaction on this side, there
was another one on that side; and so it built up.

SOURCE: Mark Tully and Zareer Masani, *From Raj to Rajiv: Forty Years of Independence* (New York: Braziller, 1988), p. 17.

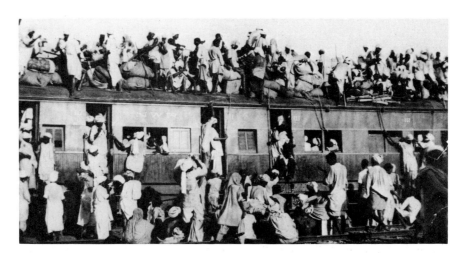

The desperation, tragedy, and hardship attending the migrations of 1947–1948 are
indicated by this photograph of a refugee train.

THE PURPOSE OF GANDHI'S SUFFERING

In his battle for Indian independence and unity, Gandhi resorted to the "fast unto death" on 17 occasions. By resolving to fast until death—or until a problem was resolved—Gandhi applied moral pressure on his opponents. This moral dilemma, he believed, would force people to think about the issues and their own actions in a new light.

The following article describes a fast that Gandhi undertook to restore peaceful relations between Hindus and Muslims in Calcutta (August 1947). His effort was successful: while other cities dissolved into communal violence, Calcutta regained its peace.

To most Indians, as to people outside, Gandhi's decision to fast as a means of changing an acute situation of social or political impasse, seemed remote, irrelevant and based on individual habit and unreason. And yet the challenge was clear; right in the heart of a brutal communal upheaval in Calcutta, resting in a broken house exposed to streets where fighting was going on, Gandhiji had chosen to impose self-suffering and penance upon his aged body, as well as on his mind. . . . His face and eyes, made luminous by suffering and controlled suffering, would show little trace of the agony that his will had mastered, but the nature of his ordeal was unmistakable to the millions. Even while repudiating his method and its efficacy, the one question in people's minds would be, "How is Gandhiji?" People would begin to feel uncomfortable; the grocer's boy, the rickshaw-puller, the office clerk, the school and

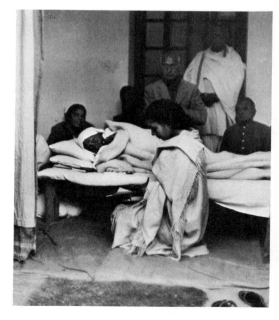

A portrait of one of Gandhi's last fasts on behalf of Hindu-Muslim unity conveys the suffering involved in the event. Gandhi's life was in danger within a matter of hours.

college students would scan the news columns early in the morning and listen to the radio throughout the day and feel more and more personally *involved* in the situation. . . .

So the fast would continue. Men would come back from their offices in the evening and find food prepared by their family, ready for them; but soon it would be revealed that the women of the home had not eaten during the whole day. They had not felt hungry. Pressed further, the wife or mother would admit that they could not understand how they could go on when Gandhiji was dying for their own crimes. Restaurants and amusement centers did little business; some of them were voluntarily closed by their proprietors. Why this total and pervasive suffering for a whole city? Why did it all begin to matter? The nerve of feeling had been restored, the pain began to be felt; the pain of the whole society, because of the pain of its members, whether Hindu, Muslim or others. Ganhiji knew when to start the redemptive process. Involvement did not merely mean pain: it was fundamentally the joy of union, and the acceptance of new responsibility which such glad assurance of united strength makes possible. An immense release filled the atmosphere when Gandhiji declared that now we had all suffered and shared, his fast would be broken. Release turned into rejoicing, the fast actually led up to feasts in which the warring communities joined heartily, while Gandhiji sipped his small glass of orange juice.

SOURCE: Amiya Chakravarty, *A Saint at Work: A View of Gandhi's Life and Message* (Philadelphia, 1950), pp. 23–24.

1. Why did Gandhi's fasting make people feel uncomfortable? Did it bring about the reforms that he intended?

C H A P T E R

T E N

MODERN INDIA

Nobody quite knew what swaraj *meant, so everyone interpreted it according to his needs.*

M. J. Akbar

In Gandhi's view, India's independence from Britain was only one step toward the goal of *swaraj,* or self-rule. To realize his vision completely, each citizen in India would have to undergo an inner transformation. "Self-rule," in Gandhi's definition, was the highest goal of human life: it meant to conquer one's personal desires and passions so that one could live in harmony with others. This individual self-restraint and cooperation, he believed, was the very basis of civilization. "Civilization," he said, "consists not in the multiplication but in the deliberate and voluntary restriction of wants."

In Chapter 9, we encountered some of the programs by which Gandhi hoped to bring about his vision. His labor campaigns, spinning wheel movement, and salt tax protests all centered on the needs of India's poorest villagers. If everyone could put aside personal interests and support these programs, Gandhi believed, the entire nation would be united and uplifted.

In Gandhi's view, a rural life of simple self-sufficiency was the basis of spirituality and of Indian civilization as a whole. By laboring on the land, peasants learned to live in harmony with nature and with other people. They did not exploit anyone else in making their livelihood but rather cooperated with their neighbors to supply the basic needs of life.

As independence approached, Gandhi hoped that programs like the spinning wheel movement would continue. Then future generations of city dwellers would live in harmony with the villagers, rather than exploit them. And their spiritual lives would be enhanced as well. For in forsaking the villages to live in large cities, Gandhi thought, people lost more than they realized: "To forget how to dig the earth and tend the soil is to forget ourselves."

Gandhi conceded that factories and large-scale industries might be a good idea in sparsely populated countries. But in India, where millions of people needed employment, he did not think it made sense to introduce labor-saving machines. The only effect, he observed, was to enrich a few factory owners, while workers were condemned to a life of low wages and mind-dulling work.

National governments, in Gandhi's opinion, had the same defects as large-scale industries: they tended to reduce people to mere cogs in the machine rather than helping them to become free and independent human beings. Moreover, because of their impersonal nature, governments were able to evade responsibility for their actions. In their relations with the rest of the world, Gandhi once declared, modern nation-states were little more than "gangs of robbers."

Gandhi's vision of independent India was of a network of self-reliant villages loosely bound together into districts and provinces. Technically, such a system would approach a state of *anarchy,* or absence of government. But of course the true government would be the conscience of each individual citizen.

THE LEADERSHIP OF JAWAHARLAL NEHRU (1948–1964)

When he chose Jawaharlal Nehru as his political heir, Gandhi was well aware that Nehru's outlook was far more "modern" and Western-oriented than his own. Nehru was confident, for instance, that Western-style technology and industry could bring many benefits to India. Also, he had less faith in people's ability to transform themselves than did Gandhi. Rather he believed that laws and a strong central government should lead the way in introducing social reforms. But despite such differences in approach, Nehru's basic goals were the same as Gandhi's. He too believed that the welfare of India's villagers must be the guiding principle of a national government. And although Nehru claimed to be an atheist, his long service to India's peoples qualified him as a religious man by Gandhi's definition. Gandhi once remarked: "While Jawaharlal always says he does not believe in God, he is nearer to God than many who profess to be His worshipers."

As independence approached, Jawaharlal Nehru commanded more prestige and authority than any other political leader. Referring to the public adulation that Nehru received, Gandhi remarked, "He is our king." In his typical fashion, however, Gandhi tempered this remark with a cautionary note: "We should not be impressed by everything the king does or does not do. If he has devised something good for us we should praise him. If he has not, then we shall say so."

Nehru himself was concerned about the harm that might befall India, and himself, if he played the role of an autocrat. Thus during his 17-year term as prime minister, he was careful to avoid such temptations. Instead, he became the first architect of India's democracy. India's present laws and institutions owe much to Nehru's guidance during the first years of independence. In two other major areas—economic policies and foreign affairs—Nehru's imprint can still be seen as well.

A PARLIAMENTARY DEMOCRACY

Under the constitution of India, which became law in 1950, each of India's state governments was given a large measure of autonomy, or independence, in such matters as public health, education, and police. However, the central government has the right to intervene in 47 local issues, including economic planning and social reforms. Also, the central government is the sole authority in such matters as national defense and foreign affairs.

The constitution established a Parliament consisting of two representative bodies. The *Lok Sabha* ("House of the People") is the more important of these. The members of this "lower house" of Parliament are chosen in general elections in which all adult citizens are eligible to vote. The "upper house" of Parliament, called the *Rajya Sabha* ("Council of State"), represents the separate states of India. Its members are elected by state legislatures and do not have as many powers as the *Lok Sabha*.

The executive branch of the government consists of the *prime minister* and the *cabinet*. They have great authority to carry out national policies but are ultimately responsible to the *Lok Sabha*.

As under the British Empire, the *judicial branch* of India's government is independent from other branches. In times of crisis, the Supreme Court may be called on to mediate disputes between the executive branch and Parliament.

The government of India also has a *president* and *vice-president*. While these offices are largely ceremonial, the president has special "reserve powers" that may be activated in times of crisis. For instance, the president may suspend India's constitution and declare a state of "President's Rule." This means that the central government (especially the prime minister) will have dictatorial powers for as long as the crisis lasts. The purpose of this special clause is to preserve the unity of the nation. However, it also has the potential to bring an end to the democracy.

The Congress Party

In theory, India's government was to be a *multiparty* democracy. However, for all practical purposes, India was a one-party state during its first few decades of independence. Because the Congress Party had been the moving force of the nationalist movement, it had a popularity and an influence that could not be matched. Although several other parties had a strong influence locally, Congress was preeminent in the nation as a whole. In the first democratic elections, held in 1952, the Congress Party captured 362 of the 489 seats in the *Lok Sabha*.

The Problem of Corruption. The question of "corruption" in the Congress Party ranks has been a major issue from 1947 to the present day. Even before Independence Day, Mahatma Gandhi had been dismayed by the "decay and decline" he saw in the party's ranks. He noted that many Congress members were using their new-found influence and power to enrich themselves, rather than working for the welfare of India's villages.

In December 1952, Indian citizens lined up to vote in the first elections held in independent India. Congress won an overwhelming victory.

To remedy this situation, Gandhi suggested that the Congress dissolve itself and form a new group called the "People's Service Organization" (*Lok Sevak Sangh*).

Ex-Congress Reformers. Although most Congress members did not take Gandhi's suggestion seriously, there were two prominent exceptions. Vinoba Bhave, one of Gandhi's closest associates, left organized politics and started his own movement for social reform. Traveling around the country on foot, Bhave appealed to large landowners to give one-fifth of their lands to the laborers who worked for them. As a result of Bhave's efforts, about a million acres of land were given to disadvantaged groups.

Another notable reformer was J. P. Narayan, who worked with Bhave's movement for several years. Unlike Bhave, however, he eventually reentered the political world. In 1974, as we will see, Narayan emerged from his "retirement" and became a prominent critic of the government of Indira Gandhi.

A SOCIALIST PROGRAM

The best way to promote the interests of India's poorest citizens, Nehru believed, was through a *socialist* economic system. This meant that the central government would control the major resources of the country. Individual entrepreneurs would be allowed to build businesses and industries, but only after obtaining licenses from the government. In this way, the government could determine if each planned business represented a wise use of the country's resources. Also, in theory, government ministers could ensure that one class of people did not grow rich at the expense of another.

The economic system that Nehru established is often referred to as a "mixed" economy. Unlike a *communist* system, the state does not claim ownership of *all* of the country's resources. And unlike a *capitalist* system, private entrepreneurs are not free to operate according to the demands of the market. Rather, strict limits are placed on the accumulation and use of private capital.

The Five-Year Plans

Using the strong central powers granted him by the constitution, Nehru set in motion three large-scale programs of rural and industrial development. The goal of each of these Five-Year Plans was to make India more self-sufficient and productive.

The first Five-Year Plan, launched in October 1952, was directed at agricultural improvement. Assisted by economic aid and expertise from the American Ford Foundation, several thousand young Indians were trained and sent to the villages to help with projects of rural "uplift." They taught the villagers about new techniques in irrigation, fertilization, and making wastelands productive. They also helped to build schools and sanitation facilities in the villages. Although some of the new agricultural methods did not have the expected results, the overall program was a success. India's agricultural output was increased by thousands of tons, enabling food supplies to keep pace with the rapidly growing population.

Nehru's second Five-Year Plan (1956–1961) continued the work of agricultural development, and also aimed to make India a major steel-producing country. Since India has large reserves of iron and coal, the major ingredients of steel, Nehru believed that steel production would be a good avenue of development. First, India would no longer have to import such products as airplanes, bicycles, cars, and refrigerators—these items could be manufactured at home. Also, steel could be sold on the world market, enabling India to earn foreign exchange for other products it needed. Nehru's decision to concentrate on this industry generally has been praised by economists. Since few other developing countries have chosen this path, India's inexpensive steel has found a ready market in the outside world.

During the third Five-Year Plan (1961–1966), India's steel-producing capacity was tripled. Nehru's enthusiasm for modern technology was also reflected in such projects as hydroelectric dams, which he termed "modern temples." Due to these efforts, electricity was brought for the first time to thousands of villages. Plants were also constructed to manufacture such products as cement, chemical fertilizers, and diesel engines.

Nehru did not live to see the completion of his third Five-Year Plan. However, his programs of modernization were continued by his daughter, Indira, who became prime minister in 1966. Her government demonstrated India's capability to use nuclear power, either as a source of energy or for military means. The nuclear device that her government tested in 1974 was the product of research set in motion by Nehru in 1956.

The strange contrasts brought into being by Nehru's Five-Year Plans have often been commented on. While India was an early member of the "nuclear club" (the 25 countries maintaining nuclear power reactors), people and animals are still the principal source of the nation's energy. On most Indian roads, the sight of farmers and their bullocks walking to or from the fields is far more common than that of a motorized tractor or trailer. The same continuity of tradition can be seen in the matter of consumer goods. Though India recently has been ranked among the

Traditional India and Modernization

Nehru's introduction of advanced technology to traditional India created many paradoxes—slightly exaggerated (*top*) by Shankar, a popular cartoonist. A French photographer captured this juxtaposition of eras in India (*bottom, left*): within yards of a nuclear power plant, laborers carry out an earth-moving project. A view of the lunch-pail distribution system in Bombay (*bottom, right*). The complex system by which office workers' lunch pails are transported from homes to offices at midday typifies the labor-intensive character of India's economy.

world's 15 largest steel producers, fewer than three percent of Indian households own a passenger vehicle, a television, or a telephone. Rather, bicycles and radios are the most visible sign of Nehru's modernization program. But handmade silk saris, bangles, and other jewelry are still, as they have long been, a favorite status symbol and family investment.

A SECULAR DEMOCRACY

The Constitution of India promises a *secular democratic republic:* that is, a society that allows complete freedom of religion yet safeguards the individual rights of each citizen regardless of caste or creed. The constitution also promises that each citizen will have "equality of status and opportunity." Yet legislation was not enough, in itself, to establish the principle of social equality. In 1958, eight years after the constitution was adopted, Nehru was asked what the most difficult part of his job was. He replied, "Creating a just state by just means. Perhaps, too, creating a secular state in a religious country."

The Status of Women

The status of women in Indian society has been a major issue since the beginning of the nationalist movement. Nationalist leaders believed that it would be impossible to build a true democracy as long as women were kept in a position of inferiority. Thus Rammohun Roy and many others had struggled to provide educational opportunities for women and to abolish the many customs that restricted their lives. Mahatma Gandhi, too, had campaigned for women's rights and had recruited women in large numbers for his noncooperation movement. One result of these efforts was that women were defined as equal citizens in the constitution: they were given the right to vote and to hold any office in the nation. But these provisions have not been enough, in themselves, to overcome age-old prejudices.

Many of the practices that stood in the way of women's improvement stemmed from ancient Hindu traditions. As we saw in Chapter 5, the Laws of Manu stated that a woman should never be independent but always subject to the authority of a male relative. Even if that husband is a drunkard or a wife beater, Manu stated, "a husband must be worshiped as God." The image of a devoted wife was so central in popular culture that a woman was considered to have no identity apart from her male relatives. A woman without a husband or sons was a nonentity in social terms.

The Hindu institution of the *joint family* helped to encourage the pattern of women's dependence. Because several related families lived together in the same household, there was no need to postpone marriage until a young couple could support themselves. Instead, marriages were commonly arranged while the couple were still children. Then, several years later, the young wife simply joined the household of her husband's family and performed domestic work under the direction of her mother-in-law. Women were not allowed to own property on their own, and upper-caste women could not remarry.

The first major women's issue addressed by the nationalists was the ancient custom called *sati*. This was an extreme act of devotion in which a widow threw herself onto her husband's funeral pyre. (The widow then became a *sati,* or "realized one.") It was believed that by committing suicide in this way, a woman could atone for her husband's sins and at the same time assure her own salvation. The idea of abolishing *sati* was controversial, for it was considered an issue of religious freedom. However, Rammohun Roy broke with the orthodox Hindu community to campaign against the practice. And in 1929, the British government of India passed a law prohibiting *sati*. Later in the century (1891), the British government passed an Age of Consent Bill prohibiting child marriages. This measure too had the support of many nationalists.

During Nehru's term of office, new laws were passed to increase the rights of Hindu women and to prolong the time of their independent life before marriage. The minimum age at which a woman could be married was raised to 15, and women were also granted the right to sue for divorce and to inherit property in their own right. These measures did not apply to the Muslim community, which continued to be guided by the *Sunna,* or Islamic tradition.

Despite legislation, incidences of age-old practices—even *sati*—have continued to occur in independent India. However, the passage of each law has had a dramatic effect on patterns of behavior.

The Long Road to Equality: Education and Living Standards

Both Gandhi and Nehru believed that universal basic education must be a primary goal in India's democracy. Among other reasons, people who have literacy skills—the ability to read and write—are better able to understand their rights and to participate in political affairs. Hence if all citizens had a basic education, the goal of social equality would be almost within reach.

The goal of universal literacy has proved difficult to achieve in India. One problem is that in an impoverished rural economy, family farms often depend on the labor of children. Consequently, millions of school-age children have not had the leisure to go to school. Also, Nehru's commitment to technology and higher education left comparatively few funds for

Education is highly prized in India. People who missed schooling in childhood often attend adult literacy classes.

elementary education. However, as living standards improved, significant gains were also made in the matter of literacy. By 1981, it was estimated that about 55 percent of adult Indian men were literate, and about 26 percent of adult women. In the population as a whole, about 41 percent of all adults were literate. (In Pakistan, the literacy rate was about 26 percent of all adults in 1981. Even this number was a significant advance over the preindependence figure of 9 percent.)

In India, as in other regions of the world, such factors as literacy rates, living standards, and birth rates are closely correlated—that is, a change in one factor will usually have an impact on the others. For instance, improvements in living standards usually lead to higher rates of literacy, since more parents have the means to send their children to school. Increased literacy in turn often leads to a decline in birth rates.[1] In an overpopulated country, a decline in birth rates will almost certainly bring an improvement in living standards, since there are fewer people to share the available resources. And quality-of-life improvements are seen as the

---

1. In the state of Kerala, a high rate of literacy—without an improvement in living standards —appears to have brought about a lower birth rate. One theory is that literate couples think about their options in greater detail and are less likely to consider their sons as necessary "security" for their old age.

most effective way to reduce communal conflicts; such conflicts, it is thought, are usually rooted in the frustrations of poverty.

During Nehru's term in office, it was assumed that if modernization programs succeeded, other gains would follow. In general, the Five-Year Plans did have a positive impact on social mobility and on living standards. Industries and factories opened up new employment opportunities for millions of people, and gains in agricultural production created a more secure food supply.

Critiques of Nehru's government have mainly focused on the issue of corruption. Though laws and policies emphasized the welfare of the poorest citizens, the ministers in charge of them often turned the system to their own advantage. The centralized economy that Nehru created tended to encourage such abuses. Government officials had the sole authority to allocate business permits, and tended to show marked favoritism toward their own friends and relations in awarding them. Before long, charges of *influence peddling, nepotism, bribe taking,* and *abuse of power* had become a regular feature of public life. Over the years such charges and countercharges have greatly reduced the prestige of politicians—particularly Congress members.

FOREIGN AFFAIRS: PEACE AND NONALIGNMENT

In foreign affairs, Nehru had three stated goals: to promote India's interests, to pursue peace when possible, and to avoid entangling alliances with foreign powers. The last two points are nearly identical to the foreign policy set forth by George Washington, founding father of the American nation. However, they were to cause much controversy in the political world of the mid-20th century.

The Policy of Nonalignment

Though war with Pakistan was an ever-present threat, Nehru wanted to avoid making any alliances with foreign powers. But in the charged atmosphere of the Cold War, India's *nonalignment* policy was not viewed with favor. In official circles of the Soviet Union, Nehru was referred to as a "Running Dog of Imperialism" for bringing India into the British Commonwealth of Nations in 1947. And in the United States, prominent officials called him a "Communist" because of his overtures to the Soviet Union. Eventually, Nehru was able to establish cordial relations with both superpowers. However, the United States came to view Pakistan as a far more reliable "friend" than India. Beginning in the 1950s, billions of

Nehru's foreign policy at first caused great puzzlement in the international community. But at last a word was found to describe it, and *nonalignment* became an
accepted principle.

dollars' worth of American military equipment was shipped to Pakistan so
that it might play a role in "containing" communism.

The policy of arming Pakistan with sophisticated military hardware
has had several major repercussions. First, it helped to make the army,
rather than the civilian population, the most important political force in
Pakistan. Also, it forced India to maintain a large standing army as part of
its basic defense. (In 1989, this army numbered 1,260,000 personnel.)

Conflict with Pakistan (1947)

India's first military conflict with Pakistan occurred shortly after Independence Day, when the violence of partition was still vivid in people's minds.
The immediate cause of the clash was the issue of Kashmir.

The combined states of Kashmir and Jammu have a Muslim-majority
population, and are adjacent to Pakistan. Thus Jinnah had reason to claim
that the region was part of Pakistan. But if Kashmir went to Pakistan, India
would be cut off from its province of Ladakh. More important, disposing of

Kashmir on the basis of religion would contradict India's claim to be a secular democracy. In Nehru's words, "Once we accept that nationality goes by religion, we break up our whole conception of India. India is a country with many religions." In addition, the prime minister may have had an emotional stake in the issue: the beautiful Vale of Kashmir was the ancestral home of the Nehru family.

When Pakistani guerrilla forces invaded Kashmir, in October of 1947, its Hindu ruler quickly acceded to India. Indian troops then forced the Pakistanis out of the region. But an election was never held, and the disposition of Kashmir has remained an issue of bitter dispute.

Internal Military Clashes

To consolidate the new nation, Nehru also found it necessary to use force in two other instances. In 1948, he sent troops to Hyderabad to force the Muslim ruler of this large Hindu-majority province to accede to India. And in 1961, troops were again used to claim Goa for India, as Portugal's king had refused to give up the colony in a peaceful manner.

A Leadership Role in Asia

Nehru hoped that India's unique struggle for independence might serve as an inspiration for other Asian countries. In March 1947, he convened an All-Asian Conference at New Delhi to discuss the problems of countries that, like India, had known the burdens of imperialism. Before long, Nehru was regarded as a leading spokesman for other Asian nations-in-the-making.

At a second meeting of Asian and African nations in 1949, Nehru worked out a deadline for Indonesia to be freed from Dutch rule. His suggestion was supported by the United Nations, and Indonesia received its independence in January 1950. Another of Nehru's projects was to bring China into the world community of nations. (Until 1972, the United States refused to recognize the existence of Communist China.) However, the project of Indo-Chinese friendship ran into major complications. In 1950, Chinese troops invaded and occupied Tibet. Since India and Tibet shared a common cultural heritage, India could hardly refuse to offer sanctuary to the Dalai Lama, Tibet's spiritual leader, and thousands of his followers. And in 1962, negotiations over the Indo-Chinese border suddenly flared into violence when a Chinese army invaded Indian territory in the Himalayas. Though the Chinese army withdrew after making its point, the episode was considered a humiliation for the Indian government. Nehru, it was said, had not foreseen that an Asian nation would carry out acts of "imperialism."

SHAPING THE POST-NEHRU ERA

Nehru's death in office, in 1964, came as a shock to India and the world. Though the prime minister was 74 years old, he had no known ailments apart from exhaustion. (His sudden death was due to a ruptured aorta.) Nevertheless, there had been much speculation about his likely successors. As millions of people came to Delhi to say their last farewells to Nehru, attention inevitably focused on one of these likely candidates: his daughter, Indira.

Talk about a "Nehru dynasty" had been commonplace for about two decades. It first arose because Nehru's father, Motilal, had been a prominent Congress leader. But there is no clear evidence that Nehru intended his only child, Indira Gandhi, to succeed him as prime minister. At the time of his death, Indira had never held elective office, nor had she taken part in cabinet meetings. (Cabinet members were required to be members of Parliament.) However, she was known to the public as an energetic Congress leader and campaigner. And from 1947 to 1964, she had served as her father's official hostess. In this capacity she had met and entertained many of the world's leaders.

Indira Nehru had acquired the surname Gandhi through her marriage to Feroze Gandhi, a Parsi journalist whom she had first met as a teenager. (Feroze was no relation to Mahatma Gandhi.) After marrying Feroze in 1942, Indira had two sons, Sanjay and Rajiv, both of whom were later to play a large part in national politics. But in June 1964, Indira was too preoccupied with her grief at her father's death—and too inexperienced in politics—to consider making a bid for high office. Instead, Lal Bahadur Shastri, a Congress leader and trusted lieutenant of her father's, became India's second prime minister.

A Second Conflict with Pakistan (1965)

Prime Minister Shastri served only 18 months as India's leader, but during this time he handled one of the worst crises that India faced in the 1960s: a second war with Pakistan.

Developments in Pakistan. In many respects, Pakistan had been less fortunate than India in its first decades of independence. President Jinnah, the founding father of Pakistan, died of tuberculosis in 1948 after just one year in office. This short term had not been sufficient to establish a constitution for the new nation or to reach a consensus on many other issues. Instead, the army came to be the most prominent force in politics: since 1958 most of Pakistan's national leaders have been military commanders.

Pakistan's citizens, like those of India, have strong regional loyalties based on factors such as geography, ethnic identity, and language. However, the central government recognizes only one factor—the Islamic religion—as the basis of nationality. Frustrated by this policy, regional and ethnic groups such as the Sindhis, Punjabis, Pathans, and Baluchis have frequently called for increased autonomy and even separation from the state. (In 1971, the largest such group, the Bengalis of East Pakistan, did secede from Pakistan to form Bangladesh.) But there is one issue on which the entire nation can agree: namely, that Muslims should claim a greater portion of the subcontinent for their own. Thus, war with India—especially over the issue of Kashmir—has been one of the surest ways to bring about national unity.

The 1965 War. The second Indo-Pakistani War began when Pakistani troops in American-built Patton tanks rolled over the border of Gujarat. Several months later, the conflict shifted to Kashmir and the Punjab. In the confused warfare that followed, neither side emerged as a clear winner. However, it was apparent that India's superiority in manpower would be more decisive in the long run than Pakistan's edge in military equipment. In a peace conference sponsored by the premier of the Soviet Union, Pakistan's leader, General Mohammed Ali Khan, agreed on a plan of peaceful coexistence between India and Pakistan. Then, several hours after the treaty was signed (on 10 January 1966), Prime Minister Shastri died of a heart attack in Tashkent, USSR.

The Rise of Indira Gandhi

Following the sudden death of Shastri, no one leader emerged as his obvious successor. Instead, the decision would be made by a coalition of powerful Parliament members, popularly known as the *Syndicate*. One of the two leading candidates for prime minister was Moraji Desai, a conservative Hindu. The other was Indira Gandhi.

Believing that the relatively inexperienced Indira Gandhi would be easier to control than Desai, the Syndicate elevated her to the prime ministership. As expected, Gandhi was a figurehead leader at first. But before long, she had learned how to assert her own ideas and win popular support for them. By 1969, she had broken the power of the Syndicate and was recognized as one of India's most capable politicians.

A Monsoon Failure. As India's leader in the late 1960s and 1970s, Gandhi faced a host of overwhelming problems. The first of these was a widespread drought that was creating famine conditions for millions of people. Soon after becoming prime minister, Gandhi sought and obtained American aid in this crisis: President Lyndon Johnson agreed to give her 12 million tons of American wheat and other valuable assistance. In April 1966, she was able to announce the beginning of India's fourth Five-Year Plan, which aimed at a "breakthrough in agriculture." Eventually, this effort achieved impressive results: the years 1968 and 1969 were the beginning of a "green revolution" brought about by new seed varieties and irrigation schemes.

Demands for New States. As soon as she took office, Gandhi faced vocal demands that state boundaries within India be redrawn. Jawaharlal Nehru had already granted several such petitions when language was the determining factor. For instance, in the 1950s, the new states of Kerala and Andhra had been created, based on the fact that the languages spoken in these regions (Malayalam and Telugu) were distinct from other South Indian languages. And in 1960, Nehru had allowed the British province of Bombay to be divided into the states of Maharashtra and Gujarat. (The majority populations in these states speak the Marathi and Gujarathi languages, respectively.) However, Nehru had balked at the idea of a separate Sikh state in the Punjab: if religion and ethnic identity were to be the criteria for statehood, the division of India might continue indefinitely.

Gandhi, however, found it expedient to concede the Sikhs' demands. In 1965, Punjab, a Sikh-majority state, was separated from the Hindu-majority state of Haryana. Though this concession did not satisfy all demands for local autonomy, it bought temporary peace.

An Increasingly Independent Leader. Despite Gandhi's successful resolution of many issues, her government grew increasingly unpopular during the 1960s. In the national elections of 1967, the Congress Party's majority in the *Lok Sabha* narrowed to a margin of only 20 seats. One reason for these losses was a widespread belief that the entire Congress government was corrupt. In 1969, Gandhi addressed this concern by calling for stricter controls on personal income and business profits. In retaliation for this move, she was expelled from the party. But this measure only helped her to forge an independent identity. In national elections held in 1971, her newly formed party, called the "New" or "Ruling" Congress, won two-thirds of the seats in the *Lok Sabha.*

A Third War with Pakistan. Several weeks after Gandhi's election victory, in March 1971, East Pakistan declared its independence from West Pakistan. The war of independence waged in East Pakistan—soon to be known as Bangladesh—could hardly fail to involve India, whose territory separated the two warring parties.

Modern India

Tensions between East and West Pakistan had been simmering for a long time. The Bengali people of East Pakistan represented the majority of Pakistan's people. In a representative system, they would have had a substantial say in how the government was run. But after the nation's first popular elections, held in 1970, the military government of West Pakistan refused to cede any power to the Bengali majority.

Following the declaration of Bangladesh's independence, 60,000 troops from West Pakistan opened fire on Bengali students and other civilians, killing many thousands of them. Within a month, about one million civilians had fled across the Indian border into West Bengal. Once in India, many of the refugees began to organize guerrilla groups to fight for the liberation of Bangladesh. By October, their efforts began to have an effect. Meanwhile, India now had about eight million refugees to feed and care for, and was also supplying arms and training to the guerrillas.

In November, India openly intervened in the struggle by sending troops, airplanes, and tanks into Bangladesh. By early December, India and West Pakistan were fully at war, with each side conducting air raids on the other's territory. On 15 December, Pakistan surrendered, and the new nation of Bangladesh came into being.

The 1971 war represented a significant victory for India and for Indira Gandhi. During the war, the United States, under President Nixon, had kept up its flow of arms to Pakistan and had cut off all aid to India. Yet India had triumphed and had brought a new democracy into being. India was now recognized as the major power of the subcontinent.

THE COMING OF THE "EMERGENCY"

Despite such major successes as the 1971 war and the "green revolution," Gandhi is mainly remembered today for the 19-month period known as the Emergency. In 1975, using the special powers outlined in the constitution, she suspended democracy and began to rule India as a virtual dictator. Her declaration of a State of Emergency was made without warning and was ushered in with unheard-of speed and efficiency. It came as a complete surprise to the nation and the world. In the words of one commentator, "India, the land of every seventh person in the world, became virtually a continent of silence on June 26, 1975."[2]

The Emergency was preceded by a rising tide of public dissent. The main issue was once again corruption. Despite many promises, the government had made little headway in disciplining its own officials. Though

---

2. Ved Mehta, *The New India* (New York: Viking Penguin, 1978), p. 31.

numerous anticorruption laws had been enacted, tax evasion and other abuses continued to flourish. Moreover, a continuing population boom had helped to widen the gap between rich and poor. A high rate of inflation also added to peoples' financial woes, for wages were not keeping pace with prices.

In 1975, the diverse groups opposing the government—socialists, communists, conservatives, and religious splinter groups—coalesced into a new party known as the *Janata Morcha* ("United Front"). The foremost leaders of the new party were Moraji Desai and J. P. Narayan. Desai was the conservative leader who had narrowly missed becoming prime minister in 1964. J. P. Narayan represented the opposite end of the political spectrum: he had resigned from Congress in 1948 to work for the cause of social justice.

Public protests came to a climax on 12 June 1975, when a Supreme Court judge convicted Gandhi of two campaign law violations. The charges were four years old, and concerned her use of government vehicles and other equipment during a campaign race. Though the infractions were rather minor, India's stern campaign laws required that Gandhi must resign from office if her conviction was upheld. On 25 June, a mass rally was held in Delhi to demand that she step down. Early the next morning, the Emergency went into effect.

A New Constitution

During the first hours of the Emergency, Gandhi ordered the arrests of her opponents, including Narayan and Desai, who had been among her father's closest associates. In all, as many as 200,000 people are thought to have been imprisoned under the Emergency. Gandhi then began to amend the constitution so that her own powers were broadened and those of the Parliament and the judiciary reduced. She was able to push these amendments through the Parliament because her party still had a large majority there. Also, many opposition members were now in jail.

The new constitutional amendments granted immunity to a prime minister for all criminal and civil offenses, and also barred any legal challenges to the Emergency. Strict controls were placed on the press, and on radio and television broadcasts, so that only "good news" about the government could be published. The laws of *habeas corpus* were also revoked, so that the government could arrest and imprison any citizen for up to two years before filing charges.

Gandhi termed the Emergency a "disciplined democracy," and called upon people to "work more, talk less." The centerpiece of her new government was a 20-point program of economic and social reform. Many of the points—such as laws against tax evasion, anticorruption measures, and inflation controls—had been announced many times before. This time, however, they were enforced. Prices immediately began to fall, and productivity rose. In economic terms, the Emergency was an overwhelming success.

The Sanjay Issue

In analyzing why Gandhi had overturned India's 28-year-old democracy, together with most of the principles her father had fought for, many people focused their attention on her son Sanjay. Unlike his older brother, Rajiv, 29-year-old Sanjay Gandhi had shown a keen interest in politics. And his enormous influence over his mother was evident to all. In light of Sanjay's actions during the Emergency, commentators found it easy to believe that he had been its foremost advocate.

Sanjay's program for social improvement was almost as prominent during the Emergency as his mother's 20-point program. The most controversial part of his program was an energetic campaign on behalf of population control. To implement this program, temporary clinics, in tents, were set up on the sidewalks of Delhi. Thousands of indigent men were then pulled from the streets to be given a five-minute vasectomy operation. The rule was that any man who had three children must be sterilized. But in their haste to fulfill quotas, government employees often did not pay much attention to the family history or youth of their "customers."

During a six-month period, it was estimated, about two million men were sterilized under Sanjay's program. However, it is doubtful that these efforts had any lasting impact on the problem of overpopulation. Rather, the fear and hostility that his methods inspired set back the cause of family planning.

Another part of Sanjay's program was slum clearance, or "beautification." This effort was carried out in the same impatient, autocratic fashion as the sterilization campaign. Slum dwellers were loaded into vans and taken to encampments set up outside the city. As soon as they had departed, bulldozers rolled in and leveled their homes. Sanjay had advertised the encampments as idyllic, modern developments. But in practice, he did not trouble to supply them with sanitation facilities, water, or electricity.

Sanjay's autocratic methods and evident lack of sympathy for the slum-dwellers erased many of the public relations gains that his mother's economic plan had brought about. When elections were held once again, the government was brought down by the votes of these poorer citizens.

A RETURN TO DEMOCRACY

In January 1977, Indira Gandhi announced that elections would be held in two months and that political prisoners would be released so that they might campaign against her. Many reasons have been advanced to explain this surprising decision. It is not known whether she was motivated by regret for past actions, by confidence that the Emergency had become popular, or by other considerations.

In the event, the government and the Congress Party suffered an overwhelming defeat in the March elections. Indira Gandhi, Sanjay, and every candidate associated with them were rejected at the polls. When the results were in, Gandhi quietly repealed the Emergency and resigned her office. Moraji Desai then became prime minister.

A Brief Interlude

During Desai's two-year term in office, India's democratic form of government and original constitution were restored. But Desai, who represented the interests of the wealthy middle classes, was not able to maintain his ruling majority for long. As corruption again flourished and inflation climbed, the fragile coalition of the Janata began to fall apart.

At first, it seemed unlikely that Indira Gandhi would ever again hold public office. Following her devastating defeat, the newly freed press began to publish a flood of new accounts concerning her misdeeds during the Emergency. Such accounts ranged from stories of high-handed or petty, vindictive actions to charges that Sanjay had murdered one or more of his critics. But despite hundreds of allegations, government investigators were not able to substantiate the more serious charges.

Desai's failure to bring the Gandhis to account in a court of law contributed to his growing unpopularity. And as the economy deteriorated, public outrage concerning the Gandhis gave way to a more nostalgic view of the Emergency. Just a year after her resignation, Gandhi won a seat in Parliament, in a by-election held in South India. Two years later, in January 1980, she was again prime minister of India.

The Gandhi Dynasty in the 1980s

When Indira Gandhi was swept back into office, Sanjay too was elected to Parliament. But just five months after this triumph, Sanjay was killed while flying a private stunt plane. Sanjay's sudden death caused an outpouring of public lament, even though he had once been the most criticized man in India.

Following Sanjay's death, a "palace intrigue" seemed to be in the making as Maneka, Sanjay's widow, began to show interest in pursuing a public career. But Indira Gandhi had no intention of allowing her outspoken daughter-in-law to inherit the family mantle. Instead, she prevailed on her elder son, Rajiv, to take his brother's seat in Parliament. Though Rajiv was reluctant to give up his career as an airline pilot, he finally agreed.

Increasing Sikh Militancy. In 1983, a group of Sikh militants began to demand a fully independent state in the Punjab. To give weight to their demand, they began to carry out terrorist killings of Hindus and other non-Sikhs, who comprised nearly half the population of Punjab state. In 1984, the militants occupied the Golden Temple at Amritsar—the center of the Sikh religion—and vowed to fight to the death for their dream of Sikh independence. At this point, Prime Minister Gandhi felt compelled to take a strong stand. In June 1984, troops were sent to Amritsar to retake the temple. But as they had promised, the Sikh defenders fought to the death rather than surrender. The retaking of the temple cost the lives of more than 400 Sikhs.

Following the massacre at Amritsar, Sikh demands for an independent homeland became even more vocal.

The Assassination. The martyrdom of the Sikh militants at Amritsar stirred fierce passions, even among moderate Sikhs. On 31 October 1984, Prime Minister Gandhi was murdered by two of her Sikh bodyguards. In the aftermath of this shocking event, communal fighting between Sikhs and Hindus cost the lives of more than 2500 people.

In the difficult months following the assassination of the prime minister, Congress leaders turned to Rajiv Gandhi as their best hope to restore national unity and order. Rajiv accepted the post of prime minister and called for national elections. In these elections, the Congress Party won its largest victory ever. The public, it was clear, was solidly in favor of Rajiv, who had become famous for his disinterested attitude toward politics.

Disaster at Bhopal. Two months after Indira Gandhi's assassination, another disaster struck the nation. Around midnight on 3 December 1984, a Union Carbide plant at Bhopal, in central India, suddenly emitted a deadly pesticide known as methyl isocynate (MIC). In all, about 40 tons of the chemical drifted over the sleeping city. At least 2500 residents died immediately, and 17,000 suffered permanent injuries such as blindness and breathing difficulties. It was at the time the largest known industrial accident in history. (Only the 1986 nuclear accident at Chernobyl, in the Soviet Union, produced more casualties.)

The Bhopal disaster aroused widespread resentment of foreign companies. Here, demonstrators protest Union Carbide's settlement with the Indian government.

An increased awareness of environmental issues has been evident in recent years. These demonstrators are protesting a dam project that, if completed, will inundate thousands of acres of land.

The Bhopal disaster came to be a central symbol in several debates that have continued to the present day. Prior to Bhopal, political leaders had often remarked that India did not have the "luxury" to worry about environmental problems. But since Bhopal, environmental issues have become a national concern, and awareness of them extends even to the most remote villages. The disaster also caused people to question whether multinational corporations should be allowed to do business in India. The Union Carbide Company had been granted an exemption from India's strict licensing rules, on the grounds that it was providing advanced technology. But in 1985, the company admitted that it had not followed the same safety standards in India as it did in the United States.

The Downfall of Rajiv Gandhi. In 1987, a growing corruption scandal rocked Rajiv's government. Like the Bhopal disaster, the new scandal had to do with foreign companies. The Bofors Co. of Sweden, it appeared, had paid $50 million in kickbacks to high officials in return for a contract to sell armaments to the Indian government. V. P. Singh, Gandhi's finance minister, investigated the allegations. He soon uncovered evidence that the Bofors allegations were well founded. Furthermore, he discovered, the pattern of taking kickbacks extended back at least to 1980, when Indira Gandhi had been prime minister. Singh could not determine whether the funds had gone into the Congress Party's coffers or into the private Swiss bank accounts of high officials. He did not get a chance to find out, because he was abruptly dismissed from the cabinet.

Rajiv's cover-up of the Bofors scandal resulted in a precipitous decline in his popularity. In national elections held in November 1989, the Congress lost its majority in Parliament. V. P. Singh, now a member of the Janata Party, became the new prime minister.

SUMMARY

The democracy shaped by Jawaharlal Nehru embodied all of the central ideals of the centurylong nationalist movement. Events have shown that the great majority of India's people understand and believe in these ideals. Hence it is unlikely that the nation will ever abandon its "adventure in democracy."

The centralized, socialist economic system that Nehru created was intended to uphold the principle of *equality of status and opportunity*. But like similar experiments in the Soviet Union and elsewhere, the centralized system has tended to create its own privileged class of bureaucrats and politicians. Thus a new *oligarchy* has been shaped, in which economic power is shared by just a few citizens.

In Rajiv Gandhi's last two years as prime minister, one possible avenue of development was indicated. By loosening some of India's strict economic controls, Gandhi succeeded in opening new business and investment opportunities for thousands of citizens. Since government control of industry has proved to be ineffective in many cases, such private-sector growth may provide an answer for some of India's most pressing problems.

DISCUSSION AND ESSAY QUESTIONS

1. What was Mahatma Gandhi's vision of *swaraj*? How did his vision differ from that of most Congress members?
2. What was the significance of having a strong and popular leader during India's first years of independence?
3. What were the most overwhelming problems that Nehru faced when India became independent? What were his solutions to these problems?
4. How did Indira Gandhi's outlook differ from that of her father?
5. What qualities do India's voters look for in their leaders? Give examples of successful and unsuccessful election campaigns.

SUGGESTED READINGS

M. J. Akbar, *India: The Siege Within* (Harmondsworth, Eng.: Penguin, 1985). A prominent journalist and historian surveys some of the political movements that have posed a threat to India's unity.

Anees Jung, *Unveiling India* (New York: Viking Penguin, 1987). A member of India's growing feminist movement describes the traditional role of women and the conflicts that have arisen as women strive to reform their image.

Ved Mehta, *The New India* (New York: Viking Penguin, 1978). The 11 essays in this book concern Indian life and politics during the 1970s.

JAWAHARLAL NEHRU: THE MAKING OF A NATIONAL LEADER

As the only son of a prominent brahman family, Jawaharlal Nehru had grown up with all the luxuries and advantages that money could provide. After completing his education in England, Jawaharlal was well positioned to become a wealthy and influential lawyer like his father, Motilal. However, in 1920, both father and son were caught up in Gandhi's noncooperation movement.

In the first passage below, Nehru describes his first visit to the "real India" as a new Congress recruit. In the second passage, written in 1954, Nehru describes how his ashes should be disposed of after his death. In the process, he describes his great attachment to India and her peoples.

Visit to an Indian Village, 1920

The sun scorched and blinded. I was quite unused to going out in the sun and ever since my return from England [1912] I had gone to the hills for part of every summer. And now I was wandering about all day in the open sun with not even a sun-hat. . . .

We found the whole countryside afire with enthusiasm and full of a strange excitement. Enormous gatherings would take place at the briefest notice by word of mouth. One village would communicate with another, and the second with the third, and so on, and presently whole villages would empty out, and all over the fields there would be men and women and children on the march to the meeting place. . . . They were in miserable rags, men and women, but their faces were full of excitement and their eyes glistened and seemed to expect strange happenings which would, as if by a miracle, put an end to their long misery. They showered their affection on us and looked on us with loving and hopeful eyes as if we were the bearers of good tidings, the guides who were to lead them to the promised land. Looking at them and their misery and overflowing gratitude, I was filled with shame and sorrow, shame at my own easygoing and comfortable life and our petty politics of the city which ignored this vast multitude of semi-naked sons and daughters of India, sorrow at the degradation and overwhelming poverty of India.

India and Her Peoples

My desire to have a handful of my ashes thrown in the Ganga at Allahabad has no religious significance, so far as I am concerned. . . . The Ganga, especially, is the river of India, beloved of her people, round which are intertwined her racial memories, her hopes and fears, her songs of triumph, her victories and her defeats. She has been a symbol of India's age-long culture and civilization, ever-changing, ever-flowing, and yet ever the same Ganga. . . . And though I have discarded much of past tradition and custom, and am anxious that India should rid herself of all shackles that bind and constrain her and divide her people, and suppress vast numbers of them, and prevent the free development of the body and the spirit; though I seek all this, yet I do not wish to cut myself off from that past completely. I am proud of that great inheritance that has been, and is ours. . . .

The major portion of my ashes should, however, be disposed of otherwise. I want these to be carried high up into the air in an aeroplane and scattered from that height over the fields where the peasants of India toil, so that they might mingle with the dust and soil of India and become an indistinguishable part of India.

SOURCE: M. J. Akbar, *Nehru: The Making of India* (New York: Viking Penguin, 1988), pp. 129–130; 583–584.

AN EXPERIMENT IN DEMOCRACY

The first experiments in democracy took place in ancient Greece, where the philosophers Socrates, Plato, and Aristotle (among others) observed and described the process. But after the classical world collapsed (c. A.D. *450), their writings—and the concept of democracy—were lost to the European world. They were not rediscovered until the late Middle Ages.*

The next large-scale experiments in democracy took place in 18th-century Europe (England, France, and Holland) and in the United States. By the 19th century, most thinkers agreed with Aristotle's basic premise about democracy—that it works best when most citizens have a "middle and nearly equal condition." Modern theorists also added other requirements. They decided, for instance, that the citizens of a democracy must share a common religion and culture; only then would they have the mutual understanding necessary to make a democracy work.

Indian nationalists were, of course, aware of these theories. Yet they decided that the best way to bring about the requirements of democracy was to establish democratic institutions. The following article describes their experiment.

In 1947, independent India, flying in the face of this philosophical tradition— and, indeed, of its own long history of oligarchy—dared to set up a democratic form of government consciously modeled on that of Great Britain and the United States, and thus began what its first Prime Minister, Jawaharlal Nehru, along with his Western admirers, liked to call an "adventure in democracy." People who had never learned to sign their names and who were so backward that in some cases they had scarcely heard of the wheel or the nail would journey by yak or on foot for several days to vote by secret ballot in ballot boxes that they could identify only by means of party ideographs [picture symbols]. To insure that everyone who wanted to vote could vote, the government went to such lengths that general elections sometimes took as much as three months to complete. However inefficient and imperfect the system was, it helped to keep the country united by allowing political expression to India's diverse races, regions, religions, castes, cultures and languages. The people

For the benefit of voters who cannot read, each political party in India is identified by a pictograph symbol. In the elections of 1967, Indira Gandhi's Congress party symbol was a pair of bullocks.

elected to the Parliament and to the state legislatures were as diverse as the people they represented. They wore everything from Savile Row suits to tribal dress, and spoke in Oxford accents or in languages known only in remote villages. The people and their representatives all paid homage to Nehru, whose self-restraint, patriotism, and lifelong devotion to British socialist ideas of democracy had made the "adventure" possible in the first place.

SOURCE: Ved Mehta, *The New India* (New York: Viking Penguin, 1978), pp. 43–44.

PROS AND CONS OF THE EMERGENCY

Supporters of the Emergency argued that India was not ready for democracy. Thus, Prime Minister Gandhi had been correct in suspending it. Her Emergency had reestablished the concept of law and order, and had made it possible to introduce true economic reforms.

Opponents of the Emergency did not deny that democracies are inefficient. Yet they believed that democracy best represented the ideals and principles of the Indian people. Despite a long tradition of despotic rule, India's peoples have always understood the concept of freedom of conscience, they argued. And the leaders of the national-

ist movement—including Vivekananda, Tagore, Gandhi, and Nehru —had struggled all their lives to uphold this principle.

In the first passage quoted here, a woman from Delhi testifies about the benefits of the Emergency. In the second and third, J. P. Narayan pleads for the restoration of democratic values and describes the real roots of "corruption."

In Favor of the Emergency

Things in Delhi had come to such a pass before the Emergency that hooligans would set fire to public buses. . . . Hoarders and black marketeers were everywhere. They were creating artificial scarcities and inflation. I once went into a respectable shop to pick up a tin of Postman vegetable oil. The shopkeeper said he didn't have any. I pleaded with him—I'd been buying at that shop for 20 years—and he finally said, "All right, sister, I will do you a favor. Sixty-five rupees. Sixty-five rupees! That was double the price of my last tin of Postman vegetable oil. But at least I had the vegetable oil. Everything was breaking down. My daughter would go to her classes at college and the professors would be out on strike. If you visited government offices, you found that the clerks and underlings had had their heads so turned by unscrupulous politicians that they were out on the lawn playing cards for all to see. Government officials never arrived at their offices on time. When you tried to ring up a public service, like the railway station or the telephone office, nobody would bother to answer, or if somebody did he was so rude and offensive that you were sorry you rang up. As for using public services, to ride a city bus was to take your life in your hands. . . .

And now, what calm and discipline Mrs. Gandhi has brought over the land! . . . Mrs. Gandhi has devised all kinds of ways to catch hoarders and black marketeers. Anyone, young or old, who helps to catch one of them gets a percentage of whatever is found. . . . As a consequence of all this vigilance, all the prices have come down. The hoarded foodstuffs have been delivered to the markets. The tins of vegetable oil are now in the front of the shops, properly marked. I bought a tin of Postman vegetable oil just the other day for 32 rupees. . . . Everything works now. Classes in universities meet regularly, and examinations are held on the appointed days; buses and trains run on time. . . . Everyone in public service picks up the telephone immediately and greets you politely with a sweet tongue, in a disciplined way. Conductors are posted at bus stops, and no one can get on the bus without a ticket, and practically everyone who has a ticket can find a seat. . . .

The truth is that we Indians . . . have a very bad character. The British knew that the only way to rule us was with a stick. Mrs. Gandhi understands that and has now taken hold of that stick. She is very clever. She has even managed to control the youth. She makes them all sit down around her and ask her questions. She answers all their questions and imbues them with the spirit of nationalism, national pride and national discipline. She says things like, "Now you have to make this nation. You have to take the work of building this nation onto your shoulders." And when children all across the country read these remarks, they feel thrilled and inspired.

A Letter to Indira Gandhi   —J. P. Narayan

If Justice, Liberty, Equality and Fraternity have not been rendered to "all its citizens" even after a quarter of a century of signing of that Constitution, the fault is not that of the Constitution or of democracy but of the Congress Party that has been in power in Delhi all these years. . . .

You know I am an old man. My life's work is done. . . . Would you listen to the advice of such a man? Please do not destroy the foundations that the Fathers of the Nation, including your noble father, had laid down. There is nothing but strife and suffering along the path that you have taken. You inherited a great tradition, noble values and a working democracy. Do not leave behind a miserable wreck of all that. It would take a long time to put all that together again. For it would be put together again, I have no doubt. A people who fought British imperialism and humbled it cannot accept indefinitely the indignity and shame of totalitarianism. The spirit of man can never be vanquished, no matter how deeply suppressed. . . .

You have accused the opposition and me of every kind of villainy. But let me assure you that if you do the right things—for instance, take the opposition into confidence, heed its advice—you will receive the willing cooperation of every one of us. For that you need not destroy democracy. The ball is in your court. It is for you to decide.

With these parting words, let me bid you farewell. May God be with you.

On Bureaucracies and Corruption   —J. P. Narayan

It might be useful to turn for a moment to what is perhaps one of the most serious problems of the present day: the problem of bureaucracy and corruption. Some think that one solution of corruption is dictatorship. But even dictatorship is no solution of bureaucracy. To the contrary, we know that dictatorship breeds bureaucracy faster than other systems of government, and, in the bargain, makes it all-powerful.

Even as regards corruption, it is not generally realized that there is corruption on a gigantic scale in the dictatorships—only its form is changed. Instead of corruption in the sense of bribery and the like, there is grosser corruption in the form of lying, deceit, intrigue, terror, enslavement of the human mind, crucifixion of the dignity of man. All this corrupts human life far more than bribery and similar other things.

The only true solution of the problem both of bureaucracy and corruption is direct self-government of the people and direct and immediate supervision and control over the civil servants by the people and their elected organs.

SOURCES: Ved Mehta, *The New India* (New York: Viking Penguin, 1978), pp. 38–41, 91–92; Ainslie T. Embree, ed., *Sources of Indian Tradition,* 2d ed., vol. 2 (New York: Columbia University Press, 1988), p. 376.

1. What are the main concerns of each writer?
2. What opinion does each writer have about his or her fellow citizens? How has this opinion helped to shape their ideas on government?

GLOSSARY

ahimsa. Nonviolence, or noninjury; absence of violence.

anthropology. The study of humankind. There are two main branches of anthropology. *Cultural anthropologists* examine and compare human societies, focusing on their myths, institutions, and values. *Physical anthropologists* study the process of evolution over millions of years, often by analyzing skeletons.

archeology. The study of ancient societies through excavation, classification, and dating of their material remains (e.g., buildings, artworks, coins, and inscriptions). Also spelled *archaeology*.

artha. Prosperity; well-being; worldly success. *See also* Four Ends of Life.

ascetic. *n.* A person who practices self-denial and strict self-discipline. *adj.* Austere, without frills.

Ashoka. (Reigned c. 269–232 B.C.) A king of India during the Mauryan Empire period; generally considered to be the greatest of India's ancient kings.

atman. The soul, or spirit, of living beings.

autocracy. A dictatorship or despotic government. An autocratic ruler is not bound by laws or answerable to anyone for his or her actions.

avatar. The incarnation, or embodiment, of a god in human or animal form.

Bhagavad Gita. The dialogue between Krishna and Arjuna in the *Mahabharata;* one of the central texts of the Hindu religion.

bhakti. Devotional. The message of bhakti religion is that any person may attain spiritual liberation through devotion to a personal god. Individual striving is emphasized, and caste status is considered unimportant.

Bharata. A dynasty who ruled an ancient kingdom in northern India and were central characters in the epic *Mahabharata*. Bharata is now the official name of India.

Brahma. A god who played a major role in the original creation of the universe. Brahma, Shiva, and Vishnu together make up the *triad* of classical Hinduism. Each is considered to be an aspect of Brahman.

Brahman (deity). The Supreme Being; creator and sustainer of the universe; all-pervading and all-powerful spirit.

brahman (caste). The priestly caste of Hindu society; highest-ranking of the four *varnas*. The duty of brahmans is to preserve the ancient scriptures, and to uphold the highest standards of ethical conduct and ritual purity in daily life.

Buddhism. The religion founded by Siddhartha Gautama (c. 563–483 B.C.), better known as the Buddha ("Enlightened One").

caste dharma. The duties and obligations that each caste of Hindu society owes to society as a whole.

Chakravartin. "He who turns the wheel." A world ruler.

civil disobedience. Noncompliance with a law perceived as unjust, usually with the expectation of receiving a jail term or other punishment. Mahatma Gandhi and other reformers have used this technique to focus attention on a particular issue and so create a dialogue. The idea is to bring about change in a nonviolent way.

darbar. Reception or royal audience.

dharma. Duty; social law; right conduct.

Dravidians. A group of people who spoke a non-Aryan language and were among the earliest inhabitants of the Indian subcontinent. The languages spoken today in South India (Tamil, Telugu, Kannada, Malayalam) are Dravidian in origin.

Four Ends of Life. The four ends of life described in Hindu scriptures are *dharma* (social duty), *artha* (worldly success), *kama* (pleasure), and *moksha* (spiritual liberation). In the Four Stages of Life (*see below*), a person correctly balances the first three ends in order to attain the fourth.

Four Stages of Life. The four stages of life described in Hindu law books are *student, householder, forest-dweller* or *hermit,* and *ascetic.* In the first two stages, a person fulfills social obligations and enjoys the pleasures of family life. In the last two stages, the focus is on individual spiritual realization.

Gandhara. An ancient kingdom that extended from Afghanistan to the northern Indus valley. At times, Gandhara was a crossroads of international trade, linking India to central Asia, China, and the Western world.

Gandhi, Indira. (1917–1984.) Prime minister of India (1966–1977; 1980–1984). Gandhi was the daughter of Jawaharlal Nehru and wife of Firoze Gandhi.

Gandhi, Mohandas K. (1869–1948.) Usually called *Mahatma,* or "Great Soul." The focus of Gandhi's life and teachings was the spiritual development of the individual. As leader of the Indian nationalist movement from 1920 to 1948, Gandhi advocated *nonviolent resistance* and *self-reliance* as methods to enhance people's spiritual development and win India's independence from Britain.

ghat. A staircase leading to the water.

Gupta Empire (A.D. 320–550). An empire in northern India, ruled by the Gupta dynasty for 230 years. The hallmarks of this era were religious tolerance, artistic achievement, and advances in scientific knowledge. The Gupta Empire period is also known as the *classical age* of Hinduism.

Guru. One of the ten teachers who shaped the Sikh religion during the first two centuries of its history (c. 1500–1708).

guru. A guide or teacher. The spiritual and practical guidance of a guru is considered indispensable in yoga and in many other pursuits.

Hanuman. A monkey god who plays a major role in the epic *Ramayana.*

Harappan. The name given to the earliest known civilization of India. The Harappan civilization flourished from about 2300 to 1750 B.C.

harijans. "Children of God." Mahatma Gandhi's name for the untouchables, or outcasts, of Hindu society.

Islam. "Submission" (to Allah). The religion founded by the prophet Mohammed (A.D. 570?–632).

Jainism. The religion founded by Vardhamana Mahavira (c. 540–468 B.C.), originally a sect of Hinduism. The central creeds of Jainism—nonviolence and reverence for all life—are of great antiquity.

jati. A subcaste in Hindu society. The members of a jati are often related by blood and share an occupational specialty.

Kali. A Hindu goddess with both creative and destructive traits; consort of Shiva.

karma. Actions. According to the law of karma, every action leaves a residue on the soul. As a result, the soul is enchained to the physical world and must go through continuing rebirths.

karma yoga. The concept that actions, when carried out in a spirit of duty and unselfishness, do not incur the usual ill effects of karma. In the Bhagavad Gita, Krishna explains that such actions are a path to spiritual liberation. In modern times, Mahatma Gandhi is the best-known example of a *karma yogi*.

khadi. Homespun cloth. Also called *khaddar*.

Koran. The recitations of the prophet Mohammed, believed to have been divinely inspired; the sacred book of the Islamic religion. Also spelled *Quran*.

Kosala. An ancient kingdom in the Ganges region. In the *Ramayana*, Rama ruled Kosala from his capital at Ayodhya, 75 miles east of present-day Lucknow.

Krishna. One of the most important gods in the Hindu pantheon. The story of Krishna's life on earth is described at length in sacred literature.

kshatriya. The warrior caste; second highest in rank of the four *varnas* described in Hindu scripture.

Mahabharata. "Great Bharata." The story of a dispute between two branches of the Bharata family, with hundreds of subplots illustrating diverse aspects of Hindu religion and culture. The *Mahabharata* is the longest epic ever composed.

maharaja. A "great king;" usually Hindu or Buddhist.

Mauryan Empire (c. 334–184 B.C.). The empire founded by Chandragupta Maurya and continued under his successors; the largest empire in Indian history. The Mauryan Empire reached its greatest extent under Ashoka, who practiced religious tolerance and tried to govern according to Buddhist precepts.

maya. "Magic." Many schools of Indian philosophy think of the physical world as *maya*, an illusion that conceals the underlying reality of Brahman.

Moghul Empire (1526–1857). The empire founded in northern India by Babur, a Muslim conqueror of Turkish-Mongol descent. The empire reached its greatest extent during the reign of Akbar (1560–1605), an emperor who championed religious tolerance. After 1707, Moghul influence began to decline. The empire ended in 1857, when the last Moghul emperor was exiled by the British.

moksha. Release of the soul from its bondage to the physical world; spiritual liberation.

nawab. "Deputy" (of a sultan). A prince or governor of a province under a Muslim government.

Nehru, Jawaharlal. (1889–1964.) Prime minister of India (1947–1964) and longtime disciple of Mahatma Gandhi. Nehru differed from Gandhi in advocating a strong central government for independent India.

nirvana. "Blowing out." A Buddhist term meaning release from karma and rebirth; enlightenment.

nizam. A military commander or prince under a Muslim government.

panchayat. A council of five elders, often recognized as a court of justice in self-governing villages.

Plassey. A village north of Calcutta, scene of Robert Clive's battle against Siraj-ad-daula in 1757. Clive's victory at Plassey laid the foundation for the British empire in India.

purdah. The seclusion of women, often by means of curtains, veils, or screens. In Muslim law, also adopted by many Hindus, the face and figure of a married woman must be concealed from all males not related to her.

Radha. A Hindu goddess, chief consort of Krishna.

Raj. Empire or rule.

Rama. Legendary king of Kosala in a golden age of antiquity; hero of the *Ramayana*. The expression "kingdom of Rama" refers to an ideal state in which the highest standards of justice and morality prevail.

Ramayana. The story of Rama's battles against the evil forces threatening his family and kingdom; one of the two great epics of India. (The other is the *Mahabharata*.)

Rig Veda. A collection of the earliest hymns composed by the Aryans after their invasion of India; one of the central texts of the Hindu religion.

samadhi. The final stage of yoga, when the soul (atman) realizes its identity with Brahman.

sannyasin. A wandering ascetic; religious seeker.

Sanskrit. The Indo-European language spoken by the Aryan invaders of India; the classical language of Hindu scriptures and also of many literary writings. Most northern Indian languages have Sanskrit roots.

satyagraha. "Soul force," or "holding fast to the truth." Mahatma Gandhi's term for his tactic of nonviolent resistance.

Shiva. A central god of Hinduism, noted for his powers of creation and destruction.

Sikhism. A religion founded about 1500, originally as a refuge for people dissatisfied with Hinduism and Islam. Generally, Sikhs reject caste distinctions and religious rituals, and seek divine revelation by meditating on the name of God. The Sikh religion was guided by a succession of ten Gurus (teachers) in its formative stages. The capital of Sikhism is the Golden Temple of Amritsar, in the Punjab.

Sita. Wife of the god-king Rama in the *Ramayana.*

sudra. The servant caste, lowest-ranking of the four *varnas* described in Hindu scripture. Traditional jobs of the sudras include farming, leather-working, and laundering.

Sufism. A mystical sect of Islam, similar in some respects to bhakti Hindu religion. For Sufi Muslims, a person's individual relationship with God is more important than the ceremonies and doctrines of organized religion.

svadesh. One's own locality or country. *Svadeshi* goods are those made in the home country.

Tamil. The classical language of South India; forebear of most languages spoken in South India today. Also, a speaker of either the ancient or modern Tamil languages.

Upanishads. A group of philosophical texts composed by forest-dwelling yogis between the eighth and sixth centuries B.C. The central message of the Upanishads is that Brahman and atman are identical.

vaishya. The caste of merchants and artisans, third in rank of the four *varnas* described in Hindu scripture.

varna. The division of Hindu society into four *varnas*, or classes, is described in the *Rig Veda.* The four *varnas* are: the *brahmans,* the *kshatriyas,* the *vaishyas,* and the *sudras.*

Vishnu. A central god of Hinduism. According to many theologians, Vishnu has entered the world nine times in his role as the humanity's preserver and rescuer. The nine *avatars* of Vishnu are: Fish; Tortoise; Boar; Lion-Man; Dwarf; Rama with an axe; Rama, the hero of the *Ramayana;* Krishna; and the Buddha. (A tenth avatar is still to come.)

yoga. "Yoking," or "Harnessing." There are numerous disciplines of yoga. Some are a quest for religious enlightenment, while others are intended to produce a feeling of physical well-being. In *raja yoga,* a yogi practices rigorous self-discipline to achieve detachment from material needs. Then, using techniques of meditation and concentration, the yogi explores the relationship between the individual soul (atman) and the World Soul (Brahman).

INDEX

Abu Bakr, 130
Afghanistan, 2; British Empire and, 184, 200; geography of, 2
Agriculture, 151, 241
Ahimsa, 23, 86
Akbar, 149–154
Albuquerque, Affonso, 143, 144
Alexander the Great, 95–97
All-Asian Conference, 238
Allahabad, 13
Alvars, 123
Ambedkar, B. R., 214, 216
Amritsar: massacre at, 208; as sacred site of Sikhs, 162, 247, 248
Appar, 123–124
Architecture, of Mogul period, 153, 156–157
Arcot, siege of, 172
Art: Hindu themes in, 30; of Moghuls, 153
Arthashastra (Kautilya), 97–99
Arya Samaj, 198
Aryabhata, 113
Aryans: culture of, 43, 49–50, 71; early society of, 51–52; gods of, 52–53
Ashoka: Buddhist views of, 103–104; reign of, 100–103, 105
Atman, 22–26
Aurangzeb (Alamgir), 159–163

Babur, 139, 146–148
Bangladesh: boundary with, 9; independence of, 243; language spoken in, 10
Benares, 14
Bengal: and British East India Company, 176–177; partition of, 202
Bhagavad Gita, 58, 66–67
Bhakti movement: explanation of, 118, 123–124; poetry of, 134–135
Bhave, Vinoba, 230
Bhopal disaster, 248–249
Bindusara, 99, 100, 105
Black Hole incident, 174–175

Bodhisattvas, 81
Bofors scandal, 249–250
Brahma, 27
Brahman caste, 32–33; criticisms of, 72–73; emigration to South India, 122; Manu's laws regarding, 110, 112, 232; rituals and ceremonies of, 53–54, 195
Brahman (deity), 22, 24, 26, 199
Brahmanas, 53–54
Brahmo Samaj, 197–198
British East India Company: British interests in, 177–180; establishment of, 168–175; exploitation of Bengal by, 176–177; under Wellesley, 182
British Empire in India: beginning of, 175–180; expansion of, 180–184; imperialism of, 167–168; and rebellion of 1857–1858, 187–189, 195; system of government in, 184–187, 191, 192; views of, 192–193
Buddha: depictions of, 106, 107; life of, 71, 87–91, 94; teachings of, 73–80, 88–91
Buddhism: art of, 106, 107; Christianity and, 83, 91; doctrines and teachings of, 76–80, 87–91; origins of, 70–71; sects of, 80–82, 103; shrines of, 76, 77; views of Ashoka, 103–104
Burke, Edmund, 178–179

Caste dharma, 35
Caste system: continuity of, 35–36, 195; four varna of, 31–33; subcastes within, 34–35; in Tamilnad, 122–123; untouchables and, 33–34, 38–39, 112, 215–216
Chakravartin, 71, 94
Chandra Gupta, 110
Chandra Gupta II, 110–111
Chandragupta Maurya, 96–99
Chera dynasty, 121, 122
China, 238
Chola era, 121, 122, 124–125
Christianity: Buddhism and, 83, 91–92; early